Palgrave Studies in Creativity and Culture

Series Editors
Vlad Petre Glăveanu
School of Psychology
Dublin City University
Dublin, Ireland

Brady Wagoner
Communication and Psychology
Aalborg University
Aalborg, Denmark

Both creativity and culture are areas that have experienced a rapid growth in interest in recent years. Moreover, there is a growing interest today in understanding creativity as a socio-cultural phenomenon and culture as a transformative, dynamic process. Creativity has traditionally been considered an exceptional quality that only a few people (truly) possess, a cognitive or personality trait 'residing' inside the mind of the creative individual. Conversely, culture has often been seen as 'outside' the person and described as a set of 'things' such as norms, beliefs, values, objects, and so on. The current literature shows a trend towards a different understanding, which recognises the psycho-socio-cultural nature of creative expression and the creative quality of appropriating and participating in culture. Our new, interdisciplinary series Palgrave Studies in Creativity and Culture intends to advance our knowledge of both creativity and cultural studies from the forefront of theory and research within the emerging cultural psychology of creativity, and the intersection between psychology, anthropology, sociology, education, business, and cultural studies. Palgrave Studies in Creativity and Culture is accepting proposals for monographs, Palgrave Pivots and edited collections that bring together creativity and culture. The series has a broader focus than simply the cultural approach to creativity, and is unified by a basic set of premises about creativity and cultural phenomena.

Francesco Arese Visconti

The Invisible Diaspora

Rethinking Photographic Portraiture of 21st Century Italian Migrants on the Arc Lémanique area

palgrave
macmillan

Francesco Arese Visconti
School of Communications
Webster University, Geneva Campus
Geneva, Switzerland

ISSN 2755-4503 ISSN 2755-4511 (electronic)
Palgrave Studies in Creativity and Culture
ISBN 978-3-031-74924-7 ISBN 978-3-031-74925-4 (eBook)
https://doi.org/10.1007/978-3-031-74925-4

This Palgrave Macmillan imprint is published by the registered company Springer Nature Switzerland AG.
The registered company address is: Gewerbestrasse 11, 6330 Cham, Switzerland

To Lucia, Andrea and Niccolò

Preface

In January 2007, my first son Andrea was born, and my wife and I were living and working in Italy. We had an intensive life which didn't really give us the possibility to spend the necessary amount of time with our son. Did we have to outsource what we, as parents, had the desire and obligation to do? Did we have to ask our parents, relatives or institutions to grow and educate our son? We decided that it was the time to migrate and find a place where we could work and earn enough money to improve the quality of our life. By 'quality' I mean having more time to spend with Andrea and build a family based on human relationships. As many other Italians had done in the past and were still doing in 2007, we basically had to migrate. I had to leave the city where I was born and lived my entire life. By August 2007, we had moved to the French-speaking part of Switzerland and started our migrants' journey which in 2023 also gave us a second nationality. It all seems a smooth transition, considering that we did not have to struggle to migrate as our ancestors had in the 1960s and 1970s. As explained further in some parts of this book, in the period after the Second World War until the 1970s, migrants who had decided to migrate to Switzerland had to go through a process which was very demanding from a bureaucratic, physical and emotional point of view. Compared to those years, our migration has been easy. However, when people change the landscape of their lives there is a sense of displacement that arises. There are psychological consequences that grow and influence their life (Bolzman et al. 2003; Juhasz and Mey 2003; Mey et al. 2005; Ortner 1973: 1339). Like me, many other Italians have moved since 2007 and are still doing so while I am writing. Is this kind of migration still considered to be worth narrating today? In times of globalization and space/time compression, when you can easily eat a good pizza and drink an Italian 'aperitivo' in the centre of Geneva or Lausanne, when arguably Switzerland and Europe have gone through a process of *méditérranéisation* (Maiolino 2013: 154), when we all dress in the same way and look similar, can we still talk about Italian migration as an impactful phenomenon on Swiss society? Since I have always been interested in doing research that relates to issues of migration, I decided that this recent process of which I was an active part deserved to be investigated and photographed. In this regard, this book is not only about the process of how I produced photographic portraits of recent Italian migrants in the French-speaking part of Switzerland. This book is also about me and my experience as an Italian migrant.

Webster University, Geneva Campus
Geneva, Switzerland

Francesco Arese Visconti

References

Bolzman, C., Rosita Fibbi and Marie Vial. (2003). *Secondas – Secondos: le processus d'intégration des jeunes adultes issus de la migration espagnole et italienne en Suisse*. Zürich: Seismo.

Juhasz, A. and Eva Mey. (2003) *Die zweite Generation: Etablierte oder Aussenseiter? Biographien von Jugendlichen ausländischer Herkunft*. Wiesbaden: Westdeutscher Verlag.

Maiolino, A. (2013). "La construction des identités dans le débat politique." In La Barba et al. (ed.). *La migration italienne dans la Suisse d'après-guerre*. Lausanne: Editions Antipodes.

Mey, E., Miriam Rorato and Peter Voll (2005) 'Die soziale Stellung der zweiten Ausländergeneration', in Bundesamt für Statistik (ed.) Die Integration der ausländischen zweiten Generation und der Eingebürgerten in der Schweiz: Eidgenössische Volkszählung 2000, Neuchâtel: Bundesamt für Statistik, 61–138.
Ortner, S. B. (1973) 'On key symbols', American Anthropologist, 75, 1338–45.

Acknowledgements

First and foremost, I want to thank my life's pillar, Lucia, for her immense love, support and patience and my sons, Andrea and Niccolò, for their inexhaustible source of energy.

I am extremely grateful to Dr. Margherita Sprio for her fundamental guidance and experience. Without her, I would have not started and completed this journey.

Thanks go to my father and my mother, always next to me, one physically, the other one spiritually.

This project would have not been possible without the support of the Italian community of the *arc lémanique* area and my Webster University colleagues.

Competing Interests The author has no conflicts of interest to declare that are relevant to the content of this book.

Ethics Approval This study was performed in line with the principles of the Declaration of Helsinki. Approval was granted by the Ethics Committee of the University of Westminster (25th January 2017 / ETH1617-0048).

Contents

Abbreviations

AIRE	Anagrafe degli Italiani Residenti all'Estero
EFTA	European Free Trade Association
EU	European Union
FDFA	Federal Department of Foreign Affairs
FIBA	Fédération Internationale de Basketball
IOC	International Olympic Committee
IOM	International Organization for Migrations
ISTAT	Istituto Nazionale di Statistica
SEM	Secrétariat d'État aux migrations
UEFA	Union of European Football Associations
UN	United Nations

List of Figures

Introduction

Contemporary history has identified three big Italian migration movements to Switzerland: the big diaspora of the end of the nineteenth century, the period between the First and the Second World Wars and the diaspora movement from the end of the Second World War until the 1970s. After the Schwarzenbach initiatives and the oil crisis of the 1970s, Italian migration to Switzerland has decreased. However, with the beginning of the 2007–2008 global economic crisis, Italy has witnessed a large new diaspora movement to the traditional countries of migration. Academic studies have found that the most diffused narrative on the *brain drain* phenomenon is over-simplistic and needs to be re-examined and updated; notably that this diaspora in the age of globalization has new and complex layers.

The final goal of this research is to re-think photographic portrayals of the cultural identity of Italian migrants of the twenty-first century in the area between Lausanne and Geneva in Switzerland (*arc lémanique*) following a unique creative process. The work reflects on issues related to the formation of cultural identity formation of the migrant as a continuing experience and to the sense of belonging to a space which becomes a known place after years of residency. How can an image capture a complex, ineffable, and un-representable notion of modern Italian cultural identity? Furthermore, how can an image represent the cultural identity of a group of people whose lives have been changed by the experience of physically migrating to a *terra incognita*?

To answer to these questions, I have applied a wide range of multiple primary methods.

I have used a semiotic approach to understand the image (Barthes 1977; Joly 2015) and based my study of texts in the titles and in the articles of the magazines on rhetorical analysis (Berger 2014: 81–101). I have used interviews (Berger 2014: 157–176) and surveys (Berger 2014: 247–271) with my subjects and in the analysis of my own work as a photographer, I have applied the 'reflective practitioner' method (Walker 2004). As explained by Shön (1996: 4), 'it is rare that the designer has the design all in her head in advance, and then merely translates it. Most of the time she is in a progressive relationship-as she goes along, she is making judgments. Sometimes the designer's judgments have the intimacy of a conversational relationship, where she is getting some response back from the medium.' The practice part of the research has been an ongoing process. Following Walker's definition (2004: 9–10), I developed my photographic work as an 'artmaking process with openness to seeking new solutions rather than relying upon more obvious and normative possibilities for expressing the big idea'.

Research conducted in the archives of Swiss-French illustrated magazines (*L'Illustré* and *L'Hebdo*) and other online publications has highlighted distinctive photographic representations of Italian migrants in Switzerland from the 1960s–1970s to the period between 2006 and 2019. The analysis of pictures of Italian migrants made possible to understand on a larger scale how the public imagination is shaped, how it impacts on the politics of the 'other' and how society reacts to the phenomena of migration. This process has supported and influenced the development of the photographic practice of this research in its attempt to render visible the complex notion of this new migratory identity.

The aim of each chapter is to answer to specific questions. Starting from the definition of 'migrant', Chap. 1 reflects on the differences of the Italian diasporas in Switzerland in the 1960s–1970s and in the twenty-first century and the complex concept of *Italianity*. This chapter also argues how the cultural identity of contemporary Italian migrants of the *arc lémanique* in Switzerland can be represented by photographic portraiture. Chapter 2 describes how the Italian migrant was visually represented in the 1960s–1970s illustrated magazine *L'Illustré*. Following the identical methodology, Chap. 3 investigates how the contemporary Italian migrant is visually represented on illustrated magazines (including online platforms) in the years between 2006 and 2019 in the French-speaking part of Switzerland. To have a better understanding of the profile of the new Italian migrant of the twenty-first century in the Swiss confederation, Chap. 4 offers a series of selected interviews conducted with the protagonists of this research. Before the closing conclusions of Chap. 6, Chap. 5 unveils the methodology used to represent the cultural identity of contemporary Italian migrants in photographic portraits and the final outcome of this work: the photographic portraits and their display in exhibitions.

References

Barthes, R. (1977). *Image, Music, Text.* London: Fontana Press.

Berger, A. A. (2014). *Media and Communication Research Methods.* Los Angeles, London, New York, Singapore and Washington D.C.: SAGE.

Joly, M. (2015). *Introduction à l'analyse de l'image.* Paris: Armand Colin.

Schön, D.A. (1996). "Learning through reflection on conversations." In O'Reilly, D. (Ed.), "In conversation with Donald Schon." In *Capability, the HEC Journal*, vol. 2 (2).

Walker, S. (2004). "Understanding the Artmaking Process: Reflective Practice." In *Art Education*, 57:3, 6–12.

1

The Recent Italian Migration in Switzerland and the Concept of *Italianity*

Abstract Contemporary history has identified three big Italian migration movements to Switzerland: the big diaspora of the end of the nineteenth century, the period between the First and the Second World Wars and the diaspora movement from the end of the Second World War until the 1970s. After the Schwarzenbach initiatives and the oil crisis of the 1970s, Italian migration to Switzerland has decreased. However, with the beginning of the 2007–2008 global economic crisis, Italy has witnessed a large new diaspora movement to the traditional countries of migration. Academic studies have found that the most diffused narrative on the *brain drain* phenomenon is over-simplistic and needs to be re-examined and updated; notably that this diaspora in the age of globalization has new and complex layers.

The aim of this chapter is to introduce the reader to the understanding of the recent Italian migration in Switzerland and the complex, ineffable notion of *Italianity*.

Keywords Italian migration • Diaspora • Switzerland • Globalization • Italianity • Cultural identity

F. Arese Visconti, *The Invisible Diaspora*, Palgrave Studies in Creativity and Culture,
https://doi.org/10.1007/978-3-031-74925-4_1

According to the United Nations (2021), migrants are all those people who moved from their country of residence to another one or within a state away from the place of residency.[1] Following this definition, all Italians who permanently moved abroad should be considered migrants. Migration discourses, however, tend to include recent Italian migration in a different context of European mobility (Smith and Favell 2006; King and Skeldon 2010; Recchi 2013; McKay 2015; Dubucs et al. 2016). There are two lines of reasoning for this: the first one deals with migration from extra-European countries and the second one with European migrants within Europe. In the first case, the attention is on migration from the South to the North of the world, populations which are culturally different ones from the ones of the hosting countries. In this case the main point is the integration process of these different cultures. In the case of European mobility, the pivotal point is about the possibility for Europeans to move easily and find job opportunities otherwise not available in their country of origin. This mobility justifies the existence of the European Union and supports the work industry of the hosting countries. This kind of mobility has been supported since the beginning of the 1990s with programs like Socrates and Erasmus,[2] which help students to have experience abroad and reinforce mobility of possible qualified workforce. In this sense we could argue that we are talking about a certain type of individuals: European people who have the right to travel and settle down in hosting countries where they are accepted with almost the same rights as the local citizens without any specific discrimination. Apparently, it seems that there are two different kinds of migrations which are called by different names: extra-European migrants without a large variety of rights and European migrants who have the advantage of all the European

[1] 'The UN Migration Agency (IOM) defines a migrant as any person who is moving or has moved across an international border or within a State away from his/her habitual place of residence, regardless of (1) the person's legal status; (2) whether the movement is voluntary or involuntary; (3) what the causes for the movement are; or (4) what the length of the stay is' (United Nations 2021). I am aware of the different meanings that the term migrant can assume (see the case of refugee, expat, immigrant, emigrant) but I included all these categories in the UN definition of 'migrant' to maintain consistency and clarity in the reasoning.

[2] The Erasmus (later substituted by Erasmus +) (Erasmus + 2021) and the Socrates (Cordis 2014) Programs were developed by the European Commission starting in 1987 and in 1994. Both programs intended to facilitate the students' mobility within the European Union.

equivalencies. In the second case, these individuals recall a different kind of European mobility which is not led by work necessity but rather by other choices. Pichler (2006) and Quadrelli (2014) call these migrants 'cittadini mobili' (mobile citizens). They are migrants who are more educated than migrants of the past, moving abroad for choices which differ from the economic one. These people are still connected with their country of origin and also easily integrate in the society of the hosting country. Caneva (2016: 202) states that they are representatives of a new kind of migration (Smith and Favell 2006; King and Skeldon 2010) which is a transnational *habitus* (Bourdieu 1986). These migrants are not listed in the group of traditional migration as it was known in the past or in these days from the Southern to the Northern part of the world.

Contemporary historiographical scholarship production has identified three big Italian migration processes: the big diaspora of the end of the nineteenth century, the period between the First and the Second World War and the diaspora from the end of the Second World War until the 1970s. Scholars research the analogies and differences between the diasporas of the past and contemporary migrations. Pelaggi (2011) claims that in the past Italians migrated for economic reasons and the country to where they wanted to migrate was chosen based on the facility to access it and the presence of *catena migratoria* (chain migration) (Pugliese 2018: 1688).[3] Modern migration is multifaceted and characterized by different typologies of causes which bring people to migrate (better quality of life, study, family, work) (Tirabassi and del Prà 2014; Caneva 2016). These elements make it different from migration of the past which was mainly economic (Ricciardi 2018). While the migrant of the past was, following the public opinion's stereotype[4] poor, with a suitcase at the train station, the new diaspora seems to be more fluid, with a larger mobility, more open to move in search of a higher quality of life.

[3] 'Chain migration can be defined as that movement in which prospective migrants learn of opportunities, are provided with transportation, and have initial accommodation and employment arranged by means of primary social relationships with previous migrants' (MacDonald and MacDonald 1964: 82).

[4] See the photographs published on *L'Illustré* in the 1960s and 1970s.

Despite these differences, other scholars add that they find strong similarities between the old and modern diasporas. In their view, migrants were in both cases part of transnational social networks which characterized the trans-Atlantic migration of the end of the nineteenth century. In their opinion, this transnational dimension is not a specific, unique characteristic of the modern globalized society but existed already in the past (Gabaccia 2000; Corti 2011).

According to Caneva (2016), the characteristics of the global contemporary society with accessible mobility, low-cost flights and no border restrictions within the EU have modified some aspects of the modern diaspora if compared to the same one of the past. One clear aspect, also confirmed by my practice and interviews, is that it is not possible to identify the new diaspora simply as a *brain drain phenomenon*. It is important to go beyond these stereotypes and understand that the reality is more complex than one might initially think. There has been a tendency by the media to simplify the situation and identify the reasons for this new diaspora with the incompetence of Italian politicians who badly manage the country and not with a more general economic and socio-cultural crisis (Gjergji 2015: 17). While a *brain drain* phenomenon has really taken place, we have to acknowledge that there are also other aspects which are a consistent part of this new Italian diaspora.

Studies show that these migrants are representative of innovative forms of migration (Smith and Favell 2006; King and Skeldon 2010; Caneva 2016) with a larger spatial mobility which involves different social classes (Faist 2013: 1637–1638; Recchi 2013). European citizens are allowed to move within the European Union borders with an easy mobility and access to jobs and social opportunities. However, as reflected on articles published in Swiss magazines in the period between 2006 and 2019, this does not seem to be the case for migrants coming from countries less rich than the hosting nations. Romanian or Portuguese migrants, for example, while having the same rights as other EU citizens, seem to have more complicated dynamics of integration similar to those ones that Italian migrants had to face when they moved to the Swiss Confederation in the 1960s and 1970s. The migration and mobility phenomenon is more complex than we could initially think. The European Union is not a monolithic entity but more like a structure which reacts to the global migration phenomenon in different ways depending on the categories of migrants. Therefore, the recent Italian diaspora in Europe has to be studied in light of broader reflections on mobility and globalization.

According to the *Office Federal de la Statistique*,[5] in 2020 Italians were still the largest group of migrants in Switzerland and in 2022 have been passed only by Germans.[6] While the new Italian diaspora is a very complex and multifaceted process and it is not really properly visually represented through the media, the aim of this work was to find ways to creatively rethink photographic portraiture of contemporary Italian migrants who are resident in the area along the *arc lémanique* between Lausanne and Geneva. I had initially thought to develop my study on Switzerland as a whole. I then realized that planning my research on the entire Swiss confederation would have been too broad and difficult also considering all the different characteristics of each canton. On the contrary, I had to concentrate my scope on an area which is very unique for the profile of its residents in the Swiss context. The region between Geneva and Lausanne along the Geneva Lake is part of the French-speaking area of Switzerland and is comprised of the Geneva and Vaud cantons. It is populated by international organizations like the UN, the UEFA, the IOC, the FIBA and global corporations like Nestlé, Richemont, and Phillip Morris International. As a consequence of this phenomenon, during the last fifty years, these international employees have been integrated with the local Swiss population. The *arc lémanique* region is, therefore, very international and different from other Swiss regions. Like many other nationalities, Italians have massively migrated to this area. Through the case study of recent Italian migrants living in the *arc lémanique* area, this research wants to contribute to documenting an important phase of contemporary humanity when migration is still a crucial and controversial issue. It is an essential point of this practice-based work to rethink and render visible the complex notion of the cultural identity of recent Italian migrants of the French speaking part of Switzerland. These migrants hold an identity in flux, which is different

[5] https://www.bfs.admin.ch/bfs/en/home/statistics/population/migration-integration/foreign.html

[6] https://www.bfs.admin.ch/bfs/en/home/statistics/population/migration-integration/international-migration.html

from the contemporary public's understanding of migration and identity. Due to the time–space compression caused by globalization and to the *meditérranéisation* of Switzerland, the recent Italian migration in the Swiss confederation is not a highly visible phenomenon. Italians and Swiss people have become more similar today when compared to their ancestors of the 1960s and 1970s. I am referring here not only to their habits but also to their clothing and their physical aspect. It is, thus, very complicated to visually represent with photographic portraits the cultural identity of a population of migrants like Italians who are today not much visually different from the Swiss. As explained in the following chapters, this research wants to suggest a method developed through a creative practice that helps to document this transformation. An important step in this process is the reference to visual connections to the native cultural identity of Italian migrants. In the 1960s and 1970s, a small group of photographers were interested in documenting the process of Italian migration and the workers' conditions in Switzerland.[7] The majority of these photographers took images on the topic but never worked in a systematic way on a body of work with the aim of producing a book or an exhibition.[8] Migration from Italy to Switzerland in the early years of the twenty-first century has not yet been documented through photography with a systematic approach. The images produced as a result of this research are, to my knowledge, the first ones depicting the cultural identity of this new Italian diaspora and its *Italianity*. While being aware of the regional differences (and regions themselves can be vastly diverse), and the diverse minority groups that Italians are as well, I had to concentrate on a shared cultural background which could be felt as common and try to visually represent it. How could *Italianity* be visually represented? What is the meaning of *Italianity*?

[7] See for example the catalogues of the exhibitions 'Il lungo addio' (Bachmann 2003), *Ricordi e stima – Fotografia e storia orale della migrazione italiana in Svizzera dal secondo dopoguerra fino agli anni 80* (Alghisi et al. 2016) or *Nous, saisonniers, saisonnières…Genève 1931-2019* (Brux 2019) with photographs by Giambattista Colombo, Tano D'Amico, Christian Kænzig, Anita Niesz, Pia Zanetti.

[8] To my knowledge, the only case is represented by the work of Jean Mohr for the book *A Seventh Man* (Berger and Mohr 2010).

As stated by Richard Sennett (2011: 58) and confirmed by Arjun Appadurai (1996: 41, 147, 161, 163), cultural identity cannot coincide only with the ethnical, geographical and political borders of one nation: 'the food people eat, how they move when they dance, the dialects they speak, the precise forms of their prayers, these are the constituent elements of national life' (Sennett 2011: 58). All these aspects happen in one territory and, therefore, this place becomes the synonym of cultural identity. However, this concept has to be broader and linked to rituals, practices and customs connected to an imagined community (Anderson 1991). 'We need to think ourselves beyond the nation', stated Appadurai (1996: 158). The creation of a cultural unity can still exist once people move abroad like in the case of Italian migrants in Switzerland who preserve their *Italianity*. However, there are multiple aspects of *Italianity*.[9] Silvana Patriarca (2010: 6) defines this characteristic as a 'complex of predispositions that become part of the public and political attitudes of a population'. In the past, the concept of *Italianity* was linked to the idea of nation (Scaffai and Valsangiacomo 2018: 13) and influenced by politics (Patriarca 2010: 6). According to Ruggiero Romano (1997: 12), it is difficult to link the idea of *Italianity* to a nation. The concept of *Italianity* has to be found in the values of the different local practices (food, cultural, religious and social practices) more than in the consequences of important political and historical events. The title of his work, *Paese Italia*, highlights the fact that in his opinion it is better to refer to Italy as a country (*paese*) more than a nation. It is in this sense that I refer to Italians. It is then clear how complex is the concept of *Italianity*.

Valsangiacomo (Scaffai and Valsangiacomo 2018: 11–22) confirms that there are different meanings of *Italianity*. It is a concept which has changed during the years. Starting from the 1980s, Italian society has improved the welfare level. Along with it, Italian culture and Italian products have reached a high level of global diffusion. Italian communities have changed: the first old generation of migrants (like the 1960s and

[9] For other works related to the definition of *Italianity* see (Corti 2011; Balicco 2015; Bassetti 2015). While not using the term *Italianity*, Barthes (1980b: 281) gives a definition of *Italianicity* (where the adjective *Italian* becomes a noun with the suffix *-icity*): '*Italianicity* is not Italy, it is the condensed essence of everything that could be Italian, from spaghetti to painting.'

1970s in Switzerland) have integrated, the second and third generations have developed a controversial relationship with Italy but not necessarily negative with their perception of *Italianity*. Therefore, *Italianity* has a multi-layered meaning which comes from different experiences, that of one who sees Italy from outside and the other one of those who are in Italy and therefore see it from the inside. All these experiences contribute to generate a narrativity of *Italianity* which goes beyond the traditional means of literature and verbal communication and involves the concept of cultural identity. Having the same cultural identity could be interpreted as belonging to distinctive ethnic, racial, linguistic, religious and national culture and place (Hall 1996: 596). The concept of cultural identity could be associated with the feeling of being part of the same nation. When referring to Italian migrants in Switzerland, what do we specifically mean? Are Italian migrants in Switzerland identifiable as a national group?[10] It is important to understand the concept of nation under the cultural point of view in the postmodernism era of globalization. There has been a general tendency to describe the nation in restrictive ways: if, on the one hand, nation could be identified as a repressive ideological apparatus (Foucault 2014), on the other hand, it could also be defined as the 'incipient or emergent expression of the "national-popular" sentiment preserved in a radical memory' (Bhabha 1990: 3). Nation has been described not as a community given only by race or religion, dynasty, geography or language but also as a spiritual principle characterized by the same memories, the desire of living together. 'The modern nation is therefore a historical result brought about by a series of convergent facts' (Renan 1990: 12). It is probably reasonable to say that national identities are the result of the combination of the modern concept of nation state and the ancient idea of *nation* in its literal meaning of 'place of origin', 'birth' (Brennan 1990: 45). Being part of the same nation could, then, mean being member of a political state and being identified with a specific national culture (Hall 1996: 616). The national culture is built on stories and memories which are imagination constructions of the present

[10] See also in this regard literature on Italian diaspora in Britain (Sponza 1988; Colpi 1991; Sprio 2013). On the meaning of diaspora more in general and its relationship with media and society, ethnic identity, race, class and gender, globalization and immigration see (Retis and Tsagarousianou 2019).

based on the past. The distinction between national identities, then, could be identified on how these imagination constructions differ one from the other. Benedict Anderson defined national identity as an "imagined community" (Anderson 1991). With the phenomenon of globalization (in particular in recent years with the extensive use of social media), there is a compression of time and space. 'The world feels smaller and distances shorter' (Hall 1996: 619).

From the sixteenth to the nineteenth centuries, Switzerland was a country where migrants regularly moved (Arlettaz and Arlettaz 2004). After the constitution of the Federal State in 1848 and the beginning of the construction of the railway infrastructures of Gotthard, Simplon and Lötschberg, Italians started to arrive in Switzerland (Fibbi 2011: 211). From that moment, the Italian diaspora to Switzerland never stopped and in the twentieth-century Italian migrants were one of the main components of the foreigners' presence in the Swiss Confederation (Ricciardi 2018).[11] When Italians started to migrate to Switzerland after the end of the Second World War, they were the largest community of migrants in the Swiss Confederation (Cerutti 1994). They largely contributed to the prosperity of Switzerland but always as external help and hence never really integrated into Swiss society (Castelnuovo-Frigessi 1977; Castelnuovo-Frigessi 1978; Agelli 1985; Stohr 2013: 47). Italian workers were seen mostly as production elements more than people (Stohr 2013: 48). By the end of the 1970s, the protests of Italian migrants about their working conditions and rights brought Switzerland to change this unequal relationship.[12] With the 1974 oil crisis and fewer job opportunities in Switzerland, most of the Italians that were permanent residents decided to move back to Italy (Haug 1980; Maiolino 2013: 152). However at the beginning of the twenty-first century, Italians started again to migrate to the Swiss Confederation. According to official data of the Swiss Confederation from December 2018 (Statistique des étrangers à fin décembre 2018), the Italian migrants represented the biggest community of foreigners permanently resident in Switzerland, nearly 4% of

[11] See also (Halter et al. 2004).

[12] See the documentary works of Alvaro Bizzarri (1970, 1972, 1974, 1977, 1990, 2009), Alexander J. Seiler (1965), and Katharine Dominicé and Luc Peter (2010).

the Swiss population (313,725 in front of the Germans (301,548) and the Portuguese (268,067).[13] These data were confirmed in 2020 (FSO 2021) and only in 2022 Italians became the second community after the Germans.[14]

According to some scholars (Bolzman et al. 2003; Maiolino 2013: 152–158), after the massive return of Italians in their country of origin in the 1970s (Seiler 2002) and politics of integration (Niederberger 2004) applied by the Swiss institutions, there has been a growing acceptance of the Italians who have decided to stay in Switzerland. The general image of Italians has improved because of the economic growth of the country and because Italians have managed to give a different content to their presence in Switzerland. The feeling of arrogance and superiority played by the Swiss has been replaced by a sense of *meditérranéisation*. This is a term introduced by Angelo Maiolino (2013: 154) to explain the gradual acceptance by Swiss society of Italian cultural aspects (pizza, caffè espresso, fashion, lifestyle, spirit of enterprise). The *meditérranéisation* shows a gradual emancipation of the Italian community in Switzerland. Children of the first generation of migrants of the 1960s–1970s, *secondos* (Wessendorf 2007) have contributed to the improvement of the reputation of Italians in Switzerland and are also part of the managerial class (Ruspini 2010). It is probably the first generation of Italians who are not yet completely integrated. Still attached to the traditions of their country of origin, they are less well connected with the Swiss environment. They live in the memory of a country of origin which has in the meanwhile changed.[15] They live in a cultural *utopos*, a non-place (Maiolino 2013: 156). They are people in transition from one place to the other without becoming definitely permanent. The situation of the *secondos* is different. They represent a hybrid cultural model between Italy and Switzerland. They have been defined as people in *translation* (Maiolino 2013: 156). A concept introduced by Kevin Robins (1997), Hall (1996: 629) states that

[13] www.sem.admin.ch/sem/fr/home/publiservice/statistik/auslaenderstatistik/archiv/2015/12.html

[14] https://www.bfs.admin.ch/bfs/fr/home/statistiques/population/migration-integration/migration-internationale.html

[15] See (Berger and Mohr 2010).

being in *translation* 'describes those identity formations which cut across and intersect natural frontiers, and which are composed of people who have been *dispersed* forever from their homelands.' The second generation of Italian migrants are considered able to translate two different cultures (Durous 2010; Cattacin et al. 2016). Starting from 2007, data shows a constant increase of Italians who decide to migrate (ISTAT 2016b). While it is difficult to have exact measurable data because of the free circulation of people in the European Union (EU) and the EFTA (European Free Trade Association) of which Switzerland is member, in 2016 there has been an increase of migrants with a university degree compared to the year before (ISTAT 2016a). Despite the fact that mobility could cause a difficult collection of realistic data of migration in Europe, academic literature has pointed out that this recent migration has been characterized by the *brain drain, brain gain* and *brain circulation* phenomenon (Beltrame 2007; Docquier and Rapoport 2007; Dahinden 2008; Friedrich and Schultz 2008; Cassar 2010; Dequiedt and Zenou 2011; Boeri et al. 2012; Tirabassi and del Prà 2014; Minneci 2015; Tintori and Romei 2017; Cattacin et al. 2022). There might be an over-estimation of this process (Franchi 2017) but the market change, the demand for specific competences and the need of them in hosting countries have shown that migrants of the new millennium have a higher level of education than migrants of the 1960s–1970s.[16]

As demonstrated in the next chapters, the representation of the Italian migrant in Switzerland in the 1960s and 1970s was limited to the photojournalistic approach[17] for the documentation of the social and working condition of workers. Photographers like Giambattista Colombo (1921–2005), Anita Niesz (1925–2013), Pia Zanetti (1943), Tano D'Amico (1942), Fernand Rausser (1926–2016) and Christian Känzig (1952) have been involved in the process of documenting the migrants' situation for newspapers and magazines but never worked in a systematic way on a body of work. A selection of their images with work from other photographers has been collected in an exhibition curated by Dieter

[16] See also the documentary on the twenty-first-century Italian diaspora to London by Luca Vullo (2016).

[17] I use here the definition of photojournalistic approach given by Newton (2001).

Bachmann, *Il lungo addio—Die lange Abschied*, (Bachmann 2003) presented for several years in Italy and Switzerland. More recently, another collection of images called *Ricordi e Stima—Fotografia e storia orale della migrazione Italiana in Svizzera dal secondo dopoguerra fino agli anni 80* (Widmer 2016) on Italian migration in the 1960s, 1970s and 1980s was presented as a retrospective. A book was created after the exhibition (Alghisi et al. 2016). The only photographer who worked systematically as a photo-reporter on the migration process from Italy to Switzerland and back was Roger Wehrli. His work *Un viaggio per immagini: Italia—Germania—Svizzera e ritorno* (Wehrli 2006) has been exhibited in Italy in 2004 and 2006. All these works are concentrated on the Swiss–German region.

The visual representation of Italian migrants by photojournalists has followed stereotypes to underline their physical difference with the local Swiss population. The issue of the visual aspect of Italian migrants in Switzerland, the difference with the Swiss and the perception of them by the public opinion was remarkable in the 1960s. Referring to the visual dissimilarities between Italian migrants and Swiss people and to reinforce this point, it is interesting here to report the statement of a Swiss policeman from the Bern Canton in 1968: 'We, Swiss, do not easily accept that racial characteristics prevent assimilation. Physiognomy of Germans, Austrians or French does not differ much from ours, therefore we unconsciously accept them if only for their physical aspect. A Calabrian, with his short height, black and curly hair, will hardly be seen as a future Swiss. […] There are so many different kinds of Italians and Spanish, even in their second generation, that it is impossible to confuse them with a Swiss' (Fibbi 2011: 217). In the movie *Pane e cioccolata* (Brusati 1973), the main character Nino Garofalo, a migrant from the South of Italy, wants to become a member of the Swiss society regardless of all the difficulties and decides to dye his moustache and hair to look Swiss.[18] In times of globalization, cultural contamination, and *meditérranéisation*, contemporary Italian migrants in Switzerland seem visually less recognizable than before.

---

[18] See also the movie *Die Schweizermacher* ('The Swissmakers') (Lyssy 1978). In this acclaimed 1978 Swiss comedy film, the recently arrived Italian migrants throw their spaghetti away and pretend to be eating fondue when the immigration inspectors visit their home.

One of the most interesting aspects of the new Italian diaspora is its complexity and fluidity. The profile of the new Italian migrant is therefore not easy to frame. In a study conducted in 2017, sociologist Cristina Franchi (2017) has identified different profiles of the new Italian migrants in the largest city of the German part of Switzerland. At the moment of the research, the Italian community in Basel was the largest of the Swiss German part of the country (8436 individuals in 2016) and it was the main community of foreigners after the Germans.[19] After the big phenomenon of the seasonal workers of the 1960s and 1970s, there has been a decrease of Italian migrants in the region but, starting from the first decade of 2000s, Italians were massively returning. This data is in line with the data in the rest of Switzerland and with what I found in the *arc lémanique* area. Franchi interviewed twenty subjects who migrated to Basel starting from 2007. The economic crisis has had a fundamental role in the decision to migrate. In contrast with the simplified and romantic view of the media (and the above mentioned scholars), these migrants have been forced to migrate due to a lack of work or because of the objective struggle of planning a decent life without any income. These results are in contrast with the idea that migrating is a deliberate choice due to the desire of a stimulating new cultural offer in a fascinating foreign country. These people have been forced to leave for a lack of opportunities in their country of origin. Through this research, Franchi has identified three profiles which are similar with what we have found with the present research on twenty-first-century Italian migrants living in the *arc lémanique*. The first group lists migrants with a degree with a highly qualified career. In Franchi's case, five out of the twenty interviewed are part of this group. They come from Italy already with a position guaranteed. They have good work conditions which are largely better than what they had in Italy. Moving in one city in Switzerland is actually for them only one leg of their career during which they will very likely move to other countries. They seem to fit in the *brain drain* category or in the group of professionals who work for international companies in cities in different countries for a limited amount of time. Even though the migratory

[19] A similar situation exists in the French speaking part of Switzerland where the Italians are behind the French community in terms of numbers (FSO 2021).

experience was instigated by the economic crisis, for these individuals the choice of moving abroad is a formative decision and not strongly due to an economic discomfort. This cannot be said for the other two groups of migrants identified by Franchi (2017), aligned with the research presented in this book, which are migrants with a degree and an unstable working position in the hosting country and non-professionally qualified migrants with a good chain migration network. In the first category, there are individuals with a good level of education (usually humanistic degrees) who struggle to find a job corresponding to their exact qualification and, if they find one, have worse conditions when compared with their Swiss colleagues. Despite the fact that these subjects have different backgrounds, they share the same issues in getting integrated into an unknown context, the deep lack of confidence on the Italian job market and the difficulties in finding a job in Switzerland. They also share an ambiguous feeling of satisfaction for having found a job granting them financial autonomy and frustration for not having found a job corresponding to their specific qualifications. They also struggle in managing work and family (children). These are, then, Italians who leave their own country of origin to find an alternative, but despite the fact that they have a degree and a good level of education they end up working as waiters or in cleaning companies. In the second category fall individuals who have a medium-low education and have a migration experience in Switzerland in their family. Initially, taking advantage of the *chain migration* (Pugliese 2018), they are hosted by their relatives who had arrived in Switzerland from the 1960s until the 1980s as seasonal workers. Taking advantage of the family network, these subjects have immediately found a working position with a regular contract. In other cases, they are young people who have finished studying and want to have an experience abroad and take advantage of their family network in a foreign country. Family is therefore a key support, and these individuals seem to show a lower level of frustration compared to the other two groups of people. However, their working situation is not stable and permanent. This situation seems to contradict what is claimed by Lafleur et al. (2017: 202). According to them, there is no link between the older diaspora and the new one due to the massive number of returns to the countries of origin after the oil crisis. The interruption of the migratory flux in Switzerland, in their opinion, is purely symbolic considering the broken link between the migrant community in Switzerland and the country of origin. This aspect, according to Lafleur, Stanek and Veira, would not support the socio-cultural integration process of the new diaspora. On the contrary, Franchi (2017) remarks that there are similarities with the old migration system: in Switzerland many migrants have returned to Italy after the oil crisis, while almost half of them has remained. As reported by the Federal Statistical Office of the Swiss Confederation (FSO 2021), before the oil crisis there were around 600.000 Italians in Switzerland. Until the 2007 revamp of the new diaspora, the number of Italians never fell below 300.000. This aspect contributed to guarantee the continuity with the following diasporas in particular for those migrants with a low level of education and a family network in place. While some scholars (Baldassar and Pyke 2014; Coso and Ortega-Rivera 2016; Bartolini et al. 2017) still confirm that the new diaspora is only young and talented (*brain drain* phenomenon), this study by Franchi confirms what I have found also through my research and practice: the new diaspora is more complex and heterogeneous than generally thought.

The contemporary Italian migrants of the French-speaking part of Switzerland hold a cultural identity in flux. Limiting this phenomenon to the *brain drain* narrative would be simplistic (Caneva 2016; Franchi 2017; Sanfilippo 2017; Pugliese 2018; Licata 2019). While on one hand it is true that part of the new group of migrants is composed of talented, young, educated individuals who were looking for a more stimulating life experience, on the other hand there is a large, consistent part of the new diaspora composed of people with different titles and different levels of education who were struggling to find a decent job in their country of origin and felt the need to migrate. This is an aspect that has only been studied in recent years. There are some differences between the old and the new diaspora of Italians who moved to Switzerland. The level of mobility for migrants in the 1960s and 1970s was more complicated than the recent one. The rights to be resident abroad were much reduced if compared to the possibilities offered today after the bilateral agreement between Europe and Switzerland. Most of the time, the seasonal workers of the Schwarzenbach years had guaranteed work even if it was often only for nine months with the possibility of being renewed yearly. The majority of the new migrants do not seem to have a guaranteed job. While it could seem that there is a repetition of migration model of people always pushed to migrate as a consequence of an economic crisis and unemployment, starting again from 2007, Italians migrated in the same way that the earlier migrants did but the social, political and work context have changed. If compared to the 1960s and 1970s publications, the reduced quantity of articles and images related to the recent diaspora proofs that there is a different perception towards the new migration process. Italians today are photographically less visible than the earlier waves. The visual familiarity of a symbolism system evoked by Boltanski (2018) has changed if compared with the images published on *L'Illustré* in the years between 1960 and 1970. The recent image production related to the new Italian diaspora to Switzerland has changed influenced by the new political, historical and ideological context (Johnson 2011) and in photographic practice. This seems to be evident after the research conducted on recent publications of Swiss magazines. Visual signs of migration like the suitcase have disappeared in the photographs published between 2006 and 2019. Strong importance is given to the composition, the use of the light and the face. Due to the time-space compression caused by globalization and *meditérranéisation* of Switzerland, the recent Italian migration to the Swiss confederation is not a visually recognizable phenomenon. Italians are today more integrated to Swiss people if compared to their ancestors who migrated in the 1960s. They more easily connect to different worlds and contribute to sharing habits, traditions and ways of being which can eventually become part of a new living context.[20] Nevertheless, migration involves a shift of cultural identity for the individual. This situation increases the complexity of the cultural re-affirmation of the individual and is one of the reasons why it is complicated to represent the contemporary Italian cultural identity in Switzerland with photographic portraiture (Fig. 1.1).

[20] See (Cattacin et al. 2022).

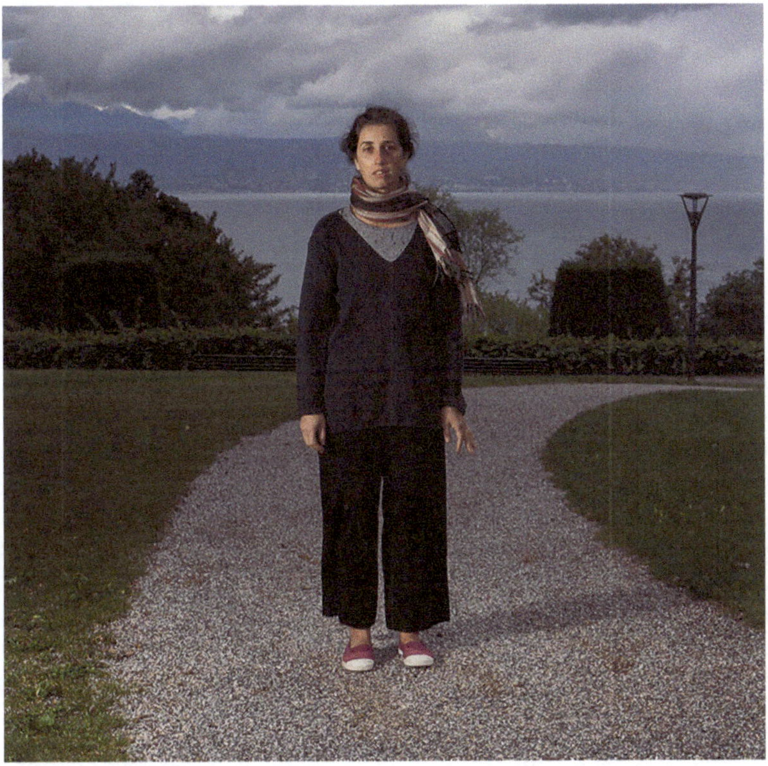

Fig. 1.1 Francesco Arese Visconti, *LP*, 2017

References

Agelli, T. (1985). *Passaporti, Prego!: Ricordi e Testimonianze Di Emigrati Italiani.* Zurigo: Zurigo : Federazione colonie libere italiane in Svizzera.

Alghisi, G. et al., eds. (2016). *Grazie a voi: ricordi e stima – Fotografien zur Italienischen Migration in der Schweiz.* Zürich: Limmat Verlag.

Anderson, B. (1991). *Imagined Communities: Reflections on the Origin and Spread of Nationalism.* London: Verso.

Appadurai, A. (1996). *Modernity at Large: Cultural Dimensions of Globalization.* Minneapolis: University of Minnesota Press.

Arlettaz, G., and Silvia Arlettaz. (2004). *La Suisse et Les Étrangers. Immigration et Formation Nationale (1848–1933).* Lausanne: Editions Antipodes.

Bachmann, D. (ed.) (2003). *Il Lungo Addio – Der Lange Abschied.* Zurich: Limmat Verlag.
Baldassar, L. and Joanne Pyke. (2014). "Intra-Diaspora Knowledge Transfer and 'New' Italian Migration." In *International Migration*, iv, 52, pp. 128–43.
Balicco, D. (2015). *Made in Italy e cultura. Indagine sull'identità italiana contemporanea.* Palermo: Palumbo.
Barthes, R. (1980b). "Rhetoric of the Image." In Trachtenberg, A. (ed.) (1980). *Classic Essays on Photography*. New Haven: Leete's Island Books.
Bartolini, L., Ruby Gropas and Anna Triandafyllidou. (2017). "Drivers of highly skilled mobility from Southern Europe: escaping the crisis and emancipating oneself." In *Journal of Ethnic and Migration Studies*, iv, 43, pp. 652–73.
Bassetti, P. (2015). *Svegliamoci italici! Manifesto per un futuro glocal.* Venezia: Marsilio.
Beltrame, L. (2007). *Realtà e Retorica Del Brain Drain in Italia. Stime Statistiche, Definizioni Pubbliche e Interventi Politici.* Torino: Università degli Studi di Trento, Dipartimento di Sociologia e Ricerca Sociale.
Berger, J. and Jean Mohr. (2010). *A Seventh Man : A Book of Images and Words about the Experience of Migrant Workers in Europe*. London and New York: Verso.
Bhabha, H. (ed.) (1990). *Nation and Narration.* London and New York: Routledge.
Bizzarri, A. (1970). *Il Treno Del Sud.* Switzerland: Bertrand Theubet, Les Amis d'Alvaro Bizzarri/TSR/AB.
———. (1972). *Lo Stagionale*. Switzerland: Bertrand Theubet, Les Amis d'Alvaro Bizzarri/TSR/AB.
———. (1974). *Il Rovescio Della Medaglia.* Switzerland: Bertrand Theubet, Les Amis d'Alvaro Bizzarri/TSR/AB.
———. (1977). *Pagine Di Vita Dell'emigrazione*. Switzerland: Bertrand Theubet, Les Amis d'Alvaro Bizzarri/TSR/AB.
———. (1990). *Touchol.* Switzerland: Bertrand Theubet, Les Amis d'Alvaro Bizzarri/TSR/AB.
———. (2009). "Accolti a Braccia Chiuse - Empfang Mit Verschränkten Armen - Accueillis à bras fermés: lavoratori immigrati in Svizzera negli anni '70." *Empfang Mit Verschränkten Armen*. Lausanne: Climage.
Boeri, T., Herbert Brücker, and Frédéric Doquier. (2012). *Brain Drain and Brain Gain: The Global Competition to Attract High-Skilled Migrants.* Oxford: Oxford University Press.
Boltanski, L. (2018). "La retorica della figura." In *Un'arte media – Saggio sugli usi sociali della fotografia*, ed. Pierre Bourdieu. Milano: Meltemi.

Bolzman, C., Rosita Fibbi and Marie Vial. (2003). *Secondas – Secondos: le processus d'intégration des jeunes adultes issus de la migration espagnole et italienne en Suisse*. Zürich: Seismo.

Bourdieu, P. (1986). "Habitus, code et codification." In *Actes de La Recherche En Sciences Sociales*, 64, 40–44.

Brennan, T. (1990). "The National Longing for Form." In *Nation and Narration*, edited by Homi Bhabha, 333. London and New York: Routledge.

Brusati, F. (1973). *Pane e cioccolata*. Italy: Lucky Red.

Brux, T. (curator). (2019). "Nous, saisonniers, saisonnières…Genève 1931–2019." http://rosabrux.org/category/saisonnier-ere-s/. Access 11.01.2021.

Caneva, E. (2016). "The New Italian Emigration: What we Know, How We Talk of It." In *Cambio - Rivista sulle trasformazioni sociali*. VI, 11. 195–208.

Cassar, L. (2010). "Should I Stay or Should I Go? An Institutional Approach to Brain Drain." 489. Zürich.

Castelnuovo-Frigessi, D. (1977). *Elvezia, Il Tuo Governo: Operai Italiani Emigrati in Svizzera*. Torino: Einaudi.

———. (1978). *La Condition Immigrée : Les Ouvriers Italiens En Suisse*. Edited by Lorette Coen, Gérard Delaloye, Jean Ziegler, and Silvia Kimmeier. Lausanne: Ed. d'En bas.

Cattacin, S., Rosita Fibbi, and Philippe Wanner. (2016). "La Nouvelle Seconde Génération. Introduction Au Numéro Spécial." *Swiss Journal of Sociology* 42 (2): 209–17.

Cattacin, S., Irene Pellegrini and Toni Ricciardi. (2022). *Dalla valigia di cartone al web. La rete sociale degli italiani in Svizzera*. Roma: Donzelli Editore.

Cerutti, M. (1994). *Un secolo di emigrazione italiana in Svizzera (1870-1970), attraverso le fonti dell'Archivio federale.*

Colpi, T. (1991). *Italians Forward: Visual History of the Italian Community of Great Britain*. Mainstrem Publishing.

Cordis. (2014). "Community action programme, SOCRATES, 1995 – 1999)." www.cordis.europa.eu. Available from https://cordis.europa.eu/programme/id/ET-SOCRATES-1. Access 11.05.2021

Corti, P. (2011). "La nuova mobilità degli italiani e le migrazioni internazionali." In Miranda, A. and A. Signorelli (eds.), *Pensare e ripensare le migrazioni*. Palermo: Sellerio editore: 120–134.

Coso, V., Elena and Enrique Ortega-Rivera. (2016). "How the Integration of Italians and Spaniards into the Swiss Labor Market Changed over Time." In *Highlights*, iv, pp. 18–31.

Dahinden, J. (2008). "Die Mobilität von Hochqualifizierten Fachkräften." Zürich.
Dequiedt, V. and Yves Zenou (2011). "International Migration, Imperfect Information, and Brain Drain." *Journal of Development Economics*, 2013, 102, 62–78.
Docquier, F., and Hillel Rapoport. (2007). "Skilled Migration: The Perspective of Developing Countries." 2873.
Dominicé, K., and Luc Peter. (2010). *Les Années Schwartzenbach*. Switzerland: Connaissance 3.
Dubucs, H., Thomas Pfirsch, Ettore Recchi and Camille Schmoll. (2016). "'Je suis un Italien de Paris:' Italian migrants' incorporation in a European capital city." In *Journal of Ethnic and Migration Studies*. 43, 4. 578–595.
Durous, R. (2010). *Des Ritals En Terre Romande*. Vevey: Editions de l'Aire.
Erasmus +. (2021). "Erasmus +." www.ec.europa.eu. Available from https://ec.europa.eu/programmes/erasmus-plus/node_en. Access 11.05.2021.
Faist, T. (2013). "The mobility turn: a new paradigm for the social sciences?." In *Ethnic and Racial Studies*, 36:11, 1637–1646.
Fibbi, R. (2011). Come siamo diventati biondi: L'immigrazione italiana in Svizzera. *Limes. Rivista Italiana Di Geopolitica (L'importanza Di Essere Svizzera. I Quaderni Speciali Di Limes)*. No. 3, Pp.211–220.
Foucault, M. (2014). *Sorvegliare e punire. Nascita della prigione*. Torino: Einaudi.
Franchi, C. (2017). "Non Solo Brain Drain : Il Caso Svizzero Di Basilea." *Altreitalie*, no. luglio-dicembre: 95–115.
Friedrich, K., and Andrea Schultz. (2008). *Brain Drain Oder Brain Circulation?: Konsequenzen Und Perspektiven Der Ost-West-Migration*. Forum Ifl. Leibniz-Institut für Länderkunde.
FSO. (2021). "Federal Statistical Office - Foreign Population." https://www.bfs.admin.ch/bfs/en/home/statistics/population/migration-integration/foreign.html. Access 11.04.2022.
Gabaccia, D. R. (2000). *Italy's Many Diasporas*. Abingdon-on-Thames: Routledge.
Gjergji, I. (ed.). (2015). *La nuova emigrazione italiana. Cause, mete e figure sociali*. Venezia: Edizioni Ca' Foscari.
Hall, S. (1996). "The Question of Cultural Identity." *Modernity: An Introduction to Modern Societies* 4: 596–632.
Halter, E., Giovanni Casagrande, Gé Arlettaz, and Silvia Arlettaz. (2004). *Gli Italiani in Svizzera : Un Secolo Di Emigrazione*. Bellinzona: Casagrande.
Haug, W. (1980). "...Und Es Kamen Menschen." Ausländerpolitik Und Fremdarbeit in Der Schweitz, 1914–1980. Basel: Z-Verlag.

ISTAT. (2016a). "Migrazioni Internazionali e Interne Della Popolazione Residente." 2016. https://www.istat.it/it/archivio/206675. Access 20.11.2016.

———. (2016b). "Migrazioni Internazionali e Interne Della Popolazione Residente." *ISTAT*, no. Novembre 2017.

Johnson, H. (2011). "Click to Donate: visual images, constructing victims and imagining the female refugee." In *Third World Quaterly*, 32:6, 1015–1037.

King, R. and Ronald Skeldon. (2010). "Mind the Gap!' Integrating Approaches to Internal and International Migration." In *Journal of Ethnic and Migration Studies*, 36, 10: 1619–1646.

Lafleur, J-M., Mikolaj Stanek and Alberto Veira. (2017). *South-North labour migration within the crisis-affected European Union. New patterns, new contexts and new challenge*. Basel: Springer Open.

Licata, D. (ed.). (2019). *Rapporto Italiani nel Mondo.* Todi: Tau Editrice.

Lyssy, R. (1978). *Die Schweizermacher*. Switzerland: Marcel Hoehen.

MacDonald, J. S. and Leatrice D. MacDonald. "Chain Migration Ethnic Neighbourhood Formation and Social Networks." In *The Milbank Memorial Fund Quarterly*, Jan. 1964, Vol. 42, No. 1 (Jan., 1964), pp. 82–97.

Maiolino, A. (2013). "La construction des identités dans le débat politique." In La Barba et al. (ed.). *La migration italienne dans la Suisse d'après-guerre.* Lausanne: Editions Antipodes.

McKay, S. (2015). "Young Italians in London and in the UK." In *La nuova emigrazione italiana. Cause, mete e figure sociali.* Venezia: Edizioni Ca' Foscari. 71–82.

Minneci, F. (2015). "If There Were a 'Highly Skilled Red Octopus'? The Case of Italian Highly Skilled Mobility at Times of Crisis." *Economics and Sociology*, III (8): 170–82.

Newton, J. (2001). *The Burden of Visual Truth: The Role of Photojournalism in Mediating Reality*. New York: Routledge.

Niederberger, J. M. (2004). *Ausgrenzen, Assimilieren, Integrieren. Die Entwicklung Einer Schweizerischen Integrationspolitik.* Zürich: Seismo Verlag.

Patriarca, S. (2010). *Italianità. La costruzione del carattere nazionale.* Bari: Editori Laterza.

Pelaggi, Stefano. (2011). *L'altra Italia. Emigrazione storica e mobilità giovanile a confronto.* Roma: edizioni Nuova Cultura.

Pichler, Edith. (2006), "50 anni di immigrazione italiana in Germania: transitori, inclusi/esclusi o cittadini europei?" In *Altre Italie*, 6–18.

Pugliese, E. (2018). *Quelli che se ne vanno: la nuova emigrazione italiana.* Bologna: Il Mulino.

Quadrelli, F. (2014), "Una nuova fase per l'emigrazione italiana?" In Livi B., Massimo and Corrado Bonifazi (Eds.). (2014). *Le migrazioni internazionali ai tempi della crisi.* Firenze: Associazione Neodemos. 100–103.

Recchi, E. (2013), *Senza frontiere. La libera circolazione delle persone in Europa.* Bologna: Il Mulino.

Renan, E. (1990). "What Is a Nation?" In Bhabha, Homi (ed.). *Nation and Narration.* London and New York: Routledge.

Retis, J. and Roza Tsagarousianou (eds.) (2019). *The Handbook of Diasporas, Media, and Culture.* Hoboken: John Wiley & Sons.

Ricciardi, T. (2018). *Breve Storia Dell'emigrazione Italiana in Svizzera.* Roma: Donzelli editore.

Robins, K. (1997). "Tradition and Translation: National Culture in Its Global Context." In *Enterprise and Heritage: Crosscurrents of National Culture,* 21–44. London: Rout.

Romano, R. (1997), *Paese Italia. Venti secoli di identità.* Roma: Donzelli.

Ruspini, P. (2010). *Second Generation Migrants in Switzerland (Including an Exploratory Fieldwork in the Ticino Canton).* Lugano: Institute of Communication and Public Policy (ICPP).

Sanfilippo, M. (2017). "La nuova emigrazione italian (2000 – 2017): il quadro storico e storiografico." In *Studi Emigrazione,* LIV, n. 207.

Scaffai, N. and Nelly Valsangiacomo (eds.). (2018). *À l'italienne. Narrazioni dell'italianità dagli anni Ottanta a oggi.* Roma: Carocci Editore.

Seiler, A. J. (1965). *Siamo Italiani – Gespräche Mit Italienischen Gastarbeitern.* Switzerland: EVZ.

———. (2002). *Vento di Settembre.* Switzerland: Filmcoopi.

Sennett, R. (2011). *The Foreigner - Two Essays on Exile* (2017th ed.). London: Notting Hill Editions.

Smith, M. P. and Adrian Favell (Eds.). (2006). *The Human Face of Global Mobility.* New Brunswick (NJ): Transaction.

Sponza, L. (1988). *Italian Immigrants in Nineteenth-Century Britain.* Leicester: Leicester UP.

Sprio, M. (2013). *Migrant Memories - Cultural History, Cinema and the Italian Post-War Diaspora in Britain.* Bern: Peter Lang.

Stohr, C. (2013). "Des représentations au aispositif de régulation." In La Barba et al. (ed.). *La migration italienne dans la Suisse d'après-guerre,* 390. Lausanne: Editions Antipodes.

Tintori, G., and Valentina Romei. (2017). "Emigration from Italy After the Crisis: The Shortcomings of the Brain Drain Narrative." In Lafleur, J. M. and Mikolaj Stanek (eds.). *South-North Migration of UE Citizens in Times of Crisis*. 49–64. Cham: Springer International Publishing.

Tirabassi, M., and Alvise del Prà. (2014). *La meglio Italia. Le mobilità italiane nel XXI Secolo*. Torino: Accademia University Press. https://books.openedition.org/aaccademia/509. Access 21.05.2018.

United Nations. (2021). "Migration." www.un.org. Available from https://www.un.org/en/sections/issues-depth/migration/index.html. Access 19.02.2021.

Vullo, L. (2016). *Influx: Documentary*. UK - Italy: IMDbPro.

Wehrli, R. (2006). *Un Viaggio per Immagini: Italia – Germania – Svizzera e Ritorno*. Genoa: Centro Culturale Europeo.

Wessendorf, S. (2007). "'Roots Migrants:' Transnationalism and 'Return' among Second-Generation Italians in Switzerland." *Journal of Ethnic and Migration Studies* 33 (7): 1083–1102.

Widmer, M. (ed.). (2016). *Ricordi e stima – Fotografia e storia orale della migrazione italiana in Svizzera dal secondo dopoguerra fino agli anni '80*. St. Gallen: Historisches und Völkerkundemuseum.

2

1960–1970 Photographic Representation of Italian Migrants on the *Arc Lémanique*

Abstract This chapter investigates how the Italian diaspora of the 1960s/1970s was represented in French-speaking illustrated Swiss magazines. The research concentrated on the archives of *L'Illustré*, the only and most popular illustrated magazine of the *Suisse Romande* in those years. This magazine often featured seasonal workers identified as migrants. The purpose of the chapter is to clarify how this visual representation was influenced by the political, sociological and economical Swiss and Italian contexts.

Keywords Photographic portraiture • Suisse Romande • L'Illustré • Migrants • Visual semiotics

Introduction

In the process of rethinking new ways of photographic portraiture of twenty-first-century Italian migrants in the *arc lémanique* area, I had to understand how the Italian diaspora of the 1960s/1970s has been represented in French-speaking illustrated Swiss magazines of those years and

F. Arese Visconti, *The Invisible Diaspora*, Palgrave Studies in Creativity and Culture,
https://doi.org/10.1007/978-3-031-74925-4_2

how it was then later photographed between 2006 and 2019. A key point of the research was to clarify how this visual representation has been influenced by the political, sociological and economical Swiss and Italian contexts, and if these images have significant dissimilarities between these two periods. This research highlights a symbolism system and demonstrates through its findings that the production and selection of these images was based on an ideological discourse (Hall 1972). The analysis of motifs and conventions of images related to the migration phenomenon in Switzerland from the 1960s to the 1970s has the purpose of showing the reasons behind the decisions taken in the production of the photographic practice of this research. The discussion on the meaning of postures, composition, lighting, clothing in these old images produced in social contexts different from today supports the reasoning to achieve the desired message of the photographic portraits of this research. Since the work is based on images published in news printed media, the main arguments draw on Stuart Hall's considerations on the determinations of news photographs. In Hall's opinion there are two aspects of significations of news: the first one is the news value of the photographic sign, the second one is its ideological level. News values are essential in the elaboration of the story following the common-sense understandings as to what constitutes the news in a newspaper discourse. What supports the reasoning here are Hall's reflections on the ideological value of images and how this aspect is part of a more general discourse.[1] Images can build attention only if there is a background consensus knowledge, the shared knowledge of social structures. The reader can understand only if there is a foreground knowledge of news stories.[2] An event which is photographed and then selected enters the domain of ideology. This process of selection is a highly ideological procedure. Ideological values are part of the moral-political discourse in society. Newspapers and magazines have editorial lines: it is how they decide to present news. This act is very ideological. In Hall's view, these two acts, the news values and the ideological value, are close. He claims that (Hall 1972: 232) 'in practice, there is probably little or no distinction between these two aspects of news production. The

[1] Hall (1972: 241) calls it ideological universe of society, an archetypical message.

[2] Boltanski (2018: 202) stresses the same point.

editor not only looks at and selects the photo in terms of impact, dramatic meaning, unusualness, controversy but the resonance of the event also signified, etc. (formal news values): he considers at the same time how these values will be treated or 'angled'—that is, interpretatively 'coded'. This is an ideological decision. The question here is if this ideological decision is somehow linked to the myth theory of Barthes (1972). Ideology contributes to build myths in modern society. In *Mythologies*, Barthes analyses myths of our contemporary society, properties and meanings that are assigned to images of things that surround us. In his view, myths are originated in society by groups controlling communications through media and language. We perceive these meanings as part of the natural order of things. It is forgotten or hidden, Barthes states, where the meaning of signs came from and the process that transformed them. These myths generated by these groups filter the political content out of signification. Stuart Hall recalls Barthes' theory of myths when referring to the ideological level of news photographs. Hall claims that, having codes of meaning which make signification possible, news images follow the ideological universe of society. In *Image, Music, Text: The Photographic Message*, Barthes (1977) states that we have to have a historical understanding of the context when images have been taken and of when images are being interpreted. However, Hall (1972: 241) argues that images are part of universal signs otherwise called archetypical messages.

In the essay in the 1965 book *Un art moyen, essai sur les usages sociaux de la photographie* edited by Bourdieu (1965),[3] French sociologist Luc Boltanski (2018: 369) refers to the different kind of photographs which illustrate daily (*France-Soir*) and weekly (*Paris-Match*) publications in France in the 1960s (Boltanski 2018). In this process, Boltanski raises issues on Barthean's semiology and symbolism in weekly magazines. The objective quality of photography is to record events as well as press does. In his view, photography is the reflection of reality. In the daily publication, photography is important if it captures the event when it happens. The general frame is not necessarily given by the other elements present in the composition (Boltanski 2018: 200). Separated from context, the action which happens in the photograph cannot be situated without the

[3] I used the revised Italian version (Bourdieu 2018).

caption. A weekly publication (like *Paris-Match* in France or *L'Illustré* in Switzerland) has a different approach. The images which illustrate the articles don't show the event itself but they present anecdotes. These anecdotes evoke the event (Boltanski 2018: 202). Photographs have to be synthetic: characters and objects which allow a story to be told must be represented in one image. Furthermore, Boltanski claims that these photographs must be symbolic: each object present in the frame has to recall the background, the memory and synthetize the Barthean connotation of meaning. Boltanski quotes Barthes' definition of connotation[4] specifying that for *Paris-Match* journalists it is synonym of symbolism. These symbols must be present in the weekly publication's photographs. To be understandable, it is necessary that the reader could refer to a symbolism system which he can recall. The key to this symbolism has to be found in the visual familiarity with the event and its actors. Boltanski associates this visual familiarity with the Sartrean *ellipsis*.[5] In the next pages we will look at the photographs and texts from the most popular French-language Swiss magazine, *L'Illustré*, keeping in mind the idea that there are editorial lines which want to generate 'familiar recognitions'. For the reader, as stated by Hall (1972: 232), it is 'by producing in the reader "familiar recognitions," that a discourse becomes ideological'. What kind of visual symbolism was adopted in the 1960s–1970s migration photographs in *L'Illustré* and to which models do they refer? While keeping in mind these questions, after an explanation of the reasons which led to the selection of this particular period of time and the research method used for the image/text analysis, the following pages will show the five findings of the research.

---

[4] Boltanski mentions that this definition was given by Barthes in a photocopy given during a seminar on semiology at the École pratique des hautes études, 6th section, 1962–1963 (Boltanski 2018: 204).

[5] Referring to literature, Sartre (1949: 68) states that 'people of a same period and collectivity, who have lived through the same events, who have raised or avoided the same questions, have the same taste in their mouth; they have the same complicity, and there are the same corpses among them. That is why it is not necessary to write so much; there are key-words.'

Why 1960–1970?

L'Illustré is one of the oldest illustrated magazines published in the French-speaking part of Switzerland. It was founded in 1921 in Lausanne and for many years it was the only significant and popular illustrated magazine in the area. *L'Illustré* is still today a weekly publication which deals with general issues related to the Swiss Romande society. In total 572 issues of *L'Illustré* from 1960 to 1970 were analysed. I found a total of eight articles which dealt with migrant workers (not only Italians). Out of these articles, six included photographs (of which one article had no matching images) and two without photographs. These articles are from 11th May, 1961, 7th March, 1963, 28th March, 1963, 5th November, 1964, 1st April, 1965, 11th May, 1967, 2nd April, 1970, and 7th May, 1970.

The decade between 1960 and 1970 was chosen for historical reasons. At the end of the Second World War, there was a new political and economic landscape in Italy. Agriculture was not the main focus of the new economic development (Barbagallo 2001: 21). The Southern part of Italy, where the economy was mainly based on agriculture was therefore heavily affected by this decision and unemployment drastically increased. Many people were unemployed. Therefore, migration became necessary to relaunch the economy in Italy and in particular in the South. The economist Manlio Rossi Doria in 1958 stated that in the post-war period (1950–1960) 'peasants' misery no longer existed in inland areas and this substantial progress was due to migration' (Rossi-Doria 1958: 100). Italian post-war Union leader, Giuseppe Di Vittorio claimed that a valid instrument for economic development of Italian post-war political strategy was inevitably migration (Di Vittorio 2012: 81). Despite the fact that the Italian economy blossomed in the 1960s,[6] Italian workers were encouraged to migrate. Differently from the diaspora of the end of the nineteenth and beginning of the twentieth century which mainly moved to United States, the post-war migration was directed to Europe. Italians elected Belgium, France, Germany, Great Britain and Switzerland as their

[6] Well represented in the 1960 movie by Federico Fellini *La Dolce Vita*, 1960 is considered the symbolic year of the boom of Italian economy from poverty (Ricciardi 2018: 1949). In January 1960, *The Financial Times* selected the Italian Lira as the most important currency and the GDP (Gross Domestic Product) of Italy reached an impressive +8% (Caruso 2016: 7).

main destinations. In 1963, Switzerland was the favorite choice of Italian migrants (about 44 %) (Cerutti 1994: 13). If successfully admitted after a medical check in Brig (close to the Italian border), these workers were allowed to stay in Switzerland for nine months only. This diaspora was not as permanent as the trans-Atlantic migration. As witnessed in *L'Illustré* articles,[7] a massive number of Italian workers moved to Switzerland, and it represented an exponential progression. The seasonal workers' (*saisonniers*) impact on Swiss society was perceived as a problematic issue (see the large number of articles published in *Journal de Genève*, *Gazette de Lausanne* and *Le Nouveau Quotidien*). *L'Illustré* dedicated two articles to this issue in March 1963 (n. 10 of 7th March and n. 13 of 28th March) by Maurice Rohrer (1963a, 1963b). The title of the first article is '*L'invasion pacifique des travailleurs étrangers*' with a significant subtitle: '*un problème Suisse à l'ordre du jour: 1 habitant sur 8 est étranger*' (Fig. 2.1).

There are no photographs to illustrate the article, but there are graphics and charts to demonstrate the big impact of this impressive diaspora. According to this article, 70% of migrants-workers in 1962 were Italians, ahead of Germans, Spanish, Austrians and French. The article underlines how 80% of migrants are coming from Southern Europe (80%) and only 17% are 'Germaniques'. The number of migrants is felt as an invasion. In the article, there is a reference to the 'latinisation' of Switzerland.[8] The article states that the 730,000 migrants are equivalent to the entire population of Canton Vaud and Geneva. There is a pessimistic approach about the possible integration: Maurice Rohrer cites what was said by Hans Schaffner.[9] Reporting the concepts expressed by Schaffner, Rohrer states that 'Switzerland never feared the influx of migrants. It managed during the years to absorb all those who arrived in the country. It seems, nevertheless, difficult to define the point of saturation of this diaspora' (Rohrer 1963a: 28). Starting from this pessimistic view, through charts and

---

[7] *L'Illustré*, 7th March, 1963 and 28th March, 1963.

[8] Maiolino writes about the *meditérranéization* of Switzerland in recent years (Maiolino 2013: 154). In Maiolino's opinion, this explains the gradual acceptance by Swiss society of Italian cultural aspects (pizza, espresso, fashion, lifestyle, spirit of enterprise). The *meditérranéization* shows a gradual emancipation of the Italian community in Switzerland.

[9] Federal Councilor from 1961 to 1969 and President of the Confederation from 1966 and Head of the Department of Public Economy from 1961 to 1969.

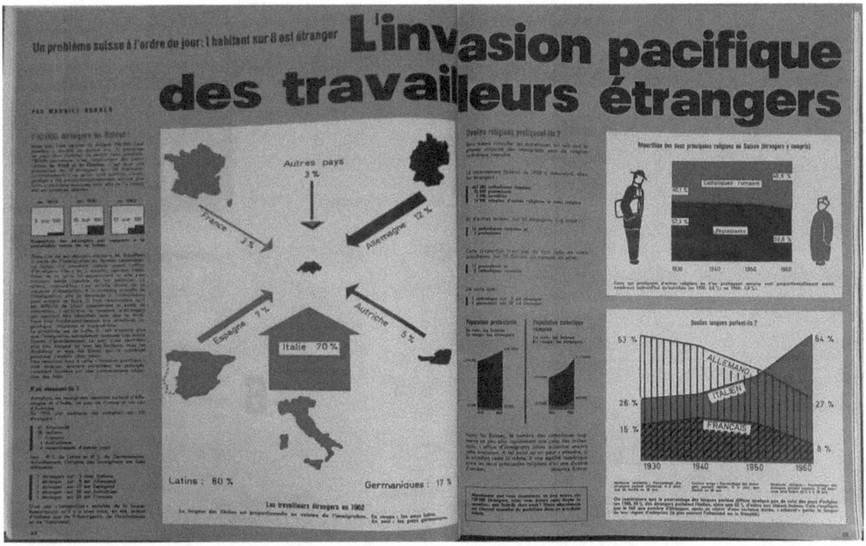

Fig. 2.1 L'Illustré – n. 10 of 7th March, 1963, pp. 28–29. With permission of L'Illustré

diagrams, the article describes the profile of these migrants. One of the aspects on which the attention is directed is religion. The majority of the new migrants were catholic. Italian journalist, Concetto Vecchio (2019: 63) in his book *'Cacciateli! Quando i migranti eravamo noi'* confirms that this mass of Catholics coming from the Southern part of Europe was a concern for Swiss people. One whole page of this article in *L'Illustré* is dedicated to this aspect. The article reports that statistics show that 467,200 foreigners of the 730,000 were catholic (coming from Italy and Spain). This number would have impacted the balance of the two main religions in Switzerland. On n. 13 of the 28th of March 1963 (Fig. 2.2), Maurice Rohrer continues his inquiry on the strangers' impact on the Swiss economy and their integration into Swiss society.

The title of the article is *'Les étrangers et notre économie'*.[10] According to Rohrer, after 1960 the number of migrant workers in Switzerland grew with a frequency of one hundred individuals per year, the majority of

[10] Interesting is also the sub-title: the use of the term *le problème* gives a very negative connotation.

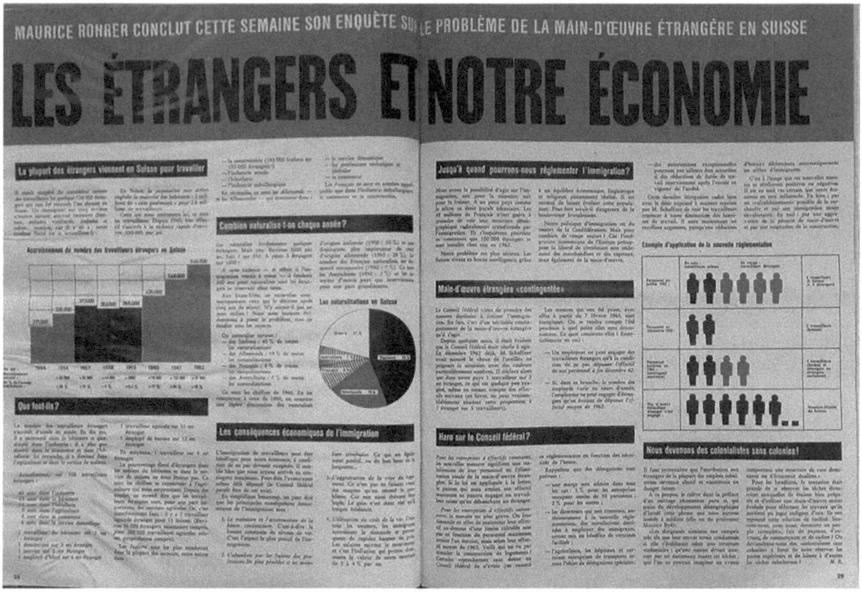
MAURICE ROHRER CONCLUT CETTE SEMAINE SON ENQUÊTE SUR LE PROBLÈME DE LA MAIN-D'ŒUVRE ÉTRANGÈRE EN SUISSE

LES ÉTRANGERS ET NOTRE ÉCONOMIE

La plupart des étrangers viennent en Suisse pour travailler

Accroissement du nombre des travailleurs étrangers en Suisse

Que font-ils ?

Combien naturalise-t-on chaque année?

Les naturalisations en Suisse

Les conséquences économiques de l'immigration

Jusqu'à quand pourrons-nous réglementer l'immigration?

Main-d'œuvre étrangère «contingentée»

Haro sur le Conseil fédéral?

Exemple d'application de la nouvelle réglementation

Nous devenons des colonialistes sans colonies!

Fig. 2.2 L'Illustré – n. 13 of 28th March, 1963, pp. 28–29. With permission of L'Illustré

them being Italians. The fear of the writer is that Switzerland will soon not be able to absorb them. The main consequences of this flow of workers in the Swiss Confederation are the stabilization of the economic boom, the possibility for Swiss citizens to avoid the most undesired and less reputable jobs, the aggravation of the housing crisis and the increase of the costs of living. The naturalization of migrants is a rare phenomenon: only three strangers over 1,000 become Swiss. Rohrer states that in the US anyone who has been resident in the country for at least five years can automatically ask for naturalization. The final conclusion of Maurice Rohrer is interesting. He wonders if Switzerland was becoming a country of colonialists without colonies, maintaining better jobs for Swiss people and leaving migrants the subaltern tasks. Like the first part of this inquiry, this appeared in the *L'Illustré* issue of 7th March, 1963, and there are no photographs to illustrate this article.

In 1965, a new agreement on workforce recruitment between Switzerland and Italy was reached. Initially signed in Rome on 10th

August, 1964 and ratified by the Federal Assembly of the Swiss Confederation on 17th March, 1965 (Ricciardi 2018: 2197), this act demonstrates that the *überfremdung* (foreign infiltration) of Switzerland was felt as a real social issue. Right-wing Swiss politician James Schwarzenbach promoted an initiative for a referendum to decrease the number of migrants in Switzerland. There was a growing fear of a loss of cultural identity. As already mentioned above, Concetto Vecchio confirms (Vecchio 2019: 63) that what scared Swiss people in the 1960s and 1970s was the impact that a large number of catholics coming from Italy would have done to alter the balance between Protestants and Catholics. Vecchio states that it was a fear of losing a typical Swiss identity, the loss of social and religious traditions. In this sense, 1970 was a significant year. Despite the fact that on 7th June the Schwarzenbach initiative was refused by the 54% of the voters, the Swiss Confederation established new laws to control the number of seasonal workers. As a consequence of that and the oil crisis of the 1970s, Italia0n migrants started returning to Italy (Ricciardi 2018: 2201).

Keeping in mind all these aspects when looking at these images, we have to make a distinction between amateur images and photographs taken by professional photographers. In Switzerland, there is a large quantity of images which represent Italian migrants abroad. They are part of associations and family archives. These images are mainly individual portraits and images related to ceremonies or scenes representing families in different contexts. They are documents which have not been commissioned by public or private institutions (including magazines or newspapers). These photographs have been used for exhibitions or events linked to Italian migration.[11] There is a considerable difference between the images by professional photographers who were assigned by public or private institutions to represent the migrant's world and the other ones taken by the migrants themselves. While the first pictures were influenced by editorial policies within the political-cultural context, the

[11] See the case of the book *Grazie a voi: ricordi e stima – Fotografien zur Italienischen Migration in der Schweiz* (Alghisi et al. 2016). This work is the final result of an exhibition which uses family and associations archives of Italian migrants from 1966 to the 1980s. The exhibition was held in 2016 in the History and Ethnology Museum of St. Gallen, the Rosenegg Museum of Kreuzlingen and the Civic Museum of Rapperswil-Jona (5th March–26th June, 2016).

second ones seem to focus more on private lives. Being aware that these amateurs' photographs play a significant role in the construction of the visual identity of migrants in Switzerland in the 1960s and 1970s, this research was mostly interested in the influence of ideology on the production of images, therefore the focus went mainly towards the images produced by professional photographers. What interested the investigation was the influence of the social context on photographers' decisions in content and composition. With social context we refer here to Barthes when he draws the attention to the properties and the meanings we attach to images of the things around us (Barthes 1972).[12]

L'Illustré: A Visual Semiotics Approach

The analysis of images and text found in *L'Illustré* draws on visuals semiotics developed by R. Barthes (1977) and M. Joly (2015). Barthes (1977: 15) stresses that press photography is a message which travels from the first point called emission (staff of the newspaper), to the point of reception (the public) through the channel of transmission (the newspaper, complex concurrent messages). The emission and reception points lay, in Barthes' view, in the field of sociology (human groups: attitudes, behaviours to be linked to the social totality). The method of analysis of the message itself is different. The message is not only a product but also an object with a structured autonomy. We need to do an 'immanent analysis of the unique structure that a photograph constitutes' (Barthes 1977: 16). Even in this context of immanent analysis, the image is not isolated. It has to be read in combination with the text (titles, article or caption) which usually is attached to the image. There are, therefore, two planes of analysis: the linguistic part and the part made of lines, surfaces and shades. First, we have to analyse them separately, and only after this we can understand how they complement each other. As stated by Martine

[12] Society with its transformations manages to direct photographers' decisions in producing images (see Bourdieu 1965: 35; Brier 2007: 11; Burke 2001). The perception of the other (understood as migrant different from us) is one of these aspects (see Belting 2013; Brier 2007: 441–454; Burke 2001: 123; Rouille 2005). Paola Corti stated that the public perception of specific events can profoundly be influenced by the media representation (Corti 2010: 15).

Joly (2015: 64), an image analysis cannot happen without interpretation of signs and symbols. There is a reference to elements relative to the culture and history of the viewer. The connotational message is symbolic and linked to the pre-existing knowledge and shared by the emission and reception parts. Stuart Hall (1972: 236) called it 'background consensus knowledge'. Without this knowledge, the reader or the writer (or photographer) could not 'recognize or understand the foreground' of stories. As a polysemic message, images can be divided into two parts: figurative or iconic signs and plastic signs. Together they are visual signs which are complementary and distinct at the same time. These elements can help in understanding the signification of the message in combination with the linguistic aspect.

Findings

Number of Photographs of Seasonal Workers in 1960s–1970s Migration in Europe

In her book *Emigranti e immigrati nelle rappresentazioni di fotografi e fotogiornalisti*, Professor of Contemporary History of the University of Turin Paola Corti claims that the production of photographs of the post-war Italian diaspora is relatively smaller when compared to the trans-Atlantic migration of the end of the nineteenth and beginning of the twentieth century (Corti 2010: 19). This involves both the private production of photographs (self-representation of migrants) and others commissioned to professional photographers by public and private institutions. This phenomenon is the consequence of the different characteristics of the two migration processes. As also claimed by Paola Corti (2010: 22), while the trans-Atlantic migration was further and more permanent (Gabaccia 2000), the same cannot be stated for the European diaspora of the 1960s and 1970s, which was characterized by the seasonal workers' phenomenon. Distances were shorter and allowed migrants to return more frequently to their homes. In the trans-Atlantic diaspora, migrants wanted to be portrayed so they could then include the photographs in the letters that they sent home.[13] Despite the fact that the post-war communication was still mainly through mail, technology partially substituted the use of letters. The need of producing photographs to be sent home was replaced by the use of telephones (Corti 2010: 21). In consideration of shorter distances, the communication of migrants with their country of origin was less frequent than in the trans-Atlantic diaspora. Living in countries like Switzerland, France or Germany allowed seasonal workers to return home more frequently; therefore, it was less needed to communicate as it was done in the trans-Atlantic migration. The small production of images on the post-war migration produced by professional photographers is also due to the policy of the hosting countries like in the case of Switzerland and of the Italian government (Gabaccia 2000; Ricciardi 2018). The provisional nature of the Italian diaspora in Switzerland meant that the Swiss government paid less attention to the phenomenon and, therefore, it didn't promote any systematic photographic documentation as happened in the United States almost a century before.[14] The massive Italian migration in the United States became a key subject in the sociological photographic research of the end of the nineteenth and beginning of the twentieth century (as in the case of L. W. Hine[15]), never replicated in the same way in Europe in the post-war period. Italian governments supported the diaspora process as part of their development strategy.[16] Encouraging Italians to migrate was indeed one of the elements which could relaunch the Italian economy in this period. This plan was never officially declared and mostly hidden from the public. It was therefore purposely never largely documented with photographs and published in magazines or newspapers. The diaspora phenomenon could find space in the newsreels of official public propaganda but in those cases only the positive aspects were highlighted (in particular the bilateral agreements

[13] For this aspect, see Blanc-Chaléard and Bechelloni (2007), Corti (2010: 256), Gibelli (1989), Ortoleva (1991: 122), Ostuni (1990), Sotelo Vásquez (2003: 488).

[14] See Riis (1971).

[15] For the work of Lewis W. Hine on Ellis Island, see Hine (1909), Rosenblum (1977), Trachtenberg (1977), Sundell (1986), Seixas (1987), Stange (1989), Kaplan (1992), Longolius (2003), Ureña (2009), Szlezák (2009, 2012).

[16] See Ricciardi (2018), Vecchio (2019).

between Switzerland and Italy).[17] Furthermore Italian post-war photojournalism was not particularly developed and was still largely influenced by how the visual communication worked during the Fascist totalitarian regime mostly based on the propaganda and always government oriented (Bollati and Bertelli 1979: 177). While on the one hand, the post-war Italian photojournalism maintained a sort of conformity of the public image, on the other hand, it partially tried to develop a new approach to visual representation with an autonomous point of view. The images produced in these years were aesthetically pleasant but often at the behest of political power (Corti 2010: 25).

Archetypical Messages of Migration

In *The determinations of news photographs*, Hall (1972: 241), images are part of universal signs, archetypical messages. Visual signs are key elements for the establishment of familiar recognitions. There are several 'familiar recognitions' in the images of *L'Illustré* from the years between 1960 and 1970. These iconic messages are the journey (health check-up point), the arrival (train station) and life conditions (working and living conditions). Iconic messages (Joly 2015: 31) like the suitcase, passports and forms to be filled are inducers of associations (Barthes 1977: 22) of the migratory experience. In this part of the chapter, it will be demonstrated how these points are confirmed in illustrated articles published in *L'Illustré* in the same years. Many images in *L'Illustré* found their communication with the reader on the visual symbolism of the journey and the arrival to the hosting land. The journey and the arrival are often represented by trains and train stations. These images recall the rhythm and rituals of the transition of migrants in the arrival areas and the forms of control of the trans-Atlantic migration. They substitute what for the trans-Atlantic diaspora were Ellis Island in New York and the *Hotel des Inmigrantes* of Buenos Aires. To find another example of this symbology, see the movie *The Immigrant* by Charlie Chaplin (Malioza 2017: 8:40–8:55). In this 1917 movie, a migrant is going from Europe to

[17] For the same situation but related to the Italian diaspora in Argentina, see the movie *Emigrantes* (Fabrizi 1949).

United States on a ship. At the entrance of the port of New York we see the Statue of Liberty while on the ship all the migrants get forced to stay behind a rope by a migration officer. The rope is the symbol of the limitation of freedom and, of course, it is in contrast with the meaning of the statue of Liberty. The images of the arrival in America are presented again in the post-war photographic iconography, with the steps and rituals of the migrant routine in being accepted. Police checks at customs are the symbol of contrast between the attempt of the migrant to reach social and financial independency and the bureaucracy of the hosting country. These police checks tried to regulate the migratory phenomenon. A good similar example is the 1963 photograph *Sottopassaggio_Unterführung* taken by Uliano Lucas (Ruppen 2003: 30).[18] In a train station, there is a sign by the Ministry of Labor and Social Security (*Ministero del Lavoro e della Previdenza Sociale*). It indicates where migrants have to stop. It is not by chance that the photographer has included that sign and placed it in the centre of the composition. It represents the bureaucratic context in which the migrant lives. It is a context constituted by rules with which the migrants struggle to eventually find the coveted economic and social independency in the country which will host them. Similar symbols related to the arrival and the journey can be seen in the article of *L'Illustré* n. 19 of the 11th of May 1961 (Olivier 1961). This is the only article related to migration in Switzerland I have found in *L'Illustré* from the years 1960, 1961 and 1962. It is a reportage by René Olivier entitled *'Habitants méridionaux des villes romandes: les italiens'* ('Southern inhabitants of the French-speaking Swiss cities: the Italians'). The first sentence is a description of how Italians look and act in the streets: they, the Italians, are 'short and dark, with black hair', they walk around in groups, stop at the corner of a sidewalk, argue loudly with a lively tone of voice and animated gesture. It is 'us' and 'them'. Italians are here defined as seasonal workers. They arrived at the train station and are described as a picturesque mass with poorly tied backpacks, boxes of food, Chianti flasks, tight pants and jackets, pointed shoes. They are, as Olivier states, in Switzerland, the land of plenty. Olivier interviews some of them. The

[18] From https://espresso.repubblica.it/foto/2013/11/21/galleria/uliano-lucas-cinquant-anni-di--scatti-1.142271/. Access 29.03.2022.

reason to migrate is always the same: the need to work. In this article, these Italians are mainly from the Northern part of Italy (from Genoa and Bergamo). There is also an interview with the owner of a restaurant who is actually in favor of this migration: Switzerland needs, he claims, workers. The last remark of the article is to support the new migrants with '*un peu plus de cœr et un peu moins d'égoïsme*'. There are three photographs to illustrate the article. The bigger one is a double-page vertical image. It represents travellers at a big train station of a city in the French-speaking part of Switzerland which could be Geneva or Lausanne. There are two men and two women standing next to their luggage. We understand that they are migrants from the content of the article and the caption. The sign behind one of the two women says that they are on a platform where a train is going to leave direction Brig-Milan. This image confirms what Paola Corti (2010: 34) states regarding the typical images produced about migration: trains and train stations are places linked to the departure and arrival of mass migration. René Olivier mentions the train station as an arrival point of their journey from Italy, after having passed through the health check in Brig.

This moment is documented by two photographs illustrating an article in *L'Illustré* no. 45 of the 5th of November 1964 (Senn 1964) (Fig. 2.3). It is an article by Renée Senn which comments on the documentary *Siamo italiani* realized by Swiss Director Alexander J. Seiler (1965) in that same year.[19] A key movie in Swiss filmography, which documents the Italian migration process to Switzerland and the *saisonnier* phenomenon, *Siamo Italiani* shows the arrival of migrants to the health check point in Brig or Chiasso, then when they continue to the city and the barracks where they will live for the next nine months, and eventually their work context.

The text of the article is very short but there are three photographs taken from the movie. The moment of the self-declaration to Swiss authorities is shown on the largest image of the article. There are migrants waiting in line in a corridor behind a glass door; they all look towards the

[19] We have to mention here the works of Alvaro Bizzarri *Il treno del sud, Lo stagionale, Il rovescio della medaglia* (Bizzarri 1970, 1972, 1974), *Braccia sì, uomini no* (Ammann and Burri 1970) on the Schwarzenbach initiative by Peter Ammann and René Burri and the documentaries of Katharine Dominice and Peter (2010).

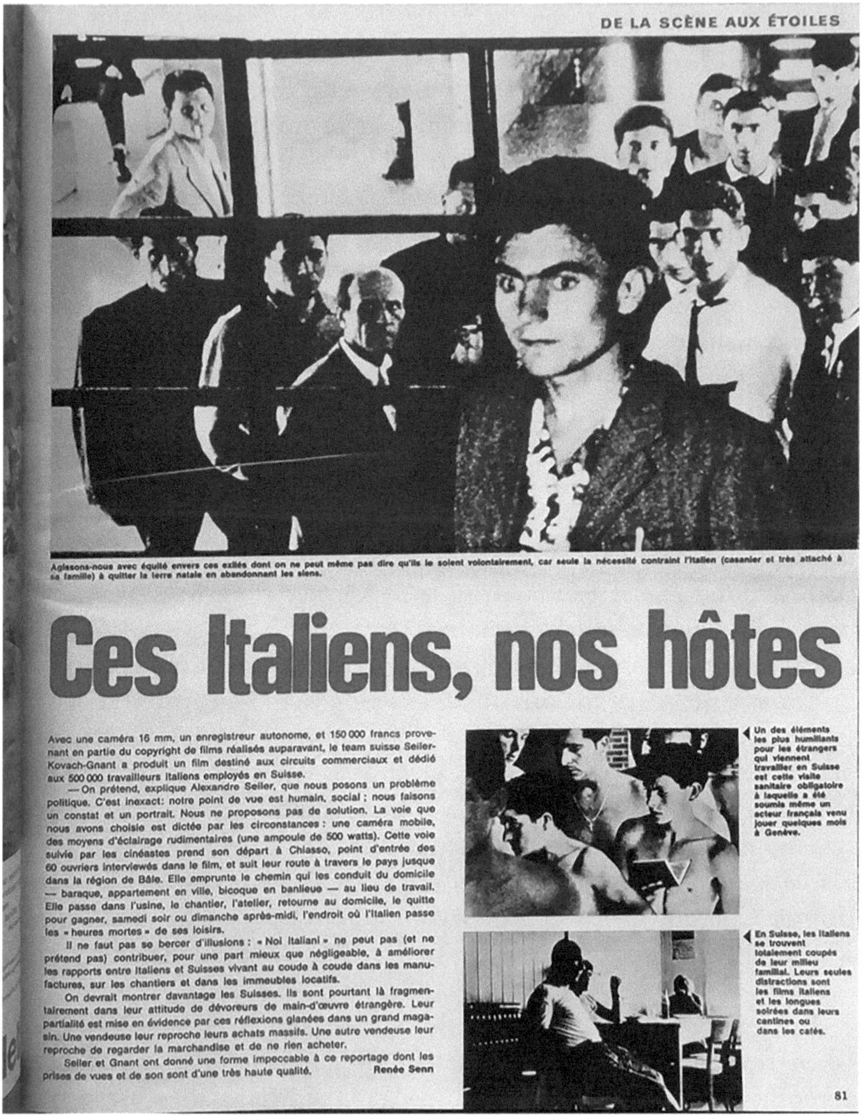

DE LA SCÈNE AUX ÉTOILES

Agissons-nous avec équité envers ces exilés dont on ne peut même pas dire qu'ils le soient volontairement, car seule la nécessité contraint l'Italien (casanier et très attaché à sa famille) à quitter la terre natale en abandonnant les siens.

Ces Italiens, nos hôtes

Avec une caméra 16 mm, un enregistreur autonome, et 150 000 francs provenant en partie du copyright de films réalisés auparavant, le team suisse Seiler-Kovach-Gnant a produit un film destiné aux circuits commerciaux et dédié aux 500 000 travailleurs italiens employés en Suisse.

— On prétend, explique Alexandre Seiler, que nous posons un problème politique. C'est inexact: notre point de vue est humain, social ; nous faisons un constat et un portrait. Nous ne proposons pas de solution. La voie que nous avons choisie est dictée par les circonstances : une caméra mobile, des moyens d'éclairage rudimentaires (une ampoule de 500 watts). Cette voie suivie par les cinéastes prend son départ à Chiasso, point d'entrée des 60 ouvriers interviewés dans le film, et suit leur route à travers le pays jusque dans la région de Bâle. Elle emprunte le chemin qui les conduit du domicile — baraque, appartement en ville, bicoque en banlieue — au lieu de travail. Elle passe dans l'usine, le chantier, l'atelier, retourne au domicile, le quitte pour gagner, samedi soir ou dimanche après-midi, l'endroit où l'Italien passe les « heures mortes » de ses loisirs.

Il ne faut pas se bercer d'illusions : « Noi Italiani » ne peut pas (et ne prétend pas) contribuer, pour une part mieux que négligeable, à améliorer les rapports entre Italiens et Suisses vivant au coude à coude dans les manufactures, sur les chantiers et dans les immeubles locatifs.

On devrait montrer davantage les Suisses. Ils sont pourtant là fragmentairement dans leur attitude de dévoreurs de main-d'œuvre étrangère. Leur partialité est mise en évidence par ces réflexions glanées dans un grand magasin. Une vendeuse leur reproche leurs achats massifs. Une autre vendeuse leur reproche de regarder la marchandise et de ne rien acheter.

Seiler et Gnant ont donné une forme impeccable à ce reportage dont les prises de vues et de son sont d'une très haute qualité.

Renée Senn

◀ Un des éléments les plus humiliants pour les étrangers qui viennent travailler en Suisse est cette visite sanitaire obligatoire à laquelle a été soumis même un acteur français venu jouer quelques mois à Genève.

◀ En Suisse, les Italiens se trouvent totalement coupés de leur milieu familial. Leurs seules distractions sont les films italiens et les longues soirées dans leurs cantines ou dans les cafés.

81

Fig. 2.3 L'Illustré – n. 45 of November 5th, 1964, p. 81. With permission of L'Illustré

viewer, waiting for their documents to be checked. A young man in the foreground is about to enter the room. He is the next person to be checked. His eyes are wide open. He seems to be living an intense, emotional moment. It is one of the key moments of a long procedure which will decide whether or not he will be admitted to Switzerland. It represents a crucial change in his life: being able to cross the border and try to change his life to a better life.[20] The entire scene is played out by the look and the face. Fifteen men are all looking in the same direction waiting to know what they have to do and what will happen to their future. The position of the young man in the foreground is dominant. He is placed by the author of the image in the right crossing line following the rule of thirds. With this trick, the viewer's attention is strongly directed on the sight of this young man, not forgetting, though, to look at what happens in the background. All these other men become like a texture, a backdrop against which the young man in the foreground is more visible. A moment of the health check is documented in one of the small images at the bottom of the page. The caption next to the image states that 'one of the most humiliating elements for the stranger who comes to work to Switzerland is the mandatory health check'. Naked men are in line. There is a person in the foreground which creates a sort of a theatrical setting. In the background, among other five migrants, a boy holds in his right hand what could guarantee his identity: a passport. The reference to these types of documents is recurrent even in photographs related to migration from the beginning of the twentieth century. Paola Corti (2010: 114) describes a photograph from the early years of 1900s which shows migrants landing on Ellis Island in New York. Loaded with baggage, these people are holding their identification documents in their mouths.

[20] It recalls here the poem by Edmondo De Amicis from 1882 'Gli emigranti' (De Amicis 1897: 87):

Cogli occhi spenti, con le guancie cave,Pallidi, in atto addolorato e grave,Sorreggendo le donne affrante e smorte,Ascendono la naveCome s'ascende il palco de la morte.

Dull-eyed, hollow-cheeked,
Pale, in sorrowful and grave act,
Supporting the distressed and dull women,
They ascend the ship
As one ascends the stage of death.
(my translation)

These forms show that these individuals have an identity which is testified on paper and that they need these documents while entering the borders of the hosting country. Passports are icons of identification.

There are other elements that function as icons related to migration narratives. The suitcase is quite recurrent in photographs of migration. Already present on one of the photographs in *L'Illustré* n. 19 of 11th of May, 1961, the suitcase is again included twice in an article published in 1965. In *L'Illustré* no. 14 of 1st April of that year, Georges Gygax (1965) presented a journalistic enquiry on seasonal workers in Switzerland in *L'Illustré*. The title was '*Travailleurs étrangers: le problème est-il résolu?*' (Fig. 2.4).

In the text, Gygax reflects on the already mentioned above 1965 bilateral pact signed by Italy and Switzerland on the status of seasonal workers. The article is illustrated with four photographs, two of which are on the first page. They represent two Italian workers, one from Calabria (Fig. 2.5) and the other one from Abruzzo (Fig. 2.6). On the denotative level, icons of travel and memories are represented on the third and the

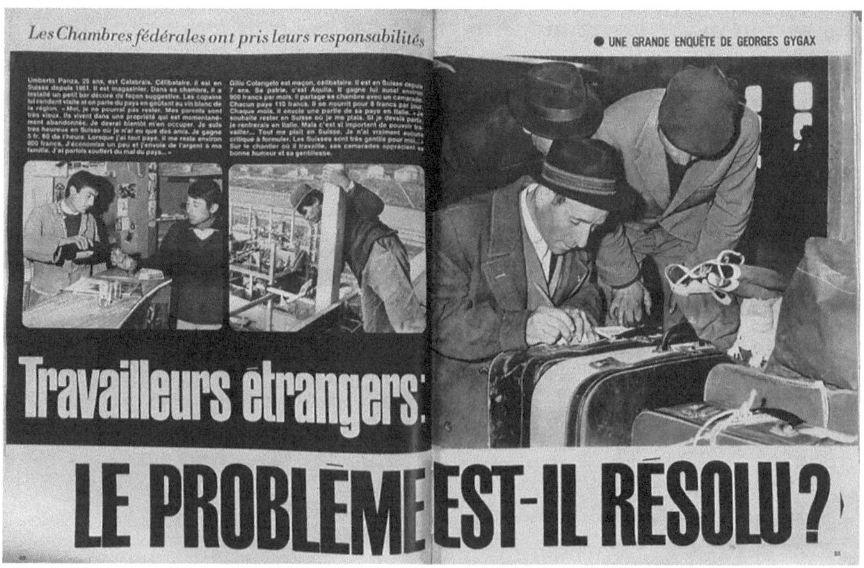

Fig. 2.4 L'Illustré – n. 14 of 1st April, 1965, pp. 22–23. With permission of L'Illustré

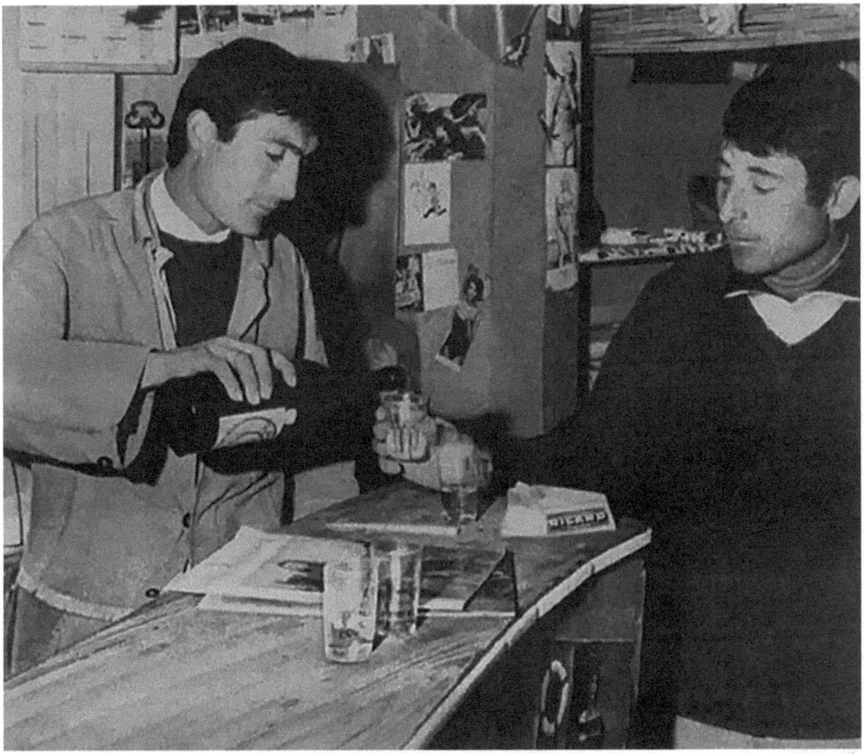

Fig. 2.5 Unknown, Travailleurs étrangers, 1965. With permission of L'Illustré

fourth images which are reproduced on the following pages (Figs. 2.4 and 2.7). On page 23, three men, well dressed, with coats and hats, are concentrated in filling a form. One man, probably on his knees, seems to be in the act of copying some information from a document.

The other two stand behind him and follow what the man is doing. The square format of the image is diagonally divided in two parts: the three men are in the upper left corner; the lower right corner is occupied by worn suitcases. These items characterize the individuals. They are props which tell us more about the three men. They tell us that they are travelling, migrating with their suitcases. The fourth image of the article includes suitcases as well. The photograph is taken in a place which seems to be a construction site (Fig. 2.7). We can see barracks on the right and

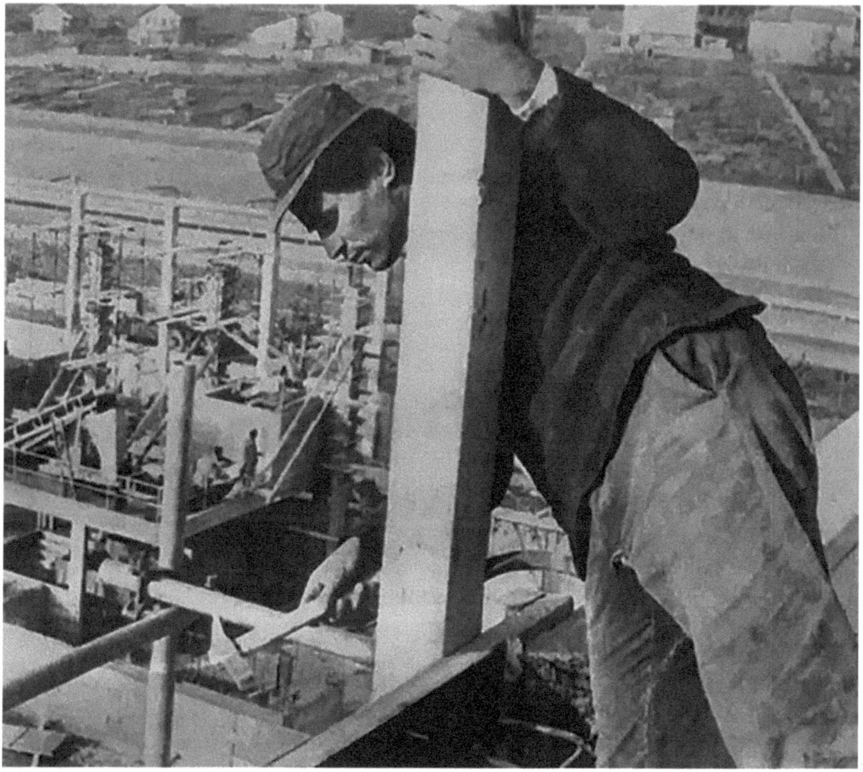

Fig. 2.6 Unknown, Travailleur étranger, 1965. With permission of L'Illustré

at the bottom of the picture. There are working tools and debris everywhere. In this desolate context, one man stands on the right-hand part of the photograph, holding a suitcase and stares at two other men who are walking away. They seem to leave because one of the two men has a suitcase in his right hand. As seen above, the suitcase is again the symbol of the migrant worker and represents his life and memory.[21] The caption at

[21] In *A Seventh Man*, Berger (Berger and Mohr 2010: 183) writes: 'In certain barracks the authorities have tried to forbid migrant workers keeping their suitcases in their sleeping rooms on the grounds that they make the room untidy. The workers have strongly resisted this, sometimes to the point of going on strike. In these suitcases they keep personal possessions, not the clothes they put in the wardrobes, not the photographs they pin to the wall but articles which, for one reason or another, are their talismans. Each suitcase, locked or tied round with cord, is like a man's memory. They defend their right to keep the suitcases.'

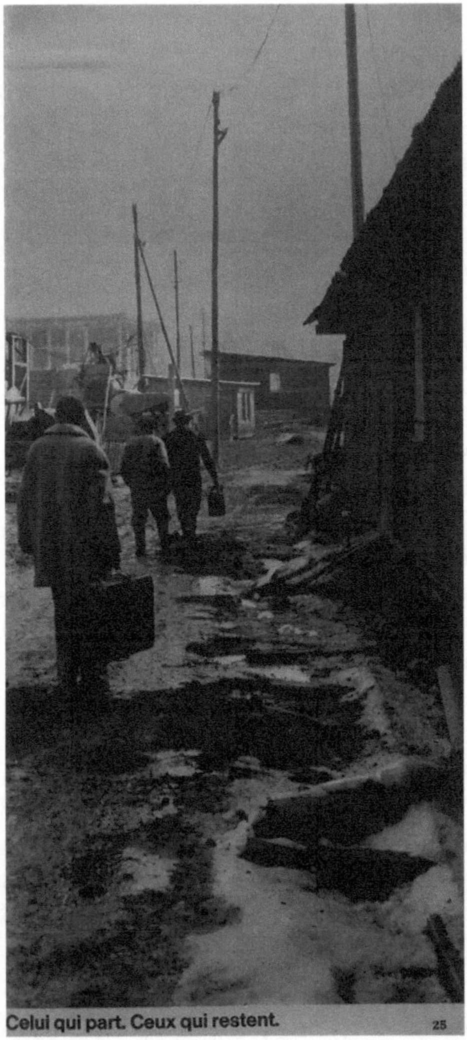

Fig. 2.7 Unknown, Celui qui part. Ceux qui restent, 1965. With permission of L'Illustré

the bottom of the image creates the links with the text of the article suggesting the interpretation of the image: '*Celui qui part. Ceux qui restent*' (Those ones who are leaving. Those ones who are staying). We don't see their faces. We witness the scene as viewers not involved in the process. As in the famous images of Lewis W. Hine from the trans-Atlantic diaspora, suitcases are icons of migration.

Photographs taken by Mauro Vallinotto in 1973, *Wolfsburg, Germany. Condominiums for the Volkswagen workers* (Corti 2009: 181) and by Uliano Lucas in 1968, *Migrant from Sardinia in front of the Pirelli skyscraper* in Milan, Italy[22] confirm this point. In the first case, a migrant is portrayed while playing an accordion in the street in Wolfsburg in front of a condominium and he is sitting on a suitcase. In the photograph taken by Lucas we see a migrant in front of Il Pirellone, the skyscraper symbol of the modern city development of Milan. He is holding a suitcase and a large box on his right shoulder. Suitcases function here again as icons with the denotation code of migration.

Similar icons were repeated in other significant works on migration in Switzerland such as *A Seventh Man* (Berger and Mohr 2010). In a section dedicated to Geneva, Jean Mohr's photographs show workers who lived in barracks with basic facilities, small rooms with four beds, acceptable heating during winter time but inadequate noise reduction. There was no real leisure after work. For most of them, the rooms were the place to meet, play cards or listen to music. In both cases, in this book and the article, this reference to music is in common. Migrants brought records from their country of origin and play them in their room. The record is, as mentioned by Berger in *A Seventh Man* (Berger and Mohr 2010: 183), a talisman, which is contained in the migrants' memory, the suitcase. The articles that the migrant has brought with himself in the suitcase are objects which are their 'personal possessions, not the clothes they put in the wardrobes, not the photographs they pin to the wall, [...]'. The suitcase is the migrant's memory. Berger mentions that the authorities had tried to forbid workers keeping their suitcases in their rooms but that they resisted this imposition. They don't want to put distance between

---

[22] From http://smargiassi-michele.blogautore.repubblica.it/2018/11/09/uliano-lucas-sognatori-ribelli-sessantotto-fotografia/. Access 21.10.2019.

themselves and the symbol of their memory. In the psychological analysis, Berger underlines the fact that the migrant worker lives mainly for his work (Berger and Mohr 2010: 175). The past and the future are represented by fixed images which do not develop. They cannot develop because migrants have no energy to do it. All their energy is dedicated to work and once they stop working all these static images haunt them. The images of their current and previous lives are very distant. He feels lost and working is the only relief. Images by Jean Mohr in the same book show the barracks (Berger and Mohr 2010: 169). He pictured bathrooms, changing rooms, washing rooms and showers. The last images of pages 172, 173 and 178 represent the rooms. They are decorated with photographs and posters pinned on the wooden walls. These images tell us something about the personality of the workers. The image *Working and living conditions of migrant workers constructing a tunnel under Geneva, Switzerland* on page 172 represents the interior of a room with a bed on the left and a small cabinet on the right. In the middle of the vertical composition, there is a cupboard. Someone has pinned two posters on it. They represent Terence Hill (born Mario Girotti, Italian actor) on the left and a naked woman on the right. Terence Hill has a gun in his right hand and looks straight into the camera. He has a cold and highly self-confident expression. He is the representation of the strong man with no fear, something that probably the migrant worker admired and dreamt to be. The girl on the right has a sexy position and looks at the viewer with a smile on her face. She has an inviting attitude. As described by John Berger on page 167 'several aspects of the self are denied by the migrant's situation. He has no natural existence as a sexual being […]'. Still Berger on page 171 defines this condition as a situation which involves absence and sexual deprivation. The co-presence of the strong man and the sexy girl is clear again on the photograph on page 173. Here are four men in a room. Two of them are sitting on a bed and one of the two has a guitar. On the wall behind them there are two posters and a calendar. The poster on the left represents Clint Eastwood in his role as the good in *The Good, the Bad and the Ugly* by Sergio Leone (1966). Next to it, there is the image of a half-naked girl. The calendar on the right shows five images of football players: the other passion of Italian migrants. All these images on the walls contribute to the representation of the physical and psychological unstable condition of the workers in their dreams, their hopes and their memories. In the majority of the cases of the photographs from the years between 1969 and 1970, sitters don't look straight into the camera. They are portrayed as they are and apparently not conscious of the presence of the photographer. It is a documentation of facts with no apparent interaction with the photographer. As it will be demonstrated in Chap. 3, the model of representation of Italian migrants of the twenty-first century in Switzerland is different. They are generally portrayed while smiling and looking straight into the lens. This gaze suggests an interaction with the subject and self-confidence of the sitters which doesn't seem to be present in these photographs from the last century. Migrants of the 1960s and 1970s in Switzerland were seasonal workers. Experiencing hard-working conditions and difficult living contexts in the barracks, they were lonely men with no families.

Au pays de la solitude: Men Without Families in a Foreign Country

As also confirmed by Berger (Berger and Mohr 2010: 62), the nineteenth-century diasporas were permanent while the 1960s and 1970s migration in Europe was temporary. Moving to a different country meant to live another life and is described as a metaphor of death (Berger and Mohr 2010: 181). The 1960s and 1970s migrations were mainly temporary (in Switzerland there were only nine-month work permits). As a consequence of being in a temporary condition, seasonal workers live in a cultural *utopos*, a non-place (Maiolino 2013: 156). Migrants have the perception of being imprisoned. They live this experience as being in a temporary space in which they are held far from their families, friends and familiar places. They know that they will eventually return to their homeland therefore they live in a state of apnea. Even the way they decorate the new space/prison where they will live for a few months is comparable to the way the prisoner decorates the jail.[23] In the articles of *L'Illustré* found

[23] 'Today the temporary migrant worker suffers a kind of imprisonment in a prison without frontiers' (Berger and Mohr 2010: 183).

from the decade between 1960 and 1970, women are not represented as much as men. In the majority of the images, we can see men alone in a non-integrated situation. In the photographs from these years, the presence of only men and clothing hanging next to them show the condition of men without family and women. Figures actually show that around 1950, women represented more than 50% of Italian migration to Switzerland, and in 1970, it was at 42% (Castro 2013: 60). Between 1945 and 1955, female Italian migrants to Switzerland constantly exceeded male immigrants.

'But after work and on Sundays it is hellish. Other facts are relevant. That he is barred from natural communication by a language barrier. That his rejection by the indigenous population as a natural inferior denies his present being, and peremptorily throws him again and again back into the past. That his living conditions are humiliating. That he is sexually deprived' (Berger and Mohr 2010: 200).

The lack of integration is confirmed by an article that appeared in *L'Illustré* n. 14 of the 2nd of April 1970 (SCOPE 1970). The title of the article, '*Les étrangers – Au pays de la solitude*', and the photographs illustrating it support the point (Fig. 2.8). As already anticipated in previous parts of this chapter, on the 7th of June 1970, Swiss citizens had to vote to decide if the number of foreigner workers in Switzerland had to be decreased down to the 10% of the entire population. This vote was the result of the so-called Schwarzenbach initiative named after James Schwarzenbach, the representative of the Swiss right-wing party, the 'Republican movement'. Started in 1968, the initiative received the support of the 46% of the voting population of Switzerland; 54% of voters didn't approve the initiative, which was, then, refused. This article was published just a couple of months before the referendum. From the text we understand that the issue of seasonal workers was relevant for Swiss society, and it is quite clear that the article was a way to let people understand the position of the magazine in relation to the Schwarzenbach initiative: '*Ils font le bonheur et le malheur de la Suisse. On les appelle "saisonniers." Ils arrivent chez nous avec le train de Pâques. Et repartent avec le train de Nöel, les valises, des cartons et des baluchons sur les épaules. Ils ne vivent pas dans les appartements les plus confortables. Ils ont de la peine à*

Les étrangers

AU PAYS DE LA SOLITUDE

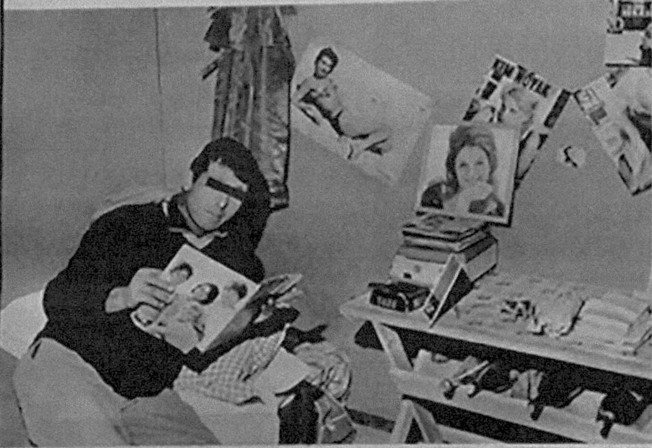

Ses loisirs? La lecture, les disques italiens qui évoquent si bien la lointaine patrie. Aux murs, des photographies qui rappellent la plage et le soleil.

Ils font le bonheur et le malheur de la Suisse. On les appelle «saisonniers». Ils arrivent chez nous avec le train de Pâques. Et repartent avec le train de Noël, des valises, des cartons et des baluchons sur les épaules. Ils ne vivent pas dans les appartements les plus confortables. Ils ont de la peine à s'intégrer à la société helvétique qui n'est pas nécessairement celle de M. Schwarzenbach. Ils ont le mal du soleil...

Questions posées :

1. Pourquoi avez-vous choisi la Suisse?
2. Ce que vous imaginiez avant de venir chez nous correspond-il à la réalité à laquelle vous êtes confronté?
3. Viviez-vous mieux dans votre pays?
4. Vous sentez-vous intégré dans la communauté helvétique?
5. Envoyez-vous de l'argent à votre famille restée au pays? En pourcentage de votre salaire, que représente cette somme?
6. A vos yeux, la Suisse est-elle un pays hospitalier?
7. Aimeriez-vous y finir vos jours?
8. Vous êtes-vous fait des amis dans notre pays?
9. Quelles sont les choses que vous possédiez chez vous et que vous n'avez pas ici?
10. Avez-vous le sentiment d'être dans un pays démocratique?

4 illustré

Fig. 2.8 L'Illustré – n. 14 of 2nd of April, 1970, p. 4. With permission of L'Illustré

s'intégrer à la société helvétique qui n'est pas nécessairement celle de M. Schwarzenbach. Ils ont le mal du soleil…'.[24]

The article is based on six interviews conducted in the French part of Switzerland. They all follow the same structure with always the same ten questions. The interviewees are asked ten questions related to their experience as migrants. The article is illustrated by two images. They are related to seasonal workers but, as stated in a note at the end of the last page, there is no connection between the images and the people interviewed. Both the images are environmental portraits. While one was taken in a domestic environment, the other one was shot during the lunch break on a construction site. The first photograph shows a man in a room (Fig. 2.9).

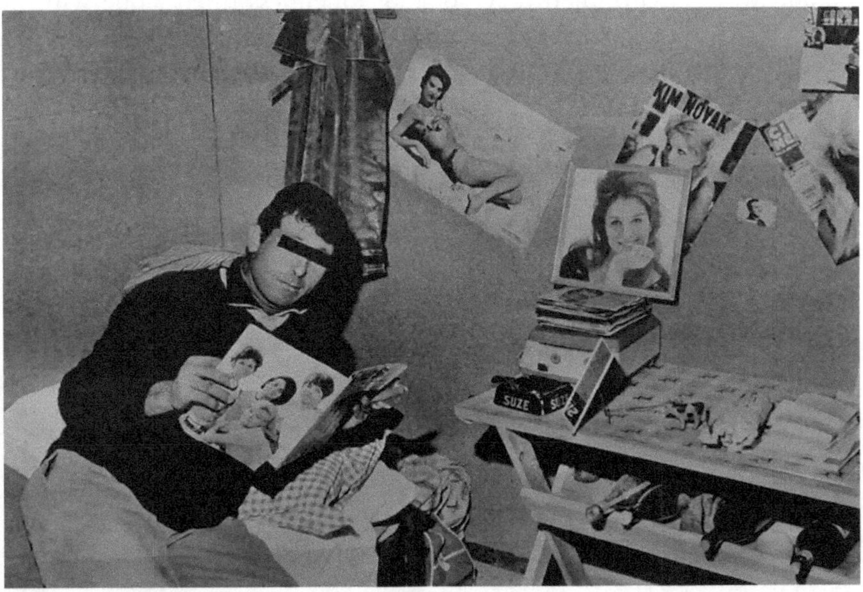

Fig. 2.9 Unknown, Au pays de la solitude, 1970. With permission of L'Illustré

[24] 'They are the happiness and the misfortune of Switzerland. We call them 'seasonal workers.' They arrive with the Easter train. And they leave with the Christmas train, with their suitcases, boxes, and backpacks on their shoulders. They do not live in the most comfortable apartments. It is difficult for them to integrate in the Swiss society, which is not necessarily that one of Mr. Schwarzenbach. They miss the sun…' (my translation).

It is the room where he lives. There is a bed and a table. On the table there is an ashtray, a record player with a stack of vinyl records, a little mirror and magazines. Under the table there are four bottles of wine. Next to his jacket, posters of actresses and models are stuck on the walls. The man is laying down on the bed in the act of reading a magazine. A black strip on the eyes is used to protect his identity. The second image represents a man during a lunch break (Fig. 2.10). He is sitting down on the ground, his back against the wall and his legs straight towards us. We understand that he is a worker from the soles of the shoes and the caption. He is chewing a bite that he gave to the sandwich he is holding in his left hand. On the ground, not far from him, there are cheese, a knife and a bottle. Both the images repeat the typical schemes of the post-war migrant representation: the context in which they are represented (domestic and work environment), symbols of loneliness (men alone with no family), their attachment to the homeland (posters, wine, records). The message is that they are human beings with feelings. They miss their land

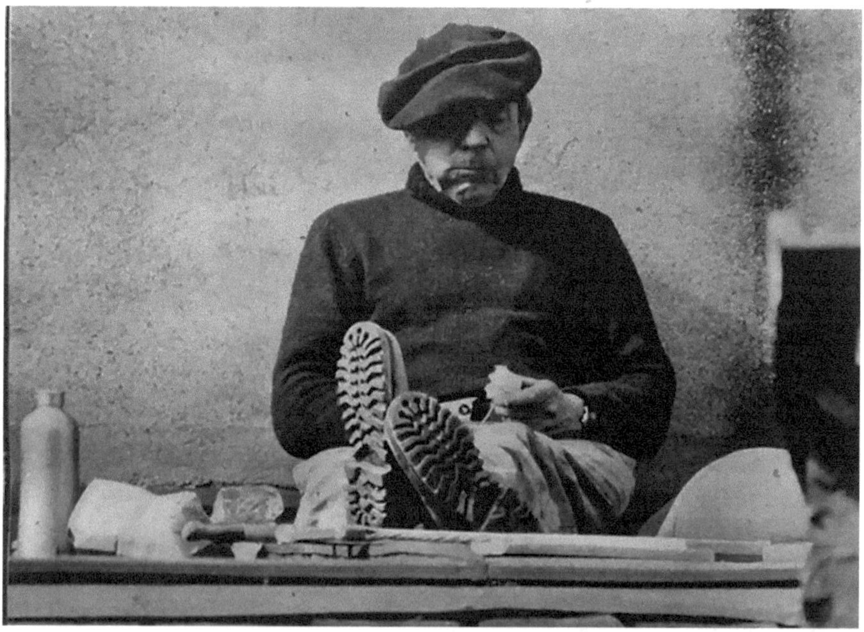

Fig. 2.10 Unknown, Au pays de la solitude, 1970. With permission of L'Illustré

and dream about it. As Max Frisch (2009) stated, 'we asked for workers, we had people instead', the suggestion of the article is for voters not to forget that the referendum is not on workers but on human beings. These migrants have their lives, their feelings, their dreams. One of the two captions claim that their spare-time activities are reading, music and photographs of the sun and the beach.

The second one states that they do not eat too often, and when they do it, they dream of their land between 12 pm and 1 pm (the lunch break). Recalling here the photographs by Hine and Sherman which documented the trans-Atlantic migration, a similar symbolism was also used by post-war photographer to narrate the migration phenomenon in Europe. However, while the American photographs showed cases part of the integration process, the same does not seem to happen for the images of the 1960s and 1970s. Corti (2010: 81–82) states that this discrepancy was a consequence on the different perception of the migratory processes by the hosting society. The characteristics of the temporary migration of the 1960s and 1970s in Europe contributed to slow down the integration process of migrant workers. The migrants' children had to be left at the borders. This separation didn't contribute to integrate migrant workers into the Swiss society since families were divided.

Les petits enfants de la frontière: Divided Families

One article from *L'Illustré* (n. 19—11th of May 1967) was dedicated to the issue of the migrants' divided families (Cascio 1967) (Fig. 2.11).[25] Five images show children at school, in the playground or simply in groups with friends (Figs. 2.12, 2.13, 2.14, 2.15, and 2.16). Children don't seem to be sad or depressed. They are actually smiling. The message delivered through these articles was that the situation was not complicated and that these kids were actually quite happy to stay in this place.

[25] This article entitled 'Les petits enfants de la frontière' by Carlo Cascio is about the situation of Italian children left at the Swiss borders by their parents, seasonal workers in Switzerland. New Swiss laws did not allow Italian seasonal workers to take their families with them. Therefore, children were left in families or in religious institutes with dorms, refectories, school and playgrounds in Domodossola. It was a hard experience for both children and parents.

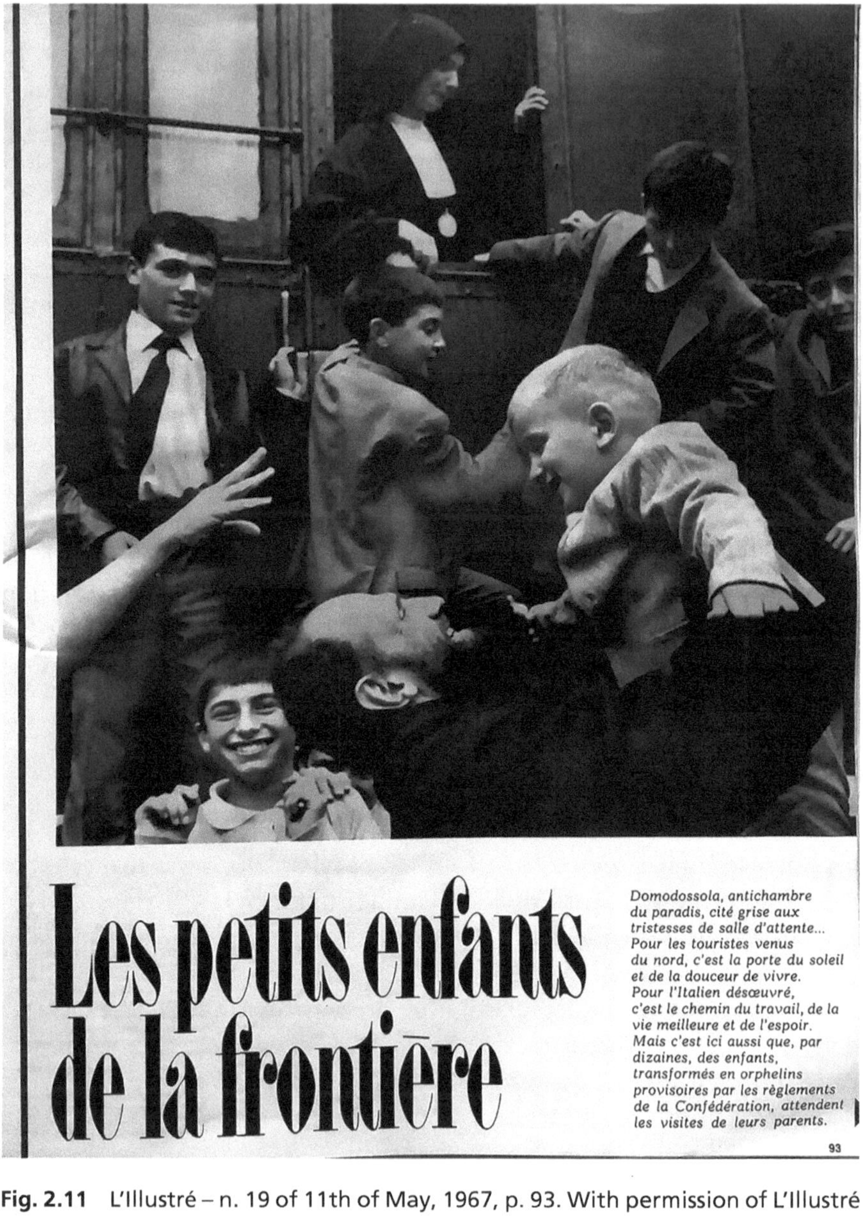

Les petits enfants de la frontière

Domodossola, antichambre du paradis, cité grise aux tristesses de salle d'attente... Pour les touristes venus du nord, c'est la porte du soleil et de la douceur de vivre. Pour l'Italien désœuvré, c'est le chemin du travail, de la vie meilleure et de l'espoir. Mais c'est ici aussi que, par dizaines, des enfants, transformés en orphelins provisoires par les règlements de la Confédération, attendent les visites de leurs parents.

93

Fig. 2.11 L'Illustré – n. 19 of 11th of May, 1967, p. 93. With permission of L'Illustré

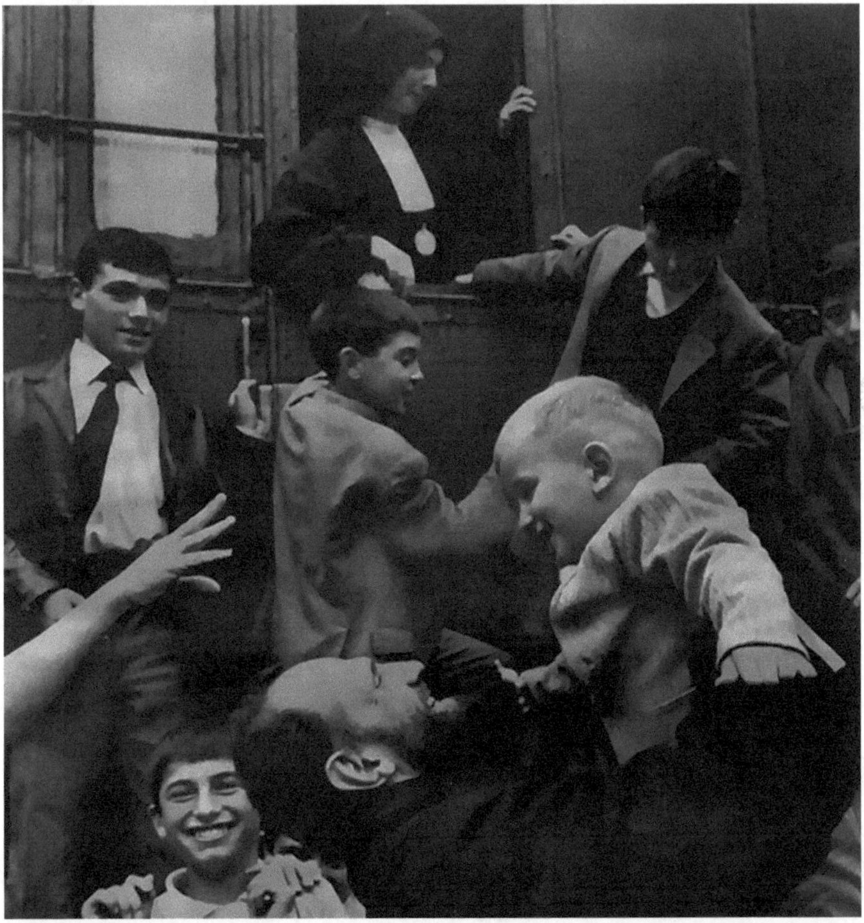

Fig. 2.12 Unknown, Les petits enfants de la frontière, 1967. With permission of L'Illustré

These five images seem to contradict the actual situation explained in the article. We don't have to forget that the article was published in a Swiss-based magazine and the message for Swiss people probably had to be softened compared to the actual situation. In all the images published here there is always at least one person looking straight into the camera. As said above for other articles, this interaction manages to shorten the

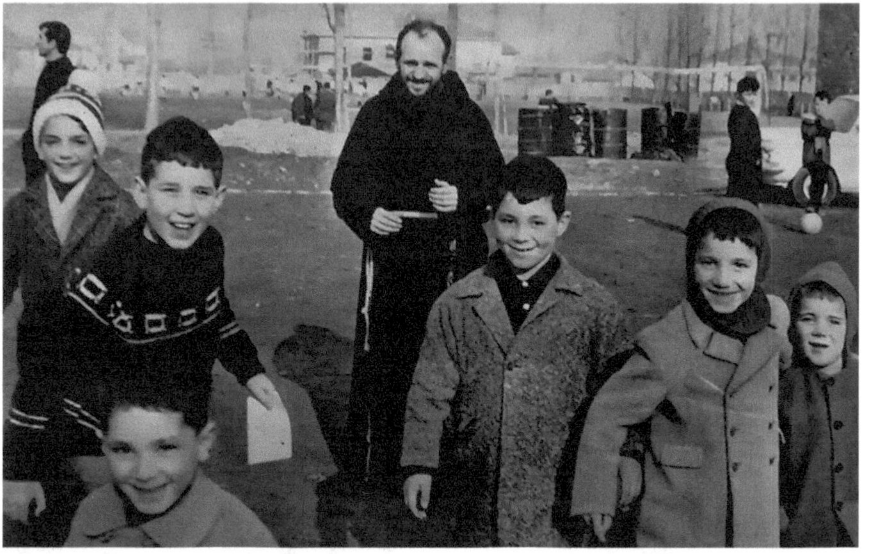

Fig. 2.13 Unknown, Les petits enfants de la frontière, 1967. With permission of L'Illustré

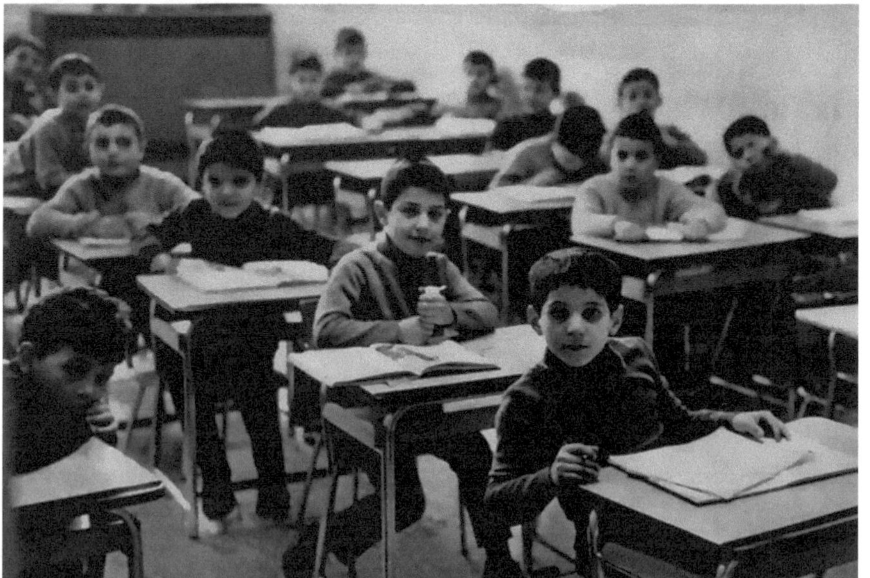

Fig. 2.14 Unknown, Les petits enfants de la frontière, 1967. With permission of L'Illustré

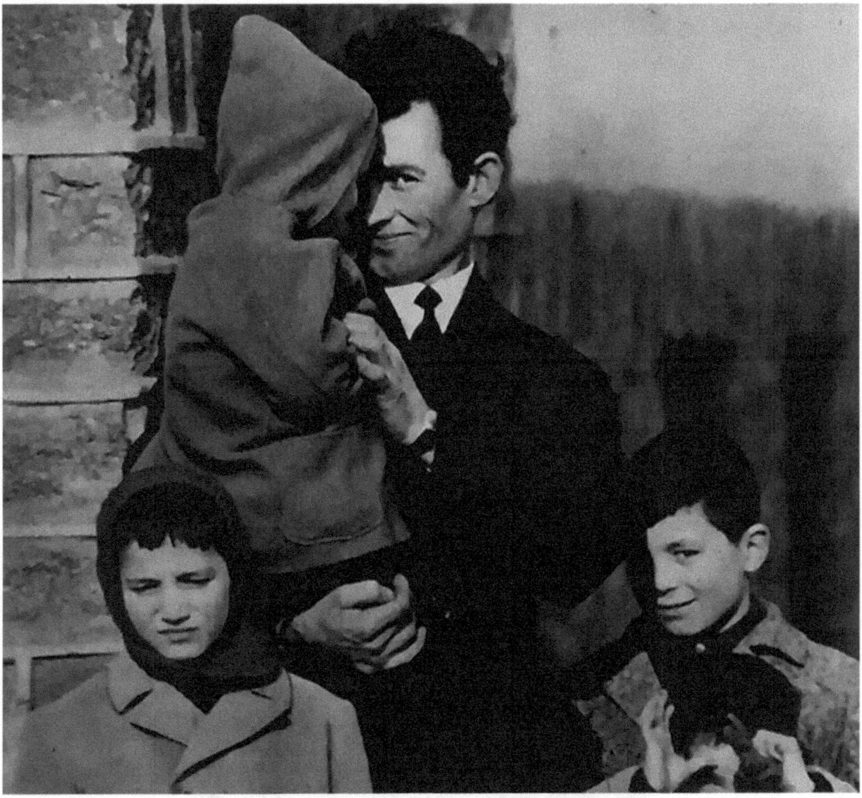

Fig. 2.15 Unknown, Les petits enfants de la frontière, 1967. With permission of L'Illustré

distance between the viewer and the photographed subjects. There are only two images where we see children with serious expressions (Figs. 2.17 and 2.18). The strongest of the two is the final image, in the last page of the article. The horizontal frame represents a boy behind a window. The window is divided in three parts and the boy is standing behind the central frame. The glass seems to be misty. Well dressed, with a tie and a jacket, this boy is looking straight into the camera. He has on his face a worried but, at the same time, accusatory expression. His gaze creates a strong connection with the viewer, a strong empathy. The glass behind which he is portrayed functions as metaphor of his condition: this transparent layer represents the separation and distance from his parents. He

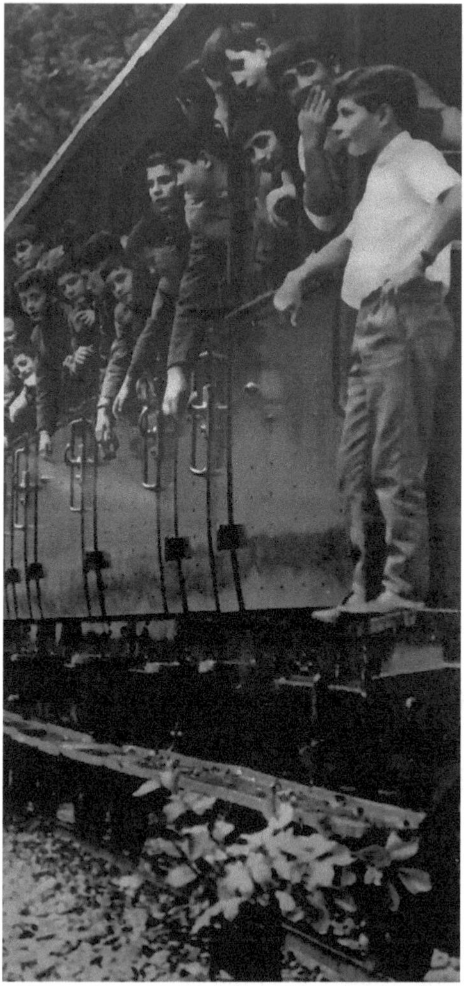

Fig. 2.16 Unknown, Les petits enfants de la frontière, 1967. With permission of L'Illustré

wants to be with them but actually has to accept this condition of being displaced following the Swiss laws.[26]

[26]As stated by Sennett (2011), 'displacement' is the feeling that is usually combined with the foreigner's experience. The foreigner who lives abroad in a condition of displacement cannot find himself. He has to construct himself a new identity and has to be creative in doing so (Sennett 2011: 76). Not moving abroad gives a sense of apparent stability (Sennett 2011: 62).

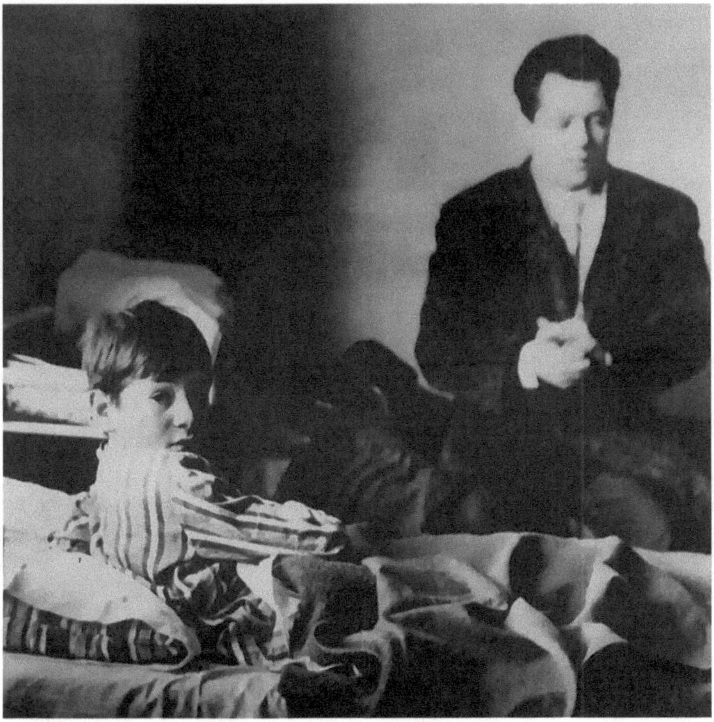

Fig. 2.17 Unknown, Les petits enfants de la frontière, 1967. With permission of L'Illustré

From the *foule bigarré et picturesque*[27] to the Schwarzenbach Years: The Shift of Perception of Italian Migrants in Switzerland

In his book *Cacciateli! Quando i migranti eravamo noi*, Concetto Vecchio (2019) narrates the story about the Schwarzenbach initiative for the 7th of June 1970 referendum on the regulated number of foreigners in Switzerland. One of the central points that Vecchio underlines is the growing intolerance towards Italian migrants from the 1960s to the 1970s. Exactly one month before the referendum on the Schwarzenbach

[27] 'Colourful and picturesque crowd' (my translation).

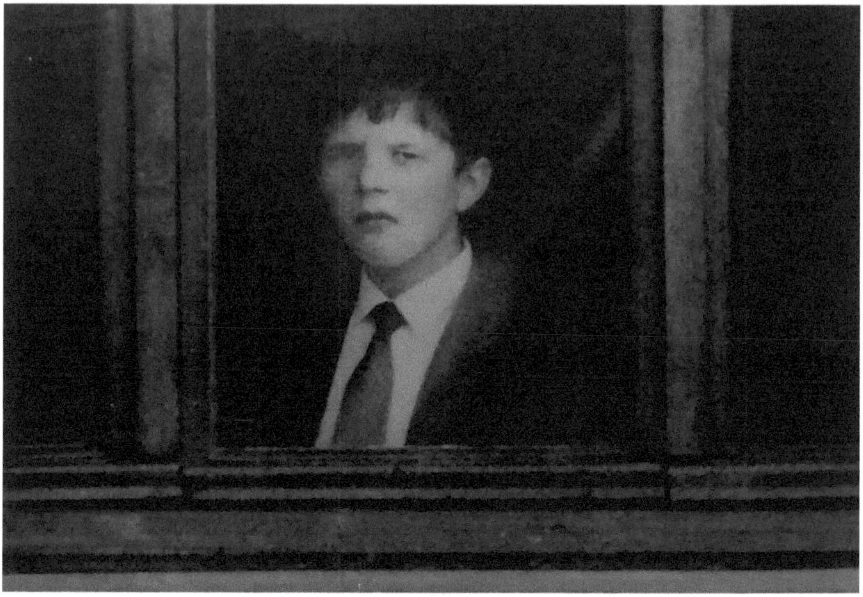

Fig. 2.18 Unknown, Les petits enfants de la frontière, 1967. With permission of L'Illustré

initiative, Paolo Frignani and John Hunger published an article on Italian migrants in *L'Illustré* n. 19 of the 7th of May 1970 (Frignani and Hunger 1970) (Fig. 2.19). It is stated in the introduction that the Swiss will soon vote on the number of seasonal workers number in the country. As a consequence of that, Frignani and Hunger claim that migrants felt uncomfortable. The journalists are wondering what the situation in the Northern part of Italy was, where migrants from the South arrived to find a job and improve their quality of life. After reading the title and the introductory text, the first thoughts one could have are that this article was published to justify the anti-Italian migration reaction of some Swiss people. If Southern Italians are not welcomed in the Northern part of Italy, their own country, how could be expected to see them well integrated in a foreign state like Switzerland? Should it be surprising, then, that the initiative Schwarzenbach was accepted? These are the core questions that seem to drive the spirit of this reportage. Images in this article are stronger than in all the other articles I have seen related to the migrants'

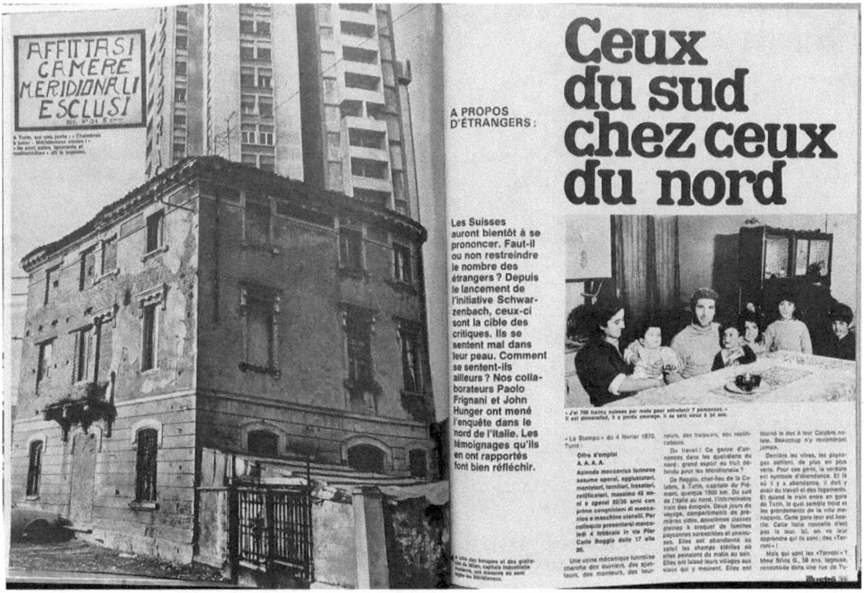
AFFITTASI
CAMERE
MERIDIONALI
ESCLUSI

A PROPOS
D'ÉTRANGERS :

Ceux du sud chez ceux du nord

Les Suisses auront bientôt à se prononcer. Faut-il ou non restreindre le nombre des étrangers ? Depuis le lancement de l'initiative Schwarzenbach, ceux-ci sont la cible des critiques. Ils se sentent mal dans leur peau. Comment se sentent-ils ailleurs ? Nos collaborateurs Paolo Frignani et John Hunger ont mené l'enquête dans le nord de l'Italie. Les témoignages qu'ils en ont rapportés font bien réfléchir.

Fig. 2.19 L'Illustré – n. 19 of 7th of May 7th, 1970, pp. 26–27. With permission of L'Illustré

condition in Switzerland. The title seems to confirm the above reasoning: '*Ceux du sud chez ceux du nord. Le débat est ouvert: comment résoudre le problème, nos envoyés spéciaux ont fait une extraordinaire enquète sur les Italiens du sud qui vivent dans le nord de leur pays.* ***Ils sont pourtant chez eux…***'.[28] The authors suggest that the solution to limit the Southern Italian migration in Switzerland is to help migrants in their own regions supporting and boosting the Southern Italian economy. In the final paragraphs of the text, Paolo Frignani and John Hunger are wondering how much time it will take for the Italian government to react to such a situation. There are seven images which illustrate the article (Figs. 2.19, 2.20, 2.21, and 2.22). Only one represents people (Fig. 2.23). It is an environmental portrait. It shows a seven-member migrant Southern Italian family. They are sitting around a table, and they are smiling. The man

[28] 'Those of the South among those ones of the North. The debate is open: how to solve the issue. Our special correspondents made an extraordinary reportage on Southern Italians who live in Northern Italy. Yet, they are at home…' (my translation).

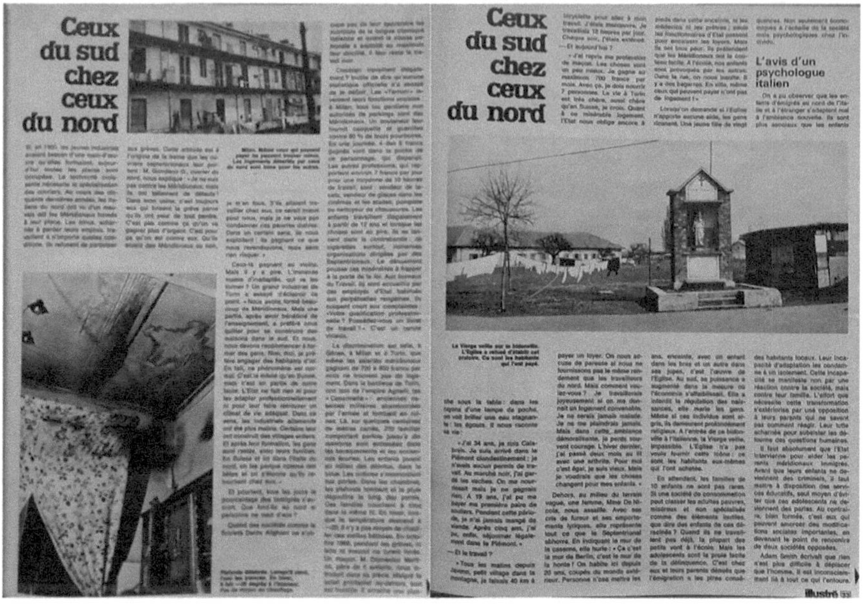

Ceux du sud chez ceux du nord

Ceux du sud chez ceux du nord

L'avis d'un psychologue italien

Illustré 33

Fig. 2.20 L'Illustré – n. 19 of 7th of May, 1970, pp. 32–33. With permission of L'Illustré

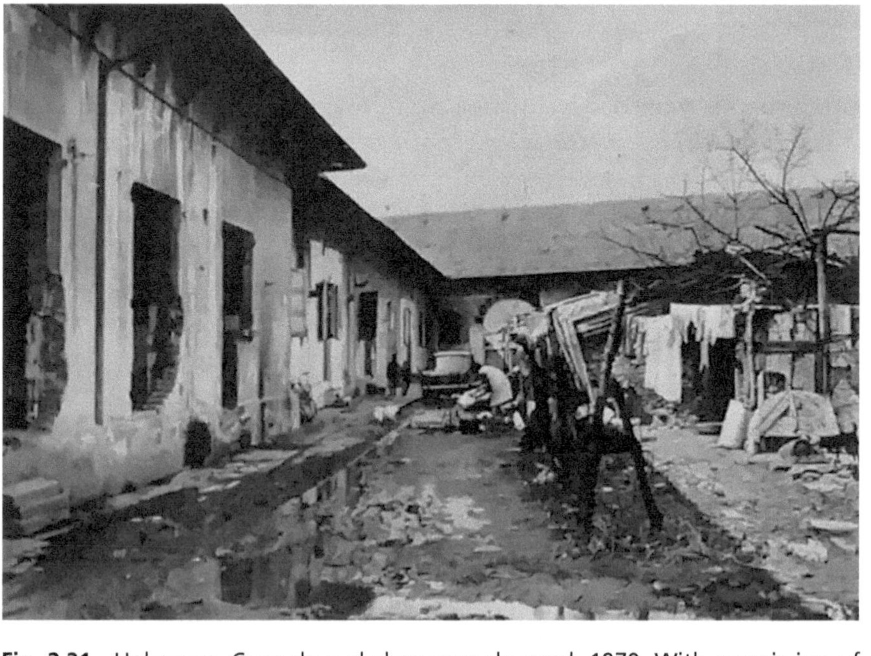

Fig. 2.21 Unknown, Ceux du sud chez ceux du nord, 1970. With permission of L'Illustré

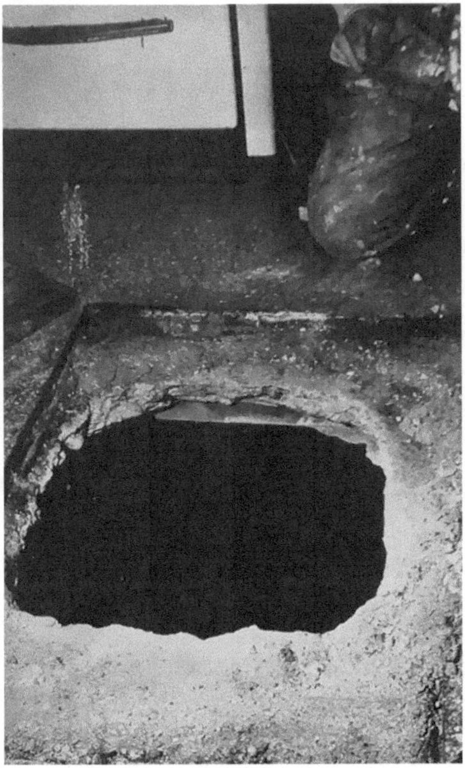

Fig. 2.22 Unknown, Ceux du sud chez ceux du nord, 1970. With permission of L'Illustré

portrayed in the centre of the frame is Domenico Martino, the worker who has to maintain the entire family with a small salary. He is described as demoralized , discouraged and old despite being only thirty-four years old. In the caption he states that he has financial difficulties maintaining seven people. The other five photographs show the living context of this family. The introductory full-page photograph shows the house where this family is living (Fig. 2.19). It is a dilapidated house surviving the 1970s Northern city expansion. We can see a skyscraper behind the old building. The caption claims that next to banks and skyscrapers in the modern and industrial Milan there are hovels (the original text literally uses the term 'masure') where Southern migrants live. In the same page,

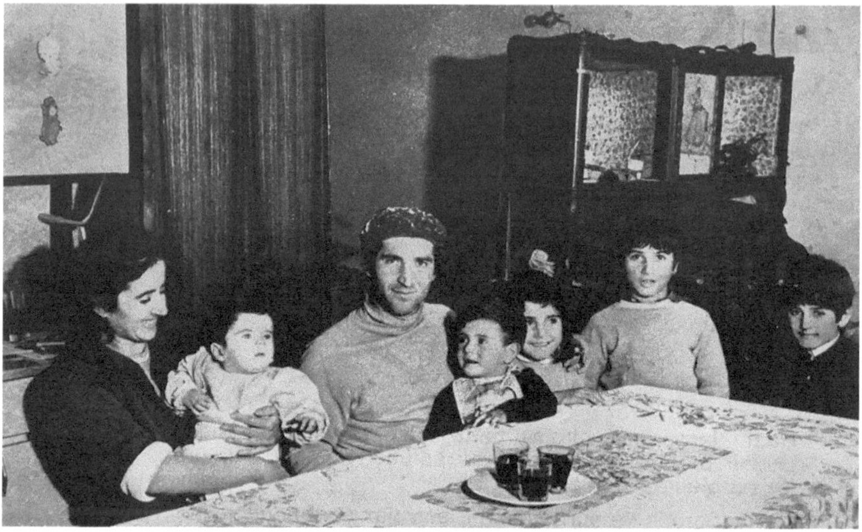

Fig. 2.23 Unknown, Ceux du sud chez ceux du nord, 1970. With permission of L'Illustré

on the top left corner, an image reproduces a sign stuck on a door in Turin, the second main city of massive migration from the South. It says: '*affittasi camera – Meridionali esclusi*'.[29] The caption reports what was said by the owner of the room: 'They are dirty, ignorant and dishonest.' This image recalls some signs which appeared in Switzerland in the same years on shop doors: 'Dogs and Italians not allowed.'[30] The rest of the images show ruined interiors with dis-repaired ceilings through which it rains. In the captions, the authors of the article underline how there is no heating system in these houses where the temperature in winter can reach -20 degrees. Another two images picture the abandoned state of a shanty-town where the local church refused even to build a chapel dedicated to St. Mary.

These photographs show how the way of representing the same kind of people over time has changed and 'that the world is not united by a smooth surface but by a complex network of frictions' (Hackett 2016:

[29] 'Room to rent - Southerners people excluded' (my translation).

[30] See Durous (2010: 105) and Mariani (2010)

14). In the articles of *L'Illustré* from 1960 to 1970, we can see this change due to this 'complex network of frictions'. They evolve because society and its perception of the issue of the migrant workers change. In the publications from the early 1960s, the migration process is represented as under control, then in the following years the situation is perceived as more critical. The first articles represented Italian migrants as *'foule bigarrée et picturesque'* (Olivier 1961: 24).[31] Photographs portray Italians working or at the train station, even smiling and chatting.[32] Approaching the years of the initiative Schwarzenbach, Italians are described as people who face serious issues in their integration process.[33] These images demonstrate what was stated in the initial part of this chapter: familiar recognitions are built and follow ideological decisions (Barthes 1972; Hall 1972). '[...] images were generally designed to appeal to the sympathies of the viewers' (Burke 2001: 22). Swiss and Italian societies have changed; the profile of the migrant has changed. Contemporary migrants are people in translation (Hall 1996) in globalized imagined communities (Anderson 1991). Drawing on these considerations, the Chap. 3 will question how Italian migrants have been represented in photographic portraiture in illustrated hard-copy and online magazines in Switzerland in the years between 2006 and 2019.

References

Alghisi, G. et al., eds. (2016). *Grazie a voi: ricordi e stima – Fotografien zur Italienischen Migration in der Schweiz.* Zürich: Limmat Verlag.

Ammann, Peter and René Burri (1970). *Braccia sì, uomini no.* Switzerland: RTS.

Anderson, B. (1991). *Imagined Communities: Reflections on the Origin and Spread of Nationalism.* London: Verso.

Barbagallo, F. (2001). *Il Sud.* Roma: Editori Riuniti.

Barthes, R. (1972). *Mythologies.* New York: Farrar, Straus and Giroux.

———. (1977). *Image, Music, Text.* London: Fontana Press.

Belting, H. (2013). *Antropologia delle immagini.* Roma: Carocci.

[31] 'A colourful and picturesque crowd who was needed by the Swiss economy' (my translation).

[32] See the central image of (Olivier 1961: 24–25).

[33] See the article of *L'Illustré*, 14th April, 1970.

Berger, J. and Jean Mohr. (2010). *A Seventh Man : A Book of Images and Words about the Experience of Migrant Workers in Europe*. London and New York: Verso.
Bizzarri, A. (1970). *Il Treno Del Sud*. Switzerland: Bertrand Theubet, Les Amis d'Alvaro Bizzarri/TSR/AB.
———. (1972). *Lo Stagionale*. Switzerland: Bertrand Theubet, Les Amis d'Alvaro Bizzarri/TSR/AB.
———. (1974). *Il Rovescio Della Medaglia*. Switzerland: Bertrand Theubet, Les Amis d'Alvaro Bizzarri/TSR/AB.
Blanc-Chaléard, M-C., and Antonio Bechelloni. (2007). *Les Petites Italies dans le monde*. Rennes: PU Rennes.
Bollati, G. and Carlo Bertelli. (1979). *Storia d'Italia. Annali 2. L'immagine fotografica 1845-1945*. Torino: Einaudi.
Boltanski, L. (2018). "La retorica della figura." In *Un'arte media – Saggio sugli usi sociali della fotografia*, ed. Pierre Bourdieu. Milano: Meltemi.
Bourdieu, P. (1965). *Un art moyen. Essai sur les usages sociaux de la photographie*. Paris: Minuit.
———. (2018). *Un'arte media*. Milano: Meltemi.
Brier, S. (2007). Raffigurare il passato. Le immagini visive e la comprensione della storia degli Stati Uniti. *Contemporanea*, 10 (3), 441–454.
Burke, P. (2001). *Eyewitnessing: The Uses of Images as Historical Evidence*. London: Reaktion Books.
Caruso, A. (2016). *1960. Il migliore anno della nostra vita*. Milano: Longanesi.
Cascio, C. (1967, May). Les petits enfants de la frontière. *L'Illustré*, 93–96.
Castro, S. (2013). "Le lavoratrici italiane in Svizzera nel secondo dopoguerra: uno sguardo statistico." In Badino, A. and Silvia Inaudi (Eds.). *Migrazioni femminili attraverso le Alpi – Lavoro, famiglia, trasformazioni culturali nel secondo dopoguerra*. Milano: Franco Angeli 2013.
Cerutti, M. (1994). *Un secolo di emigrazione italiana in Svizzera (1870-1970), attraverso le fonti dell'Archivio federale*.
Corti, P. (2010). *Emigranti e immigrati nelle rappresentazioni di fotografi e fotogiornalisti*. Foligno: Editoriale Umbra.
———. (2009). "L'emigrazione temporanea in Europa, in Africa e nel Levante." In Bevilacqua, P., Andreina De Clementi and Emilio Franzina (eds.). *Storia dell'emigrazione italiana*. Vol. 1. Roma: Donzelli. p. 181
De Amicis, E. (1897). *In America*. Roma: Enrico Voghera.
Di Vittorio, G. (2012). *Le strade del lavoro*. Roma: Donzelli editore.
Dominicé, K., and Luc Peter. (2010). *Les Années Schwartzenbach*. Switzerland: Connaissance 3.

Durous, R. (2010). *Des Ritals En Terre Romande*. Vevey: Editions de l'Aire.

Fabrizi, A. (1949). *Emigrantes*. Italy: Guaranteed Pictures Italia.

Frignani, P. and John Hunger. (1970, May). Ceux du sud chez ceux du nord. *L'Illustré*, 26–35.

Frisch, M. (2009). *Cercavamo braccia, sono arrivati uomini*. Locarno: Armando Dadò.

Gabaccia, D. R. (2000). *Italy's Many Diasporas*. Abingdon-on-Thames: Routledge.

Gibelli, A. (1989). "Fatemi un po' sapere": scrittura e fotografia nella corrispondenza tra emigrati liguri. In *La via delle Americhe. L'emigrazione ligure tra evento e racconti*. Genova: Sage.

Gygax, G. (1965, April). Travailleurs étrangers: le problème est-il résolu?. *L'Illustré*, 22–25.

Hall, S. (1972). "The determinations of news photographs." In *Working Paper in Cultural Studies*, n. 3 (autumn), pp. 53–87. Reissued: Stanley Cohen and Jock Young (eds.), *The Manifacture of News: social problems, deviance and the mass media*. London: Constable, pp. 176–190, 1972.

———. (1996). "The Question of Cultural Identity." *Modernity: An Introduction to Modern Societies* 4: 596–632.

Hackett, S. (2016). Social subjects. In *Outsiders: American Photography and Film 1950s–1980s* (pp. 9–15). Toronto: Art Gallery of Ontario.

Hine, L. W. (1909). "Social Photography: How the Camera May Help in the Social Uplift." In *Proceedings of the National Conference of Charities and Correction at the Thirty-Sixth Session*, edited by Alexander Johnson, 357. Fort Wayne: Print of Fort Wayne.

Joly, M. (2015). *Introduction à l'analyse de l'image*. Paris: Armand Colin.

Kaplan, D. (1992). "Introduction." In *Photo Story: Selected Letters and Photographs of Lewis W. Hine*, (pp. xvii–xxxvi). Washington: Smithsonian Institution Press.

Leone, S. (1966). *Il buono, il brutto e il cattivo*. Italy: Produzioni Europee Associate – United Artists.

Longolius, S. (2003). *Lewis W. Hine's Social Photography - Immigrants at Ellis Island 1904–1909*. Munich: GRIN Verlag.

Maiolino, A. (2013). "La construction des identités dans le débat politique." In La Barba et al. (ed.). *La migration italienne dans la Suisse d'après-guerre*. Lausanne: Editions Antipodes.

Malioza, M. (2017). "The Immigrant - 1917 - Ft. Charlie Chaplin." https://www.youtube.com/watch?v=NxWkRgp18oM&t=579s. Accessed 28.03.2022.

Mariani, D. (2010). ""Vietato ai cani e agli italiani!"" https://www.swissinfo.ch/ita/immigrazione-da-sud_-vietato-ai-cani-e-agli-italiani%2D%2D/8959576. Accessed 21.09.2022.

Olivier, R. (1961, May). Habitants méridionaux des villes romandes: les italiens. *L'Illustré*, 24–25.

Ortoleva, P. (1991). Una fonte difficile. La fotografia e la storia dell'emigrazione. *Altreitalie*, 5 (April), 120–131.

Ostuni, M. R. (1990). Belle foto! In *C'era una volta la Merica. Immigrati piemontesi in Argentina*. Cuneo: L'arciere.

Ricciardi, T. (2018). *Breve Storia Dell'emigrazione Italiana in Svizzera.* Roma: Donzelli editore.

Riis, J. (1971). *How the Other Half Lives. Studies Among the Tenements of NY.* New York: Dover Publications

Rohrer, M. (1963a, March). L'invasion pacifique des travailleurs étrangers. *L'Illustré*.

———. (1963b, March). Les étrangers et notre économie. *L'Illustré*.

Rosenblum, W. (1977). "Foreword." In *America and Lewis Hine.* New York: Aperture.

Rossi-Doria, M. (1958). *Dieci anni di politica agraria nel Mezzogiorno*. Roma-Bari: Laterza.

Rouille, A. (2005). *La photographie. Entre document et art contemporain*. Paris: Gallimard.

Ruppen, O. (2003). *Il lungo addio: una storia fotografica sull'emigrazione italiana in Svizzera dopo la guerra. Der lange Abschied: 138 Fotografien zur italienischen Emigration in die Schweiz nach 1945. Lange Abschied.* Zürich: Limmat Verlag.

Sartre, J-P. (1949). *What is literature?* New York: Philosophical Library.

SCOPE. (1970, April). Les étrangers - Au pays de la solitude. *L'Illustré*, 4–14.

Seiler, A. J. (1965). *Siamo Italiani – Gespräche Mit Italienischen Gastarbeitern.* Switzerland: EVZ.

Seixas, P. (1987). "Lewis Hine : From "Social" to "Interpretive" Photographer." *Americana Quarterly* 39 (3): 381–409.

Senn, R. (1964, November). Ces Italiens, nos hôtes. *L'Illustré*, 81.

Sennett, R. (2011). *The Foreigner - Two Essays on Exile* (2017th ed.). London: Notting Hill Editions.

Sotelo Vásquez, R. (2003). Imágenes en la distancia: reflexiones sobre fotografia y emigración. *Estudios Migratorios Latinoamericanos*, 51 (August).

Stange, M. (1989). *Symbols of Ideal Life: Social Documentary Photography in America, 1890–1950*. Cambridge: Cambridge University Press.

Sundell, M. (1986). "Golden Immigrants at the Gold Door : Lewis Hine's Photographs of Ellis Island." *Social Text* 16 (16): 168–75.

Szlezák, K. S. (2009). "The Ellis Island Experience: Through the Eyes of Lewis Hine." *Aspeers*, no. 2: 71–89.

———. 2012. "The Issue of Americanization in Photographs by Augustus F. Sherman and Lewis W. Hine." *American Studies* 57 (1): 9–29.

Trachtenberg, A. (1977). "Ever—the Human Document." In *America and Lewis Hine*, 118–137. New Haven: Aperture.

Ureña, L. J. (2009). *Lewis Hine at Ellis Island: The Photography of Immigration and Race, 1904–1926*. Northwestern University.

Vecchio, C. (2019). *Cacciateli! Quando i migranti eravamo noi*. Milano: Feltrinelli.

3

2006–2019 Photographic Representation of the New Italian Diaspora on the *Arc Lémanique*

Abstract Italian migration to Switzerland decreased in the 1970s; however, with the economic crisis in 2007, Italians started again to move to the Swiss Confederation. From 2006 to 2019, Italians resident abroad and registered on AIRE (Anagrafe Italiana Residenti all'Estero) increased to 70.2%. This chapter summarizes the findings of research conducted in the archives of the magazines *L'Illustré* (2006–2019), *L'Hebdo* (2006–2017) and online publications.

Keywords Economic crisis • Visual semiotics • L'Hebdo • Photographic portraiture • Suisse Romande

Introduction

Following the same methodology described in Chap. 2 (research of articles and illustrations related to Italian migration to Switzerland), we will now dig into the archives of *L'Illustré*, *L'Hebdo* and other online magazines issued between 2006 and 2019. As mentioned above, the purpose of this process is to understand how contemporary Italian migrants have

F. Arese Visconti, *The Invisible Diaspora*, Palgrave Studies in Creativity and Culture,
https://doi.org/10.1007/978-3-031-74925-4_3

been visually represented in that specific time frame. The findings suggest two lines of reasoning. In the first part, the visual semiotic analysis supports the narratives of this new migration phenomenon and compares it to the former diaspora of the 1960s and 1970s. Second, the new Italian diaspora is framed in a historical and sociological context with the support of scholars' theories. The different profiles of the new Italian migrants are identified. It is within the intersection of these two reasonings that we move. The questions that the present research has tried to answer are if there is really a new Italian diaspora phenomenon, if Italians are still considered 'migrants' by the public opinion and on visual media in the French-speaking part of Switzerland, who are the new 'migrants' and how the results of this research can be reflected through my practice. While the new Italian diaspora is a very complex and multifaceted phenomenon that is not really properly visually represented through the media, the aim of the research is to find creative solutions to rethink photographic portraiture of contemporary Italian migrants who are resident in the area along the *arc lémanique*.

As stated by Valeria Lai (2014), researcher of the Università La Sapienza in Rome, on the Rapporto Fondazione Migrantes in relation to her work on photographic imagery of new Italian migrants in the media, images are part of wider debates and reflections on social and cultural phenomena. In the years of globalization, these images support messages which are able to hinder or to promote changes that are happening in contemporary society. The media manage to develop a common shared symbolic environment. Through the analysis of pictures of migrants, it is possible to understand on a bigger scale how the public imagination is shaped, the politics of the 'other' and how society reacts to certain phenomena. Are the changes in representation strategic? If we agree with Bleiker (2001: 515) that meanings are made public through representations, some constructions are made visible to the public. Representations help to develop categorizations of people and events and are part of the collective process of assigning meanings. 'They form the context for policy making and implementation' (Bleiker 2001: 1017). To build a representation is an act of power and this action is fundamentally political.[1] The symbols, icons, messages connected with images influence society and the interpretation of specific issues and subjects. In an article on the impact of images on the public opinion's perception of refugees, Heather Johnson[2] (2011) claims that the social world of symbols and signs forms knowledge which will 'enable or disable later processes of dominance and resistance' and it is, therefore, very important in the society formation process. These actions will influence how society will interact with particular categories of people. In the case of seasonal workers in the 1960s and 1970s, was the political context influenced by the perception of images or, on the contrary, the political context influenced the public perception of images? How were they produced? Are these questions still valid today? Representation is not only in spoken or written forms but also, especially in these days, through images which operate on different levels. An image communicates not only on a language level,[3] but on the perception and emotional level (Johnson 2011: 1016). One reacts immediately with emotional responses to inputs like fears, feelings of compassion, etc., that an image can provoke. These images are read by the viewer as the realistic representation of the world (Johnson 2011: 1017). The examination of visual representation of new Italian migrants combined with an analysis of the texts associated with the images allow an understanding of the change of the perception of Italian migration in Switzerland and help to frame it in a historical context. The next paragraph explains why the time frame between 2006 and 2019 has been chosen for the research of images on Italian migration to Switzerland.

---

[1] This connects with the reason why in this book we are analysing images published in magazines that usually use professional photographers and follow editorial lines in specific historical and political contexts.

[2] Heather Johnson is Senior Lecturer of International Studies at Queen's University in Belfast.

[3] R. Barthes (1977: 28–29) explains that '(…) the photograph is verbalized in the very moment it is perceived; better, it is only perceived verbalized (if there is a delay in verbalization, there is disorder in perception, questioning, anguish for the subject, traumatism, following G. Cohen-Seat's hypothesis with regard to filmic perception). From this point of view, the image - grasped immediately by an inner metalanguage, language itself - in actual fact has no denoted state, is immersed for its very social existence in at least an initial layer.'

Why 2006–2019?

The period between 2006 and 2019 witnesses a revamped activity of migration from Italy to Switzerland similar in numbers to the 1960s–1970s diaspora. After the Schwarzenbach initiatives and the oil crisis of the 1970s, Italian migration to Switzerland decreased (Ricciardi 2018: 2201). With the beginning of the 2007–2008 global economic crisis, Italy experienced a large new diaspora phenomenon to the traditional countries of migration (Cacciatore and Pepe 2019). As already affirmed before, often addressed as a *brain drain* phenomenon, academic studies (Caneva 2016; Franchi 2017; Pugliese 2018) have stated that this narrative is over-simplistic and needs to be re-examined and updated. This diaspora in the age of globalization has new and complex layers (Cacciatore and Pepe 2019: 507). From 2006 to 2019, Italians resident abroad registered on AIRE (Anagrafe Italiana Residenti all'Estero) increase of 70.2%, growing from 3.1 million to almost 5.3 million (Bonifazi 2017: 32; Sanfilippo 2017: 366). In January 2019 the exact number was 5.288.281 (Licata 2019: 4). Almost half of them came from the Southern part of Italy (48.9%). People between 35 and 49 years old were the most represented group (23.4%), the majority of them being men (57.6%). The level of education is medium-high (52.6% has at least a diploma). The largest communities of Italians resident abroad in Europe are in Germany (764.000), in Switzerland (623.000), in France (422.000) and in the UK (327.000).[4] These numbers might be higher considering that the Schengen agreement has guaranteed European citizens free circulation throughout Europe. This is not the case for extra-Schengen people moving to Europe. As a consequence of this phenomenon, the calculation of Italian migrants who decided not to register to AIRE is complicated. Many Italian migrants could actually live in foreign European countries without being officially registered on the Italian official records of residents abroad. Hosted by friends or relatives migrated before them, these not-registered Italian migrants tried to find an occupation through personal connections. In an interesting study on Italian migrants in Basel, Switzerland, conducted by Cristina Franchi (2017), one-fourth of the

[4] See (Licata 2019).

subjects involved in the research were not registered on AIRE and therefore did not appear on official data. Figures, thus, show only part of the emerged migrants, probably only those ones who had already a job once arrived in the hosting country. Despite these considerations, the public debate has tended to concentrate since 2007 on the *brain drain* phenomenon, the loss of talented, well-educated young professionals or academics.[5]

The causes are usually directed to the economic crisis and the unemployment which it generates. In general, as stated by Caneva (2016), it seems that this process is not considered as 'migration' because it doesn't have the characteristics of the past and of the global migration from Africa and Western Asia to Europe. A generally accepted opinion (Caneva 2016; Franchi 2017; Pugliese 2018) claims that there is an identification of the past migration of the 1960s and 1970s as a migration of poor people in contrast with the contemporary migration of well-educated, talented, young Italians with a distinct separation between mobility and migration.

Visual Semiotics Image Analysis

The aim of this part of the research was to find articles related to contemporary migration to Switzerland with a particular attention to the recent Italian diaspora. While considering the historical and ideological context to understand the larger frame (Hall 1972: 62; Barthes 1977: 28), Gillian Dyer's checklist for a semiotics analysis was used (Rose 2001). This list includes fundamental elements of semiotics analysis of other scholars (Barthes 1977; Boltanski 2018) and was considered quite exhaustive in all its aspects (representation of bodies, representations of manner, representations of activity, props and settings). In the process of image analysis, the position of the camera[6] was also taken into consideration. To

[5] The *brain drain* phenomenon has been studied by Docquier and Rapoport (2007), Dahinden (2008), Friedrich and Schultz (2008), Cassar (2010), Dequiedt and Zenou (2011), Boeri et al. (2012). Specifically on Italian migration, see Beltrame (2007), Tirabassi and Del Pra (2014), Minneci (2015), Tintori and Romei (2017), Franchi (2017).

[6] Lower, equal or higher position of the camera in relation to the subject's eyes.

continue the research explained in Chap. 2, recent copies of *L'Illustré* and *L'Hebdo* were included in this new study. Both weekly French-speaking general interest magazines, *L'Illustré* and *L'Hebdo* were launched in different moments by the same publisher in Lausanne.[7] While *L'Illustré* was available in its hard copies in the publisher's archives in Lausanne, *L'Hebdo* was only accessible as online archive provided by the Lausanne University. During the research, another two interesting articles which dealt with the new Italian diaspora in Switzerland were found. The first one was published in the French-speaking Swiss edition of the *Readers Digest* from 2012 and it was also illustrated on the front cover of the magazine (Favre 2012) (Fig. 3.2). The second one was written in 2016 on the Geneva newspaper *La Tribune de Genève*.[8] In her article 'Les Italiens reviennent s'installer en Suisse', journalist Lucie Monnat (2016) highlights how, after a moment of decrease, Italians were moving back in considerable numbers to the Swiss confederation. To illustrate the article, Lucie Monnat used some of my preliminary research photographic portraits of recent Italian migrants and second-generation Italian migrants in Switzerland. An online investigation through the archives of Bilan.ch (Vakaridis 2016) and Swissinfo.ch (Ottaviani 2016a, 2016b, 2016c) was also conducted.

In the case of *L'Illustré*, fourteen years of publications were analysed (from 2006 to 2019). In the 714 issues there are fifty articles dedicated to migrants, refugees and/or clandestines. The term 'refugee' was used nine times, while 'migrants' five and 'clandestines' four times. Other new ethnicities were included in the debate about migration. While Portuguese and French migrants were also involved in the old diaspora, new nationalities appeared for the first time in this magazine. The recent migration phenomenon lists people from Iraq, Kosovo, Equador, Tunisia, Nigeria, China, Erythrea, Afghanistan, Georgia, Moldovia. This is evident in the

[7] *L'Illustré* was founded in Lausanne in 1921 and is still active. *L'Hebdo* was launched in Lausanne in 1987 and closed in 2017.

[8] *Tribune de Genève*—17th of May, 2016, p. 4. 'Le Italiens reviennent s'installer en Suisse'. Article by Lucie Monnat and photographs by Francesco Arese Visconti.

articles on *L'Illustré*[9] and confirmed by the official data of the Secrétariat d'État aux migrations (SEM 2021).

Only one article was directly dedicated to Italian migration (Clot 2010). Published in the occasion of the fortieth anniversary of the Schwarzenbach initiative from the 1970s (n. 42 of 20th October, 2010, 'Les années Schwarzenbach, 40 ans après.' pp. 46–54), this article was written by Philippe Clot (2010) and illustrated with old black and white photographs taken in the 1970s by Mario Del Curto. These images repeat the symbols found on the images analysed in Chap. 2 of this research: presence of the suitcase as icon of migration (pp. 46–47), health check (p. 48), life in the barracks (p. 49—top), men alone (p. 49—middle) and without families and women (p. 49—bottom). The article insists on the difficulties that these migrants encountered once they moved to Switzerland: *honte* (shame) and *ressentiment* (resentment) are the words used by the author to explain how migrants describe their daily experiences in Switzerland. The article is completed with three stories of migrants who still live in Switzerland and eventually were naturalized Swiss. One of them, Pietro Franco Longo, is Italian. In his color portrait, he is represented standing next to a net in a tennis ground. The caption states that he is responsible for events at the local tennis club. He is photographed full body in what seems to be a comfortable and confident position. He is looking straight into the camera, positioned at a lower height. The lower position of the camera gives authority to the subject portrayed and supports the idea that he is probably integrated into the hosting society, and he is not in a weak position. The facial expression with a large smile seems to support this point.

The research on the online archives of *L'Hebdo* at the University of Lausanne was limited to twelve years between 2006 and 2017, the closing year. The analysis included, therefore, 612 issues. Eighteen articles

[9] See *L'Illustré* n. 11 of 14th March 2007, n. 14 of 4th April 2007, n. 15 11th of April 2007, n. 6 of 6th June 2007, n. 5 of 30th January 2008, n. 32 of 6th August 2008, n. 38 of 16th September 2009, n. 7 of 17th February 2010, n. 49 of 8th December 2010, n. 1 of 5th January 2011, n. 6 of 9th February 2011, n. 16 of 20th April 2011, n. 9 of 29th February 2012, n. 35 of 29th August 2012, n. 23 of 5th June 2013, n. 45 of 5th November 2014, n. 22 of 27th May 2015, n. 23 of 23rd June 2015, n. 25 of 17th June 2015, n. 16 of 20th April 2016, n. 23 of 8th June 2016, n. 23 of 7th June 2017, n. 37 of 13th September 2017, n. 11 of 14th March 2018, n. 24 of 12th June 2019, n. 44 of 30th October 2019.

related to migration (refugees, integration, foreigners) were found. Only two were dedicated to the new Italian diaspora. All the articles are illustrated with photographs. In an article from November 2012,[10] journalist Matthieu Ruf (2012) reflects on returning second-generation migrants.[11] Second-generation migrants once lived for a certain number of years in the country of origin of their parents, before deciding to return to the place where they were born and grew up, the hosting country of migration of their parents. Matthieu Ruf describes different experiences of people from Spain, Portugal and Italy. As stated by Susanne Wessendorf (2010), second-generation Italians have similar cultural and socio-economic backgrounds but have different reactions to their parents' homeland or to Switzerland. There are three different reactions. For some second-generation Italians it is not important to feel a sense of being part of this group but rather to develop their own relationships with people with different origins (Wessendorf 2007b). For others, it is fundamental to be an active part of the second-generation Italians group but they cannot see themselves living in a country which is not Switzerland. Others decide to try to move back to their parents' homeland. This last case represents a minority which is probably influenced by their parents' feeling of nostalgia. This is the group of people to which this article is related. The majority of Southern Italian migrants of the 1960s–1970s were farmers or trades people. Their children who grew up in Switzerland were well integrated in the Swiss society due to the strong support of families, the emphasis given by their parents to education and to their socio-economic achievement. These second-generation Italians have a higher level of education then their parents (Bolzman et al. 2003; Juhasz and Mey 2003; Mey et al. 2005). Italian 'nostalgia' in parents was strong and evolved in the so-called key scenario (Ortner 1973: 1339). They had strong transnational relations with the homeland, which developed through several visits every year. Second-generation Italians followed them and loved this experience since it was often part of their holidays.

[10] N. 46 of 15th November, 2012, pp. 42–45—'Immigrés de père au fille.' Article by Matthieu Ruf and photographs by Sedrik Nemeth.

[11] On this topic, see Seiler (2002), Wessendorf (2007a, 2010).

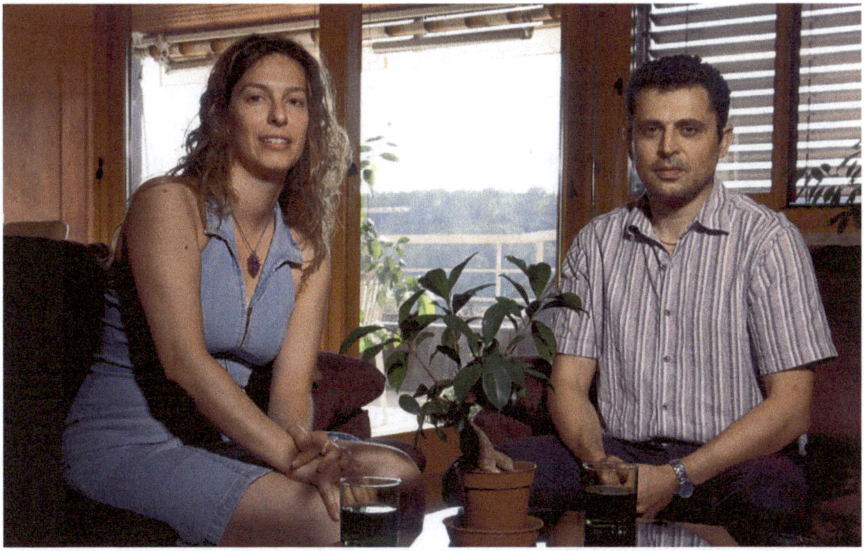

Fig. 3.1 Unknown, Filomena Giannini and Enzo Lasprogata in an interior colour portrait, 2012. With permission of *L'Hebdo*

In this way, they generated a sense of belonging. Even though they are rare cases, there are second-generation Italians who decided to move back to Italy and live there. This seems to have depended on how much they have been influenced by the feelings of 'nostalgia' transmitted through their parents and by how much they are integrated in the Italian context. These are two different kinds of experiences. In the first case, individuals had an idealized image of Italy and had difficulties integrating. This is the case of Filomena Giannini, the woman portrayed next to her husband, Enzo Lasprogata, in the article of November 2012, n. 46 of *L'Hebdo* (Ruf 2012) (Fig. 3.1). Originally from Avellino, a city in the South of Italy, Filomena and Enzo have decided to go back to Switzerland, the country which hosted her father as seasonal worker in the 1960s and 1970s. Born in Switzerland, Filomena had decided, once an adult, to move to Italy because of the strong sense of belonging to the Italian community but realized after a few years that the living and working conditions in Switzerland were better. In the photograph, Filomena and Enzo are portrayed in their apartment in Switzerland. They are sitting in their armchairs. They look straight into the camera. Filomena and Enzo have a glimpse of a smile on their faces, a sign of self-confidence and relaxation. The photograph is taken from a lower position than their eyes and puts the couple in a dominant position to the viewer. This point gives the portrayed subjects a sense of authority which supports the idea of self-confidence. The same idea returns in the portraits of Italian migrants which illustrate another article of *L'Hebdo* of July 2015 (Lietti and Tauxe 2015)[12] and on the online publications of Bilan.ch and Swissinfo.ch. On *L'Hebdo* of July 2015, the article describes the experience of foreigners who are living and are integrated in Switzerland. The texts are illustrated with twenty-two colour portraits. Italians are the most represented nationality with five images. Other migrants are from Kosovo, India, Chile, Russia, Benin, Spain, Iran, Macedonia, Australia, Turkey, United States, Greece, Cameroon, Senegal, Hungary, Algeria and Kurdistan. The research on the web on Bilan.ch and Swissinfo.ch produced three pages with articles and photographs on the new Italian diaspora. The first one is from November–December 2016 on swissinfo.ch (Ottaviani 2016a, 2016b, 2016c). This dossier is curated by Jacopo Ottaviani, Daniele Grasso, Sara Moreira and Katerina Stavroula. The photographs are by Jacopo Ottaviani. The title is *Generation E: histoires des jeunes migrants*. The article describes stories of young Italian migrants in Switzerland. The second result of the research is an article from the 20th of May 2016 on bilan.ch (Vakaridis 2016). The article is entitled *Les jeunes Italiens affluent en Suisse*. This page by Mary Vakaridis and photograph by Dominic Büttner is about the new profile of Italian migrants in Switzerland.

Special attention is deserved by the front cover and an article in the Swiss French-speaking edition of the *Readers Digest* of July 2012.[13] This article and the images (Favre 2012) which illustrate (Fig. 3.2) it summarize most of the characteristics of the new Italian migrants' profiles which will be described later in this chapter. The title of the article, which is also

[12] N. 31 of 30th July 2015, pp. 6–29, 'Ces étrangers qui nous accueillent en Suisse'—Dossier coordinated by Anne Lietti and Chantal Tauxe (Lietti and Tauxe 2015). Photographs by Nicolas Righetti, Sarah Jacquemet, Lea Kloos and Jean-Christophe Bott.

[13] July, 2012—Front cover and pp. 54–55. 'Le nouvel Eldorado.' Article by Alexis Favre—Photographs by Eddy Mottaz

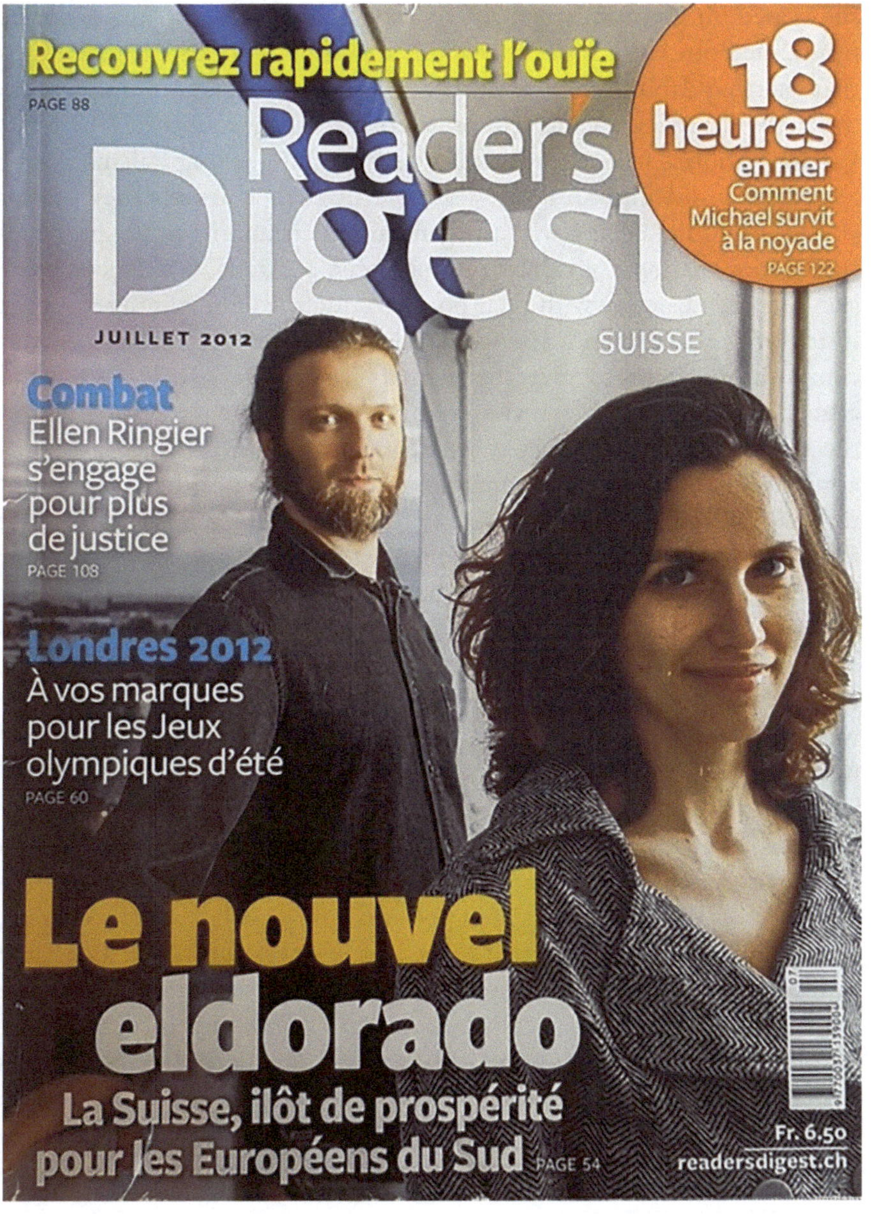

Fig. 3.2 Readers Digest—July, 2012, front cover. Photograph by Eddy Mottaz

showcased on the front page, is 'Le nouvel Eldorado – La Suisse, ilôt de prospérité pour les Européens du Sud.'[14] Journalist Alexis Favre confirms that starting from 2007 Southern Europeans decide to migrate to Switzerland in view of the economic crisis of their countries. The Swiss Confederation is seen as an island of prosperity by young Italians.

Veronica and Giovanni are a couple in their thirties. They appear young and fit in keeping with the general understanding of the profile of Italian new migrants. In these photographic portraits, both subjects are standing on a balcony with their bodies facing the light coming from the inside of the apartment. The woman is in the front of the image. This composition seems to give the woman a stronger visual impact and attracts the attention of the viewer: it goes against the traditional idea of the male-centred Italian society where women seemed to have a secondary role. In this case, the photographer communicates the evolution of the modern Italian society in which women are more conscious of their important role. We can also read in the text that Veronica is from the South of Italy and these characteristics are even more evident in that part of the country according to the traditional narrative. Giovanni and Veronica have a confident expression on their faces: the slight smile of the man in the background is repeated and reinforced on the face of the woman in the foreground. It is a smile which communicates a sense of relaxation and self-confidence. The fact that both subjects are looking straight into the camera underlines this perception and creates a direct link with the viewer. They have no props but their clothing assumes an important value in the context of the topic. In her casual jacket, the woman does not repeat the stereotype of the housewife. On the contrary, the elegant coat that she wears fits the idea of a woman who is integrated into modern society. The couple is photographed on the balcony, in a high position. From there it is possible to see the city is in the background. Veronica and Giovanni are portrayed in a position which shows that they live in an apartment and have found their place in the city. Similar concepts are expressed on the double-page image which introduces the article. In this case, the woman is on the left and has a relaxed

[14] 'The New Eldorado – Switzerland, prosperity island for Southern Europeans.'

position with her elbows on the balcony. The man has his right arm open towards his partner. This gesture creates a link between the two individuals. Giovanni has the other hand in his left pocket. As seen on the front cover of the magazine, again in this photograph the couple has a facial expression which shows self-confidence and no fear of the future. The use of the light and the signs used in these images are very similar to the photographic style of the images seen before on the recent articles of *L'Illustré* and *L'Hebdo*.

Findings

After the collection of information for this research which involves the years 2006–2019, there are four main findings that can be highlighted. In the first stance, while there are a large number of articles dedicated to the migration process of other nationalities,[15] there are not many articles which directly deal with the new Italian diaspora of the years between 2006 and 2019. This is a noticeable difference if compared with what was found in *L'Illustré* from the years between 1960 and 1970.[16] Despite the fact that the new Italian migration phenomenon was relevant in the period between 2006 and 2019 (Caneva 2016; Bonifazi 2017: 32; Franchi 2017; Sanfilippo 2017: 366; Pugliese 2018; Cacciatore and Pepe 2019; Licata 2019: 4), only six articles in total related to the recent Italian diaspora to Switzerland were found.[17] The reason of this lack of production could be understood as the general loss of interest towards the Italian diaspora. If we agree with Stuart Hall (1972: 237) and Valeria Lai (2014: 6866) that the news is interesting if dealing with new things and newsworthy, probably the Italian diaspora is not perceived by the Swiss society (including publishers of magazines) as a new thing.

[15] Fifty articles were found only in *L'Illustré* on legal and illegal migrants and/or refugees from Ecuador, Kosovo, Tunisia, Nigeria, China, Eritrea, Afghanistan, Georgia and Moldovia.

[16] As already mentioned, there were eight articles related to the Italian diaspora in *L'Illustré* between 1960 and 1970 (572 issues).

[17] The article on *L'Illustré* n. 42 of the 20th of October 2010, 'Les années Schwarzenbach, 40 ans après' concerns the former diaspora of the years between 1960 and 1970 (Clot 2010).

After the phenomenon of globalization in recent years, there does not seem to be a deep cultural difference between Italians and the hosting country. Italians don't seem to generate a negative social impact anymore, as was perceived of the former diaspora of the 1960s and 1970s. As anticipated in Chap. 2, on the articles of *L'Illustré* from the 1970s, Italians are described as people who have great issues in getting integrated with the Swiss society.[18] The bilateral agreements (FDFA 2021: 5–6) facilitate the integration process of Italians in Switzerland in the first two decades of the twenty-first century. Second, the accent of the articles still focuses on Portuguese and French. Numbers show that the Portuguese and the French migration to Switzerland has still big numbers in the first two decades of the twenty-first century (FSO 2021). This point is supported by the consistent and large presence of migrants from these European countries in the magazine taken into consideration in this research.[19] The third observation that it is possible to draw is that in the publications between 2006 and 2019 there is a different photographic style compared to the images published in the articles from the 1960s and 1970s. It seems that photographers have moved from a photojournalistic approach to portraits with a frequent use of artificial light in interiors. In these recent photographs, subjects are portrayed in a frontal position and looking straight into the camera. This direct gaze contributes to the dialogue (AA 2017) with the viewer and can substitute the meeting in the flesh (Gierstberg 2015: 12). While for the majority of the images printed in *L'Illustré* from the 1960s and 1970s the viewer was looking at migrants from a distant point of view without a visual connection (Fig. 3.3), in these images migrants establish a strong visual relationship (Bryson 1983, 1999) and are inviting the viewer to take part in their experience of identity transformation (Van Gelder 2012). This is one of the points that is repeated in the practice part of this research (Figs. 3.4, 3.5, and 3.6): the

---

[18] *L'Illustré* n. 14 of April 1970 (SCOPE 1970: 4).

[19] See the graphic on p. 58 of the Swiss French speaking edition of the *Readers Digest* of July 2012 (Favre 2012), p. 44 of *L'Hebdo* n. 46 of 15th November, 2012 (Ruf 2012), the diagram of p. 48 and pp. 54–55 of *L'Illustré* (Vassaux 2012), n. 36, 2012, p. 31 of *L'Hebdo* n. 11 of 12th March, 2015 (Dessemontet 2015).

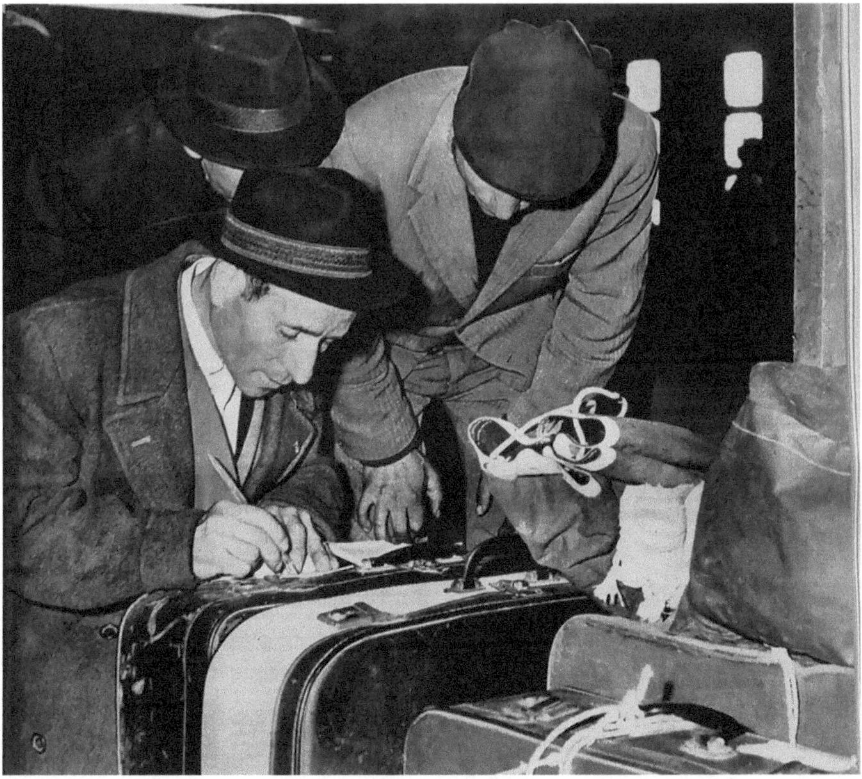

Fig. 3.3 Unknown, Untitled, 1965. With permission of *L'Illustré*

face as a mask (Barthes 1980: 35) in portraiture and the value of their interpretation in the experience of the beholder in front of a photographic image. The photographic portrait assumes the role of a mirror for recognition, self-recognition and self mis-recognition. Barthes states that photography can only achieve significance when it shows a mask. To support this point, he refers to the portrait of William Casby taken by Richard Avedon in 1963.[20] William Casby was the last man born into slavery.

[20] See (Avedon 1963).

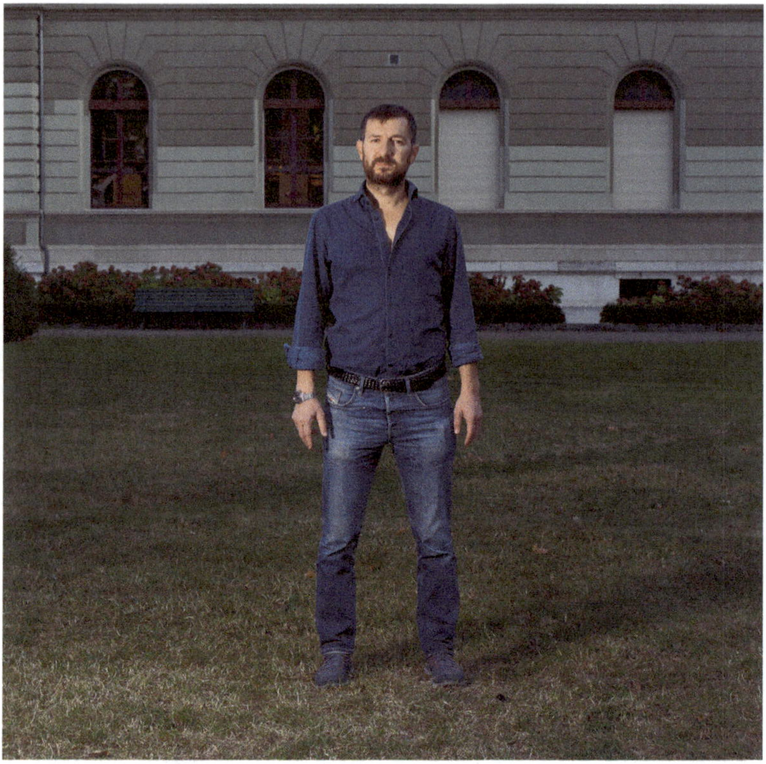

Fig. 3.4 Francesco Arese Visconti, *AA*, 2018

Barthes states that Avedon managed to portray here the essence of slavery through a theater mask in the classical sense. This mask is the product of society and its history.[21]

The first three findings lead to the last consideration. If we agree with Barthes (1977: 22) that images are inducers of associations and are part of debates and reflections on social media and cultural phenomena, it is reasonable to argue that images form the context for policy making and

[21] Italian writer Italo Calvino in his short story 'The Adventure of a Photographer' (Calvino, 1970) says that 'a mask is anything that turns a face into a product of society and its history'.

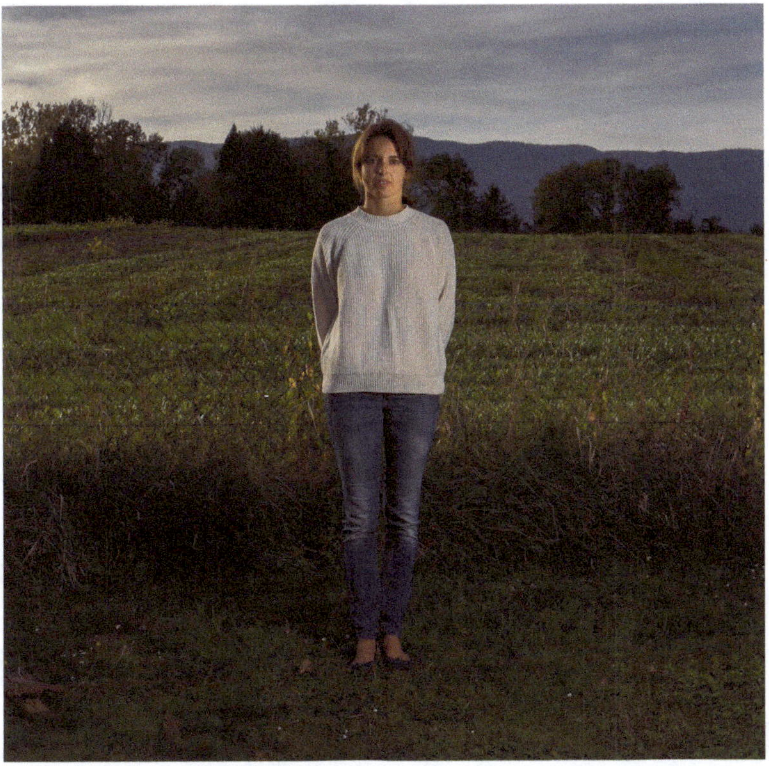

Fig. 3.5 Francesco Arese Visconti, *OM*, 2017

implementation (Lai 2014: 6841) and can be tools of political social justice (Sheehan 2018: 84). These photographs published in magazines between 2006 and 2019 deliver a narrative constructed by the selection process on the new Italian migrant. The profile of modern Italian migrants seems to be supported by their photographic representation on printed and online visual media. In the next section of the book, we have selected some of the interviews conducted with the subjects photographed. It is fundamental to read about their experience of migration.

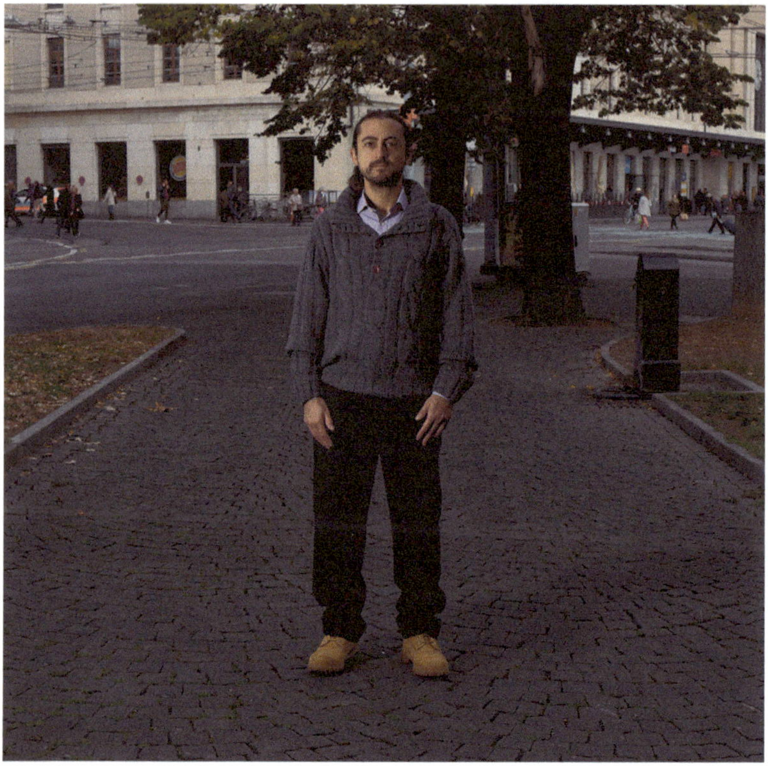

Fig. 3.6 Francesco Arese Visconti, *NC*, 2018

References

AA, S. of A. (2017). "The Face and the Body - Mark Cousins." https://www.youtube.com/watch?v=UkraaawwqKs. Access 21.04.2017

Avedon, R. (1963). "William Casby, born in slavery, Algiers, Louisiana, March 24,1963."https://www.artbasel.com/catalog/artwork/37735/Richard-Avedon-William-Casby-born-in-slavery-Algiers-Louisiana-March-24?lang=en. Access 11.01.2021.

Barthes, R. (1977). *Image, Music, Text.* London: Fontana Press.

———. (1980). *La camera chiara* . Torino: Einaudi.

Beltrame, L. (2007). *Realtà e Retorica Del Brain Drain in Italia. Stime Statistiche, Definizioni Pubbliche e Interventi Politici.* Torino: Università degli Studi di Trento, Dipartimento di Sociologia e Ricerca Sociale.

Bleiker, R. (2001). "The aesthetic turn in international political theory." In *Millennium*, 30 (30).

Boeri, T., Herbert Brücker, and Frédéric Doquier. (2012). *Brain Drain and Brain Gain: The Global Competition to Attract High-Skilled Migrants.* Oxford: Oxford University Press.

Boltanski, L. (2018). "La retorica della figura." In *Un'arte media – Saggio sugli usi sociali della fotografia*, ed. Pierre Bourdieu. Milano: Meltemi.

Bolzman, C., Rosita Fibbi and Marie Vial. (2003). *Secondas – Secondos: le processus d'intégration des jeunes adultes issus de la migration espagnole et italienne en Suisse*. Zürich: Seismo.

Bonifazi, C. (ed.). (2017). *Migrazioni e integrazioni nell'Italia di oggi*. Roma: Istituto di Ricerche sulla Popolazione e le Politiche Sociali.

Bryson, N. (1983). *Vision and Painting: The Logic of the Gaze.* New Haven: Yale University Press.

———. (1999). "The Gaze in the Expanded Field." In *Vision and Visuality*, 87–113. Seattle: Bay press.

Cacciatore, F. and Giulia Pepe. 2019. "Performing new identities: the community language post-crisis Italian migrants in London." In *National Identities*, 21:5, 507–526.

Calvino, I. (1970). *Amori difficili.* Torino: Einaudi.

Caneva, E. (2016). "The New Italian Emigration: What we Know, How We Talk of It." In *Cambio - Rivista sulle trasformazioni sociali.* VI, 11. 195–208.

Cassar, L. (2010). "Should I Stay or Should I Go? An Institutional Approach to Brain Drain." 489. Zürich.

Clot, P. (2010, October). "Les années Schwarzenbach, 40 ans après." *L'Illustré*, pp. 46–54

Dahinden, J. (2008). "Die Mobilität von Hochqualifizierten Fachkräften." Zürich.

Dequiedt, V. and Yves Zenou (2011). "International Migration, Imperfect Information, and Brain Drain." *Journal of Development Economics*, 2013, 102, 62–78.

Dessemontet, P. (2015, March). La Suisse a longtemps été une terre d'immigration pour ses voisins. *L'Hebdo*, 30–31.

Docquier, F., and Hillel Rapoport. (2007). "Skilled Migration: The Perspective of Developing Countries." 2873.

Favre, A. (2012, July). Le nouvel eldorado. *Readers Digest*, front cover and pp. 54–59.

FDFA (2021). "The Main Bilateral Agreements between Switzerland and the EU." https://www.eda.admin.ch/dam/europa/en/documents/folien/Folien-Abkommen_en.pdf. Access 18.01.2022.

Franchi, C. (2017). "Non Solo Brain Drain : Il Caso Svizzero Di Basilea." *Altreitalie*, no. luglio-dicembre: 95–115.

Friedrich, K., and Andrea Schultz. (2008). *Brain Drain Oder Brain Circulation?: Konsequenzen Und Perspektiven Der Ost-West-Migration*. Forum Ifl. Leibniz-Institut für Länderkunde.

FSO. (2021). "Federal Statistical Office - Foreign Population." https://www.bfs.admin.ch/bfs/en/home/statistics/population/migration-integration/foreign.html. Access 11.04.2022.

Gierstberg, F. (ed.). (2015). *European Portrait Photography since 1990*. Munich, London, New York: Bozarbooks and Prestel.

Hall, S. (1972). "The determinations of news photographs." In *Working Paper in Cultural Studies*, n. 3 (autumn), pp. 53–87. Reissued: Stanley Cohen and Jock Young (eds.), *The Manifacture of News: social problems, deviance and the mass media*. London: Constable, pp. 176–190, 1972.

Johnson, H. (2011). "Click to Donate: visual images, constructing victims and imagining the female refugee." In *Third World Quaterly*, 32:6, 1015–1037.

Juhasz, A. and Eva Mey. (2003) *Die zweite Generation: Etablierte oder Aussenseiter? Biographien von Jugendlichen ausländischer Herkunft*. Wiesbaden: Westdeutscher Verlag.

Lai, V. (2014). "Scatti fotografici in Rapporto Migrazione italiani nel mondo. " In Licata, Delfina (ed.). *Fondazione Migrantes – Rapporto italiani nel mondo*. Todi: Tau Editrice. 6841–7205.

Licata, D. (ed.). (2019). *Rapporto Italiani nel Mondo*. Todi: Tau Editrice.

Lietti, A. and Chantal Tauxe (eds.). (2015, July). Ces étrangers qui nous accueillent en Suisse. *L'Hebdo*, pp. 6–29.

Mey, E., Miriam Rorato and Peter Voll (2005) 'Die soziale Stellung der zweiten Ausländergeneration', in Bundesamt für Statistik (ed.) Die Integration der ausländischen zweiten Generation und der Eingebürgerten in der Schweiz: Eidgenössische Volkszählung 2000, Neuchâtel: Bundesamt für Statistik, 61–138.

Minneci, F. (2015). "If There Were a 'Highly Skilled Red Octopus'? The Case of Italian Highly Skilled Mobility at Times of Crisis." *Economics and Sociology*, III (8): 170–82.

Monnat, L. 'Le Italiens reviennent s'installer en Suisse.' *Tribune de Genève* - May 17th, 2016, p. 4.

Ortner, S. B. (1973) 'On key symbols', American Anthropologist, 75, 1338–45.

Ottaviani, J. (2016a). "Gli svizzeri dovrebbero imparare ad abbracciare il caos." www.swissinfo.ch. https://www.swissinfo.ch/ita/generazione-e-storie-di-giovani-migranti_-gli-svizzeri-dovrebbero-imparare-ad-abbracciare-il-caos/42406418. Access 05.03.2021.

———. (2016b). "Lo Stato italiano mi ha pagato gli studi, ma è la Svizzera ad approfittarne." www.swissinfo.ch. https://www.swissinfo.ch/ita/generazione-e-storie-di-giovani-migranti_-lo-stato-italiano-mi-ha-pagato-gli-studi-ma-%C3%A8-la-svizzera-ad-approfittarne/42398644. Access 05.03.2021.

———. (2016c). "Attraverso lo sport mi sono integrato nella società svizzera." www.swissinfo.ch. https://www.swissinfo.ch/ita/generazione-e-storie-di-giovani-migranti_-attraverso-lo-sport-mi-sono-integrato-nella-societ%C3%A0-svizzera/42406082. Access 05.03.2021.

Pugliese, E. (2018). *Quelli che se ne vanno: la nuova emigrazione italiana.* Bologna: Il Mulino.

Ricciardi, T. (2018). *Breve Storia Dell'emigrazione Italiana in Svizzera.* Roma: Donzelli editore.

Rose, G. (2001). *Visual Methodologies.* London, Thousands Oaks & New Delhi: SAGE Publications.

Ruf, M. (2012, November). Immigrés de père en fille. *L'Hebdo,* pp. 42–45.

Sanfilippo, M. (2017). "La nuova emigrazione italian (2000 – 2017): il quadro storico e storiografico." In *Studi Emigrazione*, LIV, n. 207.

SCOPE. (1970, April). Les étrangers - Au pays de la solitude. *L'Illustré*, 4–14.

Seiler, A. J. (2002). *Vento di Settembre.* Switzerland: Filmcoopi.

SEM. (2021). "Statistiques sur l'immigration." https://www.sem.admin.ch/sem/fr/home/publiservice/statistik/auslaenderstatistik.html. Access 19.01. 2022.

Sheehan, T. (ed.) (2018). *Photography and Migration.* London; New York: Routledge.

Tintori, G., and Valentina Romei. (2017). "Emigration from Italy After the Crisis: The Shortcomings of the Brain Drain Narrative." In Lafleur, J. M. and Mikolaj Stanek (eds.). *South-North Migration of UE Citizens in Times of Crisis.* 49–64. Cham: Springer International Publishing.

Tirabassi, M., and Alvise del Prà. (2014). *La meglio Italia. Le mobilità italiane nel XXI Secolo.* Torino: Accademia University Press. https://books.openedition.org/aaccademia/509. Access 21.05.2018.

Vakaridis, M. (2016). Les jeunes Italiens affluent en Suisse. www.bilan.ch. https://www.bilan.ch/economie/les_jeunes_italiens_affluent_en_suisse. Access 05.03.2021.

Van Gelder, H. (2012). "Aesthetic Equality." www.fotomuseum.ch. http://www.fotomuseum.ch/en/explore/still-searching/articles/26927_aesthetic_equality. Access 13.05.2018.

Vassaux, F. (2012). "Mais qui sont les nouveaux vaudois?" *L'Illustré*, pp. 48–55.

Wessendorf, S. (2007a). "'Roots Migrants:' Transnationalism and 'Return' among Second-Generation Italians in Switzerland." *Journal of Ethnic and Migration Studies* 33 (7): 1083–1102.

Wessendorf, S. (2007b) 'Who do you hang out with? Patterns of peer group association, cultural assertion and detachment among second-generation Italians in Switzerland', in T. Geisen and C. Riegel (eds) Jugend, Migration und Zugehörigkeit, Subjektpositionierungen im Kontext von Jugendkultur, Ethnizitäts- und Geschlechterkonstruktionen, Wiesbaden: VS Verlag, 111–27.

———. 'Local Attachments and Transnational Everyday Lives: Second-generation Italians in Switzerland.' *Global Networks* 10, 3 (2010). 365–382.

4

The Interviews

Abstract This chapter lists a selection of interviews conducted with all the participants in the research. These six interviews aim to give an idea of the migratory experiences undertaken by these Italians who migrated to the French-speaking part of Switzerland. To facilitate the understanding of the content of the interviews, the dialogues have been transcribed and adapted for a good understanding of the content. Due to space constraints, it has not been possible to publish all the twenty-four interviews. While recognizing the uniqueness and interest of each interview, these six interviews were selected because they are particularly representative of various migratory experiences and from different parts of Italy.

Keywords Migratory experience • Italian migration • Twenty-first-century diaspora • Switzerland • Interviews

In this chapter, we find a selection of interviews conducted with all the participants in the research. These six interviews aim to give an idea of the migratory experiences undertaken by these Italians who migrated to the French-speaking part of Switzerland. To facilitate the understanding of

F. Arese Visconti, *The Invisible Diaspora*, Palgrave Studies in Creativity and Culture,
https://doi.org/10.1007/978-3-031-74925-4_4

the content of the interviews, the dialogues have been transcribed and adapted for a good understanding of the content.

Due to space constraints, it would not have been possible to publish all the twenty-four interviews. While recognizing the uniqueness and interest of each interview, these six interviews were selected because they are particularly representative of various migratory experiences and from different parts of Italy.

All the interviews followed a basic structure with similar questions. Obviously, in some cases and following the development of the conversation, the proposed themes were explored in different ways. I found subjects who could be involved in the research through my personal connections and local associations.[1] During our first meeting, I conducted interviews with a precise set of questions about their migrant experience (Fig. 5.16). I asked them to choose where they wanted to be photographed, places which they considered important in their life in Switzerland.

The interviews do not aim to have any scientific ambition, but are simply intended to offer a glimpse into the personalities and migratory experiences of the people photographed. It is for this reason that no research with comments and conclusions connected to the interviews proposed in this book is developed.

A. A.

The 8th of October 2018

F.[2]: Age range?

A. A.: Between 40 and 49, now I'm 45 in February.

F.: Country of origin?

A. A.: Italy.

F.: Length of residence in Switzerland?

A. A.: In November it will be 15 years, if I'm not mistaken.

F.: The number of family members in Switzerland?

---

[1] Cultura Italia (https://www.culturaitalia.ch/) and COM.IT.ES. (http://comites-ginevra.ch/)

[2] 'F' stands for the interviewer, Francesco.

A A.: We are a family unit of three people.

F.: So you're not married?

A. A.: No.

F.: So you migrated to Switzerland, right?

A. A.: Yes.

F.: For what reason?

A. A.: I arrived in Geneva in 2003, for a short stay of three months initially, to do a DA, Postdoctoral Study Diploma.

F.: From where?

A. A.: From Bari, from the University of Bari, where I had started a PhD in History of Medicine, after a degree in Philosophy, and I was proposed to come to do this stay in Geneva. At that time there was an institute of History of Medicine that now has been closed, whose director was Italian and my professor was part of the commission also of the doctorate of Bari. He invited me to do at that time in Switzerland, in Geneva, a diploma that was, let's say, a kind of postgraduate master, and there was one on the History of Medicine. So I came to do this DA and stay here 3–4 months. The stay was extended to six months.

I finished my studies in Geneva. I found myself very well in Geneva, and I had also met my current partner. Let's say that I was no longer very inclined to return home. However, it seemed to me Soon, I didn't live it as a definitive choice at the time, and even today I always say that I am here in Geneva temporarily. I have been living here for 15 years. This is now my second home. Then I had a daughter who is 3 years old now. 8 years ago I started a business. After my studies I stayed here in Geneva, but I didn't find an immediate placement at the university, so I did a 2-year international master's degree between Switzerland and Italy in medical humanities. In the meantime I was preparing a project to present to the Swiss national fund for research. The proposal did not go well and at that point I started to question what to do. To be able to continue to do what I had done up to that point, perhaps I should have considered the idea of leaving, travelling, as is often done to pursue an academic career. Given that I was not very young and that I had a relationship of a few years, I thought first of all that I did not have a vocation for the university. I opened my business. A friend came from Italy proposing to do something, to invest in Apulian gastronomy. I didn't dislike the idea because I come from a family of entrepreneurs: my grandfather created a company in 1953 that still exists, for which my father worked. He retired a few months ago. My uncles and my cousins still work there. I also worked there for a short period. The entrepreneurial challenge fascinated me. With this friend who came to Geneva we discussed the possibility of doing something around Apulian gastronomy and making a cheese factory to produce mozzarella. I worked on this project for two years, two and a half years, before managing to realize it. Then it had a decent success from the start. In the meantime I also had another work experience to support myself. I worked for about two years as a freelance for a relocation company. I was responsible for accompanying people and families arriving in Geneva. Many were Italian, but there were also people arriving from all continents. I had to help them find a home, school for the children, advise them and so on. It was a job that suited me very well because I did it in a fairly autonomous and free way, and was paid quite well. A few months after the start of my business adventure I quit this job with the relocation. Now I only deal with my cheese factory.

F.: Do you often go to Italy?

A. A.: I go to Italy very often, quite often, even though I would like to go there more. I go there at least five, six times a year. I always go back for Christmas except since I had the baby. My partner is from Strasbourg so her parents' family is in Strasbourg. We alternate one year yes and one year no. Up to three years ago I always went to Italy. I never missed a Christmas. In the summer we go at least twice and then a couple more times during the year also for shorter periods.

F.: What does Switzerland mean to you?

A. A.: Switzerland means an important part of my life because being 45 years old and having spent 15 here anyway is a third of my life, and also a very important third. In the last 15 years I finished my doctorate here, I created my business, my company, I built a family and had a daughter. So even though I am strongly attached to Italy, to Puglia, to my land, to Bari, Geneva is a bit of a second home. However, I can't say that it is my home. My home is Puglia.

F.: What is Italy to you?

A. A.: I don't want to fall into nationalism, but I have a very strong Italian identity. And then I am from the south. We southerners who go abroad carry our land within us. For me Italy is culture in absolute terms. Not that it is the only country where there is a culture. My culture is that of Italy. I am strongly marked by Italian culture. I lived the era of well-being in the 80s–90s. Life was very good in Italy. I never really worked in Italy for a long time. I have never really encountered perhaps the difficulties of work that Italy is experiencing, especially in this period. I have a positive view of Italy even though, looking at it from the outside in recent years, it is quite compromised and it is very sad to see it today from outside.

F.: What does integration mean?

A. A.: I was born in Bari. In Bari, I remember in '89 the arrival of that ship called 'Flora' full of Albanians. And I also remember that with many difficulties, Puglia, Bari, had an incredible mobilisation to welcome them, doing the best they could with many difficulties. It is true that there were really many of them. If I'm not mistaken, Puglia was also nominated for the Nobel Peace Prize for how it welcomed these Albanians who arrived during that period. Puglia, like the whole Mediterranean basin, like all of southern Italy, has known many dominations: the Saracens, the Angevins, the French, the Spanish, the house of Aragon. Even our saint, Saint Nicholas, many forget, comes from Turkey and is black, he is dark. And he is the patron saint of the people of Bari. So I believe that culturally we are a land very open to the other and therefore to integration. For me, integration is that. It is also true that I arrived in Geneva for example as a research doctorate student and for me integration was very, very, very simple. I have never experienced what I think the Italians who arrived here many years ago have experienced. I believe that the real problem of integration for me today is more than anything between rich and poor. In my opinion, yes, Geneva is a city that is multi-ethnic. Many friends come from various parts of the world, but I see the only real discrimination, the only obstacle to integration, is social difference.

F.: So what does it mean when one is integrated?

A. A.: This question is complicated, yes, because it is also very current. In short, very, very current. Integration should be making sure that a person can feel at home, anyway feel welcomed in a new place. The distribution of resources is very important in this sense because it is the greatest form of discrimination that exists today in my opinion. I see in

Geneva a varied composition of the population. I see good integration. If they have a good education, they have a good job, they work in a bank, they work in the United Nations. So in my opinion access to culture, to education and to well-being, being able to have a dignified life, is anyway an essential element to promote integration. Then, obviously, there can be cultural and religious aspects in certain contexts that can represent further obstacles, but I believe that even these obstacles can be removed at a time when access to culture and education is widespread and open and promotes a process of democratisation.

F.: What is your strongest memory of your migration to Switzerland?

A. A.: It's difficult because I came to do a kind of short trip, let's say, a bit like Erasmus. I came with the carefree air of an Italian who is doing a doctorate in Bari and comes to Geneva for two, three, four months. It was to do a doctorate. I came more with the intention of having a new experience to learn a different language. I have no memories of 'packing my bags, leaving home, leaving the family'. I arrived on November 2nd in Geneva and it was cold, bitterly cold, much more than it has been in recent years at the beginning of November. I came from Bari where in recent years it has also been getting warmer. In Geneva on November 2nd there was ice on the ground. I arrived at the airport and then at the station. I already had some friends, doctoral colleagues who lived in Geneva so they had invited me to dinner and I remember that right on the pavements of Paquis there were slabs of ice. It was November 2003. It was really very cold. So that was anyway a strong impact. Switzerland is a country where I had never been. The impact with Switzerland was really grey, cold.

F.: In what way do you feel Swiss?

A. A.: Do I feel Swiss? I don't think so, not at all, no aspect. Yes, I think no aspect. It's not a negative judgement on Switzerland. There are things in which I have changed, I say, improved, because in my opinion I have improved, but it seems too banal to say for example that I have become a very punctual person. But it seems really reductive and banal to say this. I believe that it has nothing to do with the fact of having come here, but with a sense of responsibility that I have acquired over time. My father is a very punctual person so it would be really reductive to say that now I am punctual because I came to live here. I don't know. First of all, if I really had to feel something, I would feel more Genevan. Switzerland is a somewhat complex country. Switzerland is already divided into cantons with different languages, different cultures and so I have also met Swiss people from other cantons. They are profoundly different from each other. So, if I really had to say, I feel more Genevan than Swiss. But nothing else comes to mind.

F.: The last thing I ask you is in what way you think you are Italian.

A. A.: One thing in which I am Italian… Hard to say. They still tell me that: I am too Italian. Maybe too much. My partner also tells me this. In some respects, sometimes I am also a bit of a caricature of the Italian. One being abroad does not necessarily become Swiss but can lead to exaggerating the cultural characteristics that one had already acquired: the love I had for Italy, so holidays in Italy, films by great Italian directors from Fellini to Visconti. But also films, let's say, of 'b' quality, like those ones with Lino Banfi. These things here: I love Italian music. To any person I know here in Geneva I say to come to Italy: 'I have to take you to Puglia, to Polignano a Mare.' But the same thing applies to Venice, to Florence. I think I am very Italian, I hope in the positive aspects. Far be it from me to be a nationalist.

A. C.

The 10th of November 2018

F.: Age range?

A. C.: 30–39 we are just right there.

F.: Since when are you in Switzerland?

A. C.: Just over, 5 years.

F.: So, 2013?

A. C.: Yes.

F.: Family members in Switzerland?

A. C.: None, none.

F.: Single?

A. C.: Single, single.

F.: Migrated to Switzerland?

A. C.: Yes, yes, resident in Switzerland.

F.: What are the reasons for your migration to Switzerland?

A. C.: I wanted to leave the United Kingdom, where I lived quite well, and, happily, in social terms, but I did not love the context in which I worked, that of the public school. I felt gratified, teaching languages had no importance, the levels were extremely low.

F.: Did you teach languages?

A. C.: Yes, I qualified to teach in England. Initially I was not qualified to teach there and so I had to do a second pedagogical master's, because my qualification allowed me only to teach Arabic or Arabic literature. I did another master's to teach Italian abroad. That allowed me to survive in the countries where I lived, where I had scholarships, where I could to integrate the scholarships of teaching courses, for example, in studies of Italian culture abroad. I wanted to leave England and in 2012 I decided to do so. There is an international system organized by *The Times* that has a whole network on the web where there are job offers from all over the world. There was a good position in the British international school, quite renowned, in Dubai. I was interested in this opportunity to continue practising the Arabic language, to work in a context that allowed me to travel further, to learn more, and very attractive holidays, because you don't work for more than three months and half. In the meanwhile, I found also another interesting position in Switzerland. I thought about it, indeed, I already had another position in my pocket. I had told my school that I would be leaving, I applied so lightly. I immediately discovered that there were many candidates. I had the first interview in London, then two interviews on Skype. It was a very tough selection process. Then I had an interview in Geneva. The school impressed me with its beauty and also the quality of teaching. I sent my resignation letter without ever having set foot in Dubai, and I accepted this position in Switzerland with great enthusiasm. So I didn't choose Switzerland directly, but when I came for the interview that was the moment that facilitated my decision. The day I had the interview the weather was wonderful. It was March. It was 15 degrees. The sky was clear. This life seemed beautiful to me. After the interview, I had to return to the airport. I wanted to take the bus to go to the airport, but they called me a taxi. That day they were presenting the Ferrari at Palexpo because there was the Motor Show. I got stuck in traffic and missed the flight. I immediately called the UK. It was snowing there and they had closed the schools for two days. So I wasn't too worried. On the one hand, there was the disappointment of having missed the flight, on the other hand, there was this crazy joy of being able to relax and visit Geneva. I immediately looked for an Airbnb. The next day I really walked from one side of the city to the other before catching the flight to return in the evening to London.

F.: And do you travel to Italy?

A. C.: Yes, I travel a lot to Italy, once or twice a month I go to Turin, and when I can I also make quick trips to Piedmont or Val d'Aosta. These are regions of which I only had some images, because as a child I lived for a few years in Piedmont. My dad was a train driver for the state railways.

F.: Which part of Sicily are you originally from?

A. C.: Palermo.

F.: And the reason why you move to Italy today, what is it?

A. C.: For pleasure, to get to know my country. I don't think I know it well yet. It could be known better. It's nice to travel in Italy, it's a discovery. Otherwise, I travel to see my parents, my family.

F.: And what does Switzerland mean to you?

A. C.: Switzerland is a country I didn't know. I never was interested in it in certain ways. I wasn't immediately fascinated. The political horizon of Switzerland interested me. As a political activist in my own small way, Switzerland seemed to me really a reference model, with so much complexity. Perception changes when one sees things from the outside. When one then lives them, one sees the contradictions more in depth. But Switzerland for me still represents a composite model of integration, of stories that in some way have become parallel and have begun to coexist with extraordinary intelligence, something I have not seen in other realities. It really is in some way an interesting representation of integration.

F.: So, it seems that you are interested in Switzerland from a political point of view, and civic development.

A. C.: Yes. I have thought about it a few times, but I feel more attached to the Italian political reality than to the Swiss one. I feel much more connected to it, I participate much more in it. It's the only reason, probably, why I would like to return to Italy. Every time I return to Italy, and especially to Sicily, I have wounds that reopen. They are those uglinesses to which you, clearly, were not used to. Perhaps you had never seen them, but now they jump to the eye. Switzerland represents the country where I live, where now, consciously, I have chosen to live, and where for the first time, I think, I could stay for a long time. It had never happened before. For study reasons, a bit of work, I was lucky, but also willing, to be here. For almost fourteen years, after university studies, I started to have scholarships, more or less long stays abroad, between Syria, Libya, Jordan, Lebanon, Tunisia, and Egypt. It was a bit of a search for identity as well, because I didn't know what I wanted to do in my life. I wanted to be a translator a bit, but then I felt like a rat in a cage. I started to like teaching a bit by chance. I started to understand that it was something that interested me. It was not quantifiable, it was not measurable, but it made sense.

F.: And so what does Italy represent for you?

A. C.: Today? Well, Italy for me is a struggle, it is a form of individuality that is still not complete, still in progress. For me it is clearly my horizon, my country in which I know that for a long time I probably won't return to live. It is such a composite country, so varied that when I return, I do it with great pleasure. I feel I am in my country, but I don't really feel part of it, a member of that country. Instead, when I return to Sicily, yes. It's as if my cultural humus came out. Suddenly there is a sort of psychophysical well-being. Italy means many things. For me they are moments of life lived in different places. At the same time it is a creature that I do not know, at least in some of its realities. But in terms of identity, emotional and cultural, it is my country.

F.: What does integration mean to you?

A. C.: Integration for me is simply the possibility of being able to exercise one's rights in a country, to know them. This is something that often does not happen: being an active member, exercising a citizenship.

F.: What are your strongest memories of when you migrated to Switzerland?

A. C.: Initially it was difficult to live there, because when I arrived there was a limited number of people who could get the B permit. I got it after a month, I stayed at the Ibis Hotel. Then I found a house. I was quite happy, but after so many efforts they told me that I could not live for at least the first few months in Switzerland. I found myself in the situation where I said I had to go live in France. I spent two years as a cross-border worker. I also changed house, because it was a completely anonymous reality, a reality without soul. I didn't feel integrated at all, I felt with one foot in France, yes as a European citizen, but only up to a certain point, and with the other one in Switzerland. I didn't feel anywhere, so I wasn't well. My life changed significantly when I moved to Switzerland.

F.: What are the effects of living in Switzerland on you?

A. C.: I abandoned this sort of gypsy spirit. I am interested to know a bit more about Switzerland. Those few circumstances that I travelled, even the fact of moving from one region to another and not being able to communicate the language of those regions made an impression on me. Now I would like to learn a bit of German also to be able to speak even in a basic way. It is a growing interest. It doesn't take away from the fact that I feel Italian and I am.

F.: In what way do you feel Italian?

A. C.: Firstly, by sharing stories, memories, literature, poetry, a series of something that comes from the past and unites us. Then for the attitude, the attitude towards life, a kind of ability to improvise, a sort of energy, of joy, of *savoir faire* and gastronomy.

F.: Are there other things you would like to add about your experience as a migrant?

A. C.: I have never considered the possibility of being a migrant. I have worked with migrants. The only job I have done in Italy was working with migrants, with refugees who come for political asylum and unaccompanied minors. We modern Italian migrants have a right written somewhere to be able to move on this planet from one point to another almost anywhere. Many other people who migrate from other continents cannot do it legally. This should be a natural condition for each individual and it is not.

N. C.

The 31st of October 2018

F.: Age range?

N. C.: 30–39, I am 38 years old.

F.: How many years have you been living in Switzerland?

N. C.: In March I entered my eleventh year, so ten and a half years at this moment.

F.: So you arrived in March 2007?

N. C.: 3rd March, to be precise.

F.: Number of family members, if any, here in Switzerland?

N. C.: I am alone.

F.: Marital status?

N. C.: I am single.

F.: Did you migrate to Switzerland?

N. C.: Yes.

F.: What were the reasons why you migrated?

N. C.: For me it was a coincidence. In the sense that I was working after graduating in engineering. I started working in Milan. I told my boss at the time that I wanted to have an experience abroad. He proposed me to come to Geneva, where the company's headquarters was. I came here quite randomly. I wanted to have an overseas experience and I happened to arrive here. I stayed.

F.: So are they mainly work reasons?

N. C.: Yes, exclusively work-related.

F.: And do you often travel to Italy?

N. C.: Yes, I would say so.

F.: More or less how often?

N. C.: I would say that on average I return mainly to Milan, where my parents are, every month and a half.

F.: Are you originally from Milan?

N. C.: Yes, I was born and raised in the outskirts of Milan, in Pantigliata, a very small village. Milan and Geneva are really well connected. There are four trains going back and forth every day. Many times I can say that I want to go to Milan and I take a train, without major worries. I just take it and leave.

F.: What are the reasons for your trips to Italy?

N. C.: They are personal, usually they are personal, it's about going to greet the parents, to go on a bit of holiday in Italy. It is perhaps also about managing some private problems, it can be the dentist or things of this kind. However, these are paths that I had until I was 26–27 years old with that type of doctors, so I have a relationship of trust in advance. I can't turn to those who don't really know me. Sometimes it is real tourism, but generally they are private reasons.

F.: What does Switzerland mean to you?

N. C.: For me the answer is relatively simple: it was the country of opportunities. I was working in Italy with an internship contract at 512 euros per month, that is an old million of Italian Lira, and it was a salary that did not allow me to live alone. My first job contract in Geneva was an internship at about 3000 francs per month, so a salary clearly low for Switzerland, but, doing the maths, I am an engineer, I immediately understood that I could live alone. Making many sacrifices, I was careful about many things, but I said to myself 'ok, I can get by.' And so here was the opportunity to become independent. Then the opportunity also materialized in a professional career because in reality I stayed here. I have been here for ten years. It didn't take me long to realize that I could create my own small, great journey. I was immediately captivated by the many languages that are spoken here. I now speak fluently four languages: English, French, Spanish quite well, and Italian. Geneva is not Switzerland, I stayed in Geneva, which is a different nuance for me, because Geneva means internationality. It means many colours, all more or less integrated, which is not a small thing for me. It means Italian community, but not only. It means ease of getting to the city, moving around the city even on foot. It means immediately a good relationship, civic sense and quality of life. Geneva is internationality, but Switzerland is not just this. Just go outside Geneva and it already seems different to you. Yes, I could never live, I don't know, in a small village in canton X, precisely for a feeling of lack of many things. I am really convinced that Geneva is not Switzerland. Do you remember, years ago, what happened in Switzerland? In Switzerland, a vote was taken against some UN amendment that provided for the construction of mosques in Switzerland. Geneva voted in favour of the construction of mosques. Switzerland voted against. They are contemporary realities with different visions of who looks at the world from different perspectives. I could very well live in Geneva, I could not live in Mosacca, in Ciondorio.

F.: What does Italy mean to you?

N. C.: Italy is affection, affections. The country that shaped me in tastes, in smells, in the ability to understand the unsaid, the games of looks. Italy represents food for me. I am not necessarily tied to Italian food, but I like Italian food as much as I like food, let's call it exotic. It represents the country where I could spend my old age. I don't see myself becoming old or dying in Geneva, personally.

F.: Why?

N. C.: Because I have a feeling of great loneliness here. I see too many elderly and lonely people, I have this perception at least, sad. I believe there is a very hidden relationship with death. Paradoxically, in Milan where I grew up, I know my neighbours, but not because I went to introduce myself. It's because I know them naturally. In Geneva I have been living in a new place for three years. I don't know who I have next and I will never get to know. In Geneva there is the neighbours' party, in Switzerland there is the neighbours' party. The neighbours' party for me is a beautiful thing, done with a good purpose, in a context that however does not work. In Milan I know my neighbour. Need garlic, sugar in Milan, come on, go ask and the next day he will come to drink coffee at my place. There is no reason. It is so because it is my culture, especially the southern culture from which I come. Here in Geneva I don't know who I have next to me, and it seems almost absurd that I have that week in which I am allowed to speak to my neighbours. If I go on holiday, I give them the keys to water my plants. If they need bread, they knock and ask. There's no reason why. Here no, here this kind of relationship does not exist. I struggle to feel at ease in a place where I could die and no one would know until ten days later.

F.: So for you, Italy is about the food and the relationship with people?

N. C.: The relationship with people, the everyday life. In Italy, I go to the bar of my neighborhood and there I know everyone. But it's not because it's the habit of the bar. In Geneva, this doesn't exist, or, at least, I haven't seen it. In reality, maybe I can build it, but I find myself in the bar with migrants like me, people a bit more similar. The Genevan, the local culture, in my opinion, does not have this kind of thing.

F.: And so Italy only has positive sides?

N. C.: No, not at all. I don't think I'll return to Italy to create a professional path. It's not a matter of becoming rich, because I will probably never become rich in Geneva. However, I can think about being able to build something to survive relatively decently here. I struggle to think about my path in the way that my parents had. With an average salary in Italy of 1300–1400 euros per month, which would be my case, I would never buy a house. I would have great difficulty getting by. So for this type of very pragmatic aspect, I really struggle to think about returning to Italy. Then in life, no one knows what can happen. But in a rational way, I would exclude it.

F.: What does integration mean to you?

N. C.: Integration means entering into the dynamics of the place in which you are. You don't necessarily approve everything, but at least you respect what a place is. It's important to understand the mechanisms of the country in which you live. It's important to take the good that's there and maybe try to contribute to the social life of the place where you are. Integration means having people around you in the place where you are living who are not necessarily from your community of origin, so they are not necessarily Italian. I am opening the file to become Swiss and you have to find five Swiss people who will testify that you are a good person, that you are a Swiss. Integration means having these five people, having met them over the years, people you can count on. It's something that has taken me a really long time. Integration means having that kind of thing. Integration means speaking the language of the place where you are. The way I found to learn French was to sign up for my salsa course, because I needed a simple, fun mechanism to learn the language of the place where we live. I arrived here, I was working in English, from 7, from 8 to 18 I had to find a way to have fun, meet people, speak French, so with a colleague we signed up for a salsa course. So integration means language, it means knowledge of the place where you are, in a positively critical way, seeing what you like and what you don't like, contributing to the social life.

F.: What is the strongest memory you have of the moment when you migrated?

N. C.: I remember the journey, the first journey I made. I left on a Sunday at noon, if I remember correctly, it was May 3rd. During the journey, the first journey to get to Geneva, I started to chat on the train, with a little family. I didn't speak French. There were children, and so I played with the children to have them teach me the words of the face. There was this little girl who taught me. If you want, the first memory of my arrival in Geneva was this fun interaction, a bit cheeky with this little girl to whom I asked how to say the parts of the face. And she answered me. So this is perhaps one of the first memories. It's a pleasant memory. There was also a bit of melancholy. I knew what I was leaving behind, I didn't know what I was finding. I was coming from a previous Italian situation where I really struggled to see a professional future.

F.: What effect did living in Switzerland have on you?

N. C.: I became global. The fact of speaking many languages, seeing many people clearly developed a sense of tolerance for difference in me. Let me explain it in this way, I don't know if it's relevant. Over the years, I met some homosexual people in Genoa. One was a former flatmate of mine. One day I said to him: 'why don't we go to Gay Pride?'

He replied: 'why should I go to Gay Pride? I mean, I'm gay, you're vegetarian, that one supports Juventus. I don't have the duty or the right to demonstrate something that is mine'. In reality, he was clearly right. To be what I am, why should you arrogate the right to accept me? I live. And so this kind of basic tolerance, perhaps in a certain sense I didn't have it. This is the biggest thing that Geneva gave me. Switzerland is not this thing, but Geneva is. So this is perhaps the biggest lesson of tolerance. I don't have the right to accept someone else or the duty. It's paradoxically wrong that I should accept someone else. You have the right to exist.

F.: Is there anything else you want to add about your migration experience?

N. C.: It hasn't always been easy. There have been moments, even here very hard, a bit of loneliness, or maybe you lose your job. You have thoughts and you ask yourself: 'how do I live now, how do I pay the electricity bill?' So you have great things that you love and moments of great thoughts, great darkness. But that's what life gives us. In any place where you are, you can look for the beauty and solve the problems that happen. It's part of the rules of the game.

C. C.

The 3rd of July 2019

F.: Age range?

C. C.: 51. That's my exact age exact age.

F.: Country of origin? Italy?

C. C.: Florence.

F.: Years of residence in Switzerland?

C. C.: I arrived in 2006, so this year is the 13th year.

F.: And how many family members do you have here in Switzerland?

C. C.: I have my son and that's it.

F.: Did you migrate to Switzerland?

C. C.: Yes.

F.: For what reason?

C. C.: For work. I arrived in 2006 in Lugano because I found work in a company that had its headquarters in Lugano. So I actually came also because I was very tired of travelling abroad. I was in America and then in England, before I had been in Budapest, in Hungary and so on. When I had the chance to come to Switzerland, which was a place where I thought I would never come in my life, I accepted. It was not really on my world map. Maybe Hong Kong could be there, but not Switzerland. It was really among those things that I never thought of. I was trying to get away from London because I was very tired of this very intense life. So I arrived in Switzerland for work.

F.: And do you go to Italy often?

C. C.: Yes, usually once a month.

F.: And do you do it for personal reasons or work or pleasure?

C. C.: Mixed. For personal reasons because my mother is still there, all my family is in Florence. And for work reasons often in Milan.

F.: What does Switzerland mean to you?

C. C.: Switzerland for me at this moment in my life means a serene base but not a point of reference. I don't know if it's a bit of a contradiction because the base is a point of reference. In reality, it is the base because clearly my son here is very integrated. But despite living here for almost 13 years now, I don't feel it as a point of reference in my life. I don't know how to say it. It's a functional thing, but not emotional. So from this point of view, it is the base. But emotionally compared to other places where I have lived in the world, like London, it has never entered me. It's a place where I'm fine but I don't feel it sentimentally part of me. It has always remained external. It happened other times. America was a fairly significant experience but I never recognized myself in the American identity because they have certain types of values, thoughts that are too far from mine. I'm talking about the values, the basic ones, family ones, that you carry with you. London has remained inside me despite it being very distant from my environment of origin and that I come from a simple Italian family. But it's a place from which I was able to take a lot, as mental stimuli, as discovery, as people. It is very important in my opinion in which phase of your life you arrive in a place. If you go to a place when you are twenty, you have a certain experience. At thirty another, at forty another, at fifty another. When I arrived in Switzerland I was already about forty years old. I was already in that phase where you create a family, my son was born. Clearly you don't have that possibility to go out, to meet people as I did in London, where I was single. So I have a different predisposition. London, from this point of view, remains inside my personal journey in a much stronger way. The second factor is that Switzerland in my opinion is very functional, but it is not a place that welcomes you. A place that welcomes you, that embraces you. Other places, the US for example, like Albany, Upstate New York, is a place that welcomes you. They are used to the foreigner. Here my feeling is that I always feel like a migrant. I've been here for 13 years. Even when I was in Lugano, and therefore there was no language problem, they considered me Italian, therefore a separate caste. Here even more so because there is clearly the language problem: even if you speak it well, there is still the accent. Switzerland in my opinion is a place where you are very well, but you have to resign yourself to the fact of being considered a migrant. Look for example at my partner who was born in Switzerland, grew up in Switzerland, never left Switzerland. He is really Swiss, he lacks nothing compared to other people, but he is the son of Italian migrants. In his clinic that he created, he is considered the Italian, despite the fact that he honestly does not speak Italian well. This gives you an idea. This would never happen in America. If he returns to Italy he is absolutely the Swiss. Here he is considered the Italian. So he lives in this perennial limbo. Switzerland in my opinion in this is much harder compared to other countries where I have lived. Yes, definitely much harder.

F.: What does Italy mean to you?

C. C.: Italy is what I am. Not so much in the way of doing, but in the way of being. In the way of doing I am not Italian, because I left Italy when I was 23 years old. So, take into account, after almost 30 years, 27 years, clearly you absorb the way of doing from where you grow up. So Italy is the way of being, the rest is the way of doing. I work in an Anglo-Saxon way, let's put it this way. I behave outside like an expat, but I am Italian. Feeling Italian means having spontaneous socialization and not constructed. Spontaneous socialization is one of the most beautiful aspects that I still find when I go to Italy, even in the way you interact with people, whether it's the taxi driver, whether it's the friend. It gives me joy. Even in difficult cities like Rome or Milan where people are stressed, there is always that simple human connection. I call it socialising: this fact of interacting with others in a natural way.

F.: What does the word integration mean to you?

C. C.: I'm thinking about the places where I really felt integrated in my wanderings. What does integration mean? Integration has occurred when the difference is no longer distinguishable, that is, you are no longer different. Then each of us is unique, but you are not different, which is very different from saying that you have your own uniqueness. Integration is when you are no longer identified as the one who comes from outside. I'm thinking of a very banal example. In my building in Florence lives an English lady. She is my neighbour. We don't call her the English lady. She is Audrey to everyone and it doesn't make a difference that she arrived in Italy thirty years ago, rather than being born there. The fact of where you come from is no longer a discriminating element compared to others. So is she integrated? Absolutely yes. And so am I integrated? No. In Switzerland I am not integrated. Let's tell the truth: for 80% probably it's my fault, and for 20% it's the system's fault. I don't know if it's due to insecurity or lack of interest, or my arrogance. Certainly, I have never made an extra effort to integrate with the Swiss.

F.: What is your strongest memory of your move to Switzerland?

C. C.: The strongest memory is the sensation of silence that I felt arriving from London. There was no noise of children in the street, there was no noise of an ambulance. Nothing. I was really shocked for a while. Now I have got used to it, and it's the opposite maybe if I go to a noisy city. I was shocked by the silence that reigns. It's not just the silence and the lack of noise of cars, sirens, children shouting, people talking, but a silence almost like a way of life, people who speak softly. I say: where is a bit of chaos, a bit of vitality? It's a thing that clearly struck me. I was coming from the centre of London. Another thing I find a bit strange is this unnecessary formality of people. It is taken for politeness, and if you don't do it too, you are accused. I found this a somewhat superficial and false way of saying that there is kindness, but in reality it doesn't mean absolutely nothing.

F.: What effects does Switzerland have on you?

C. C.: It has made me a bit sadder. Switzerland has made me much more solitary, especially these last four years. I have radically changed. I used to, every Saturday and Sunday, have dinners. I have become much, much more solitary. But not only in facts, clearly those are evident, but really in personality. I have become, honestly also, yes, a bit more, perhaps, sad. No, it's not the right word, because it's a heavy word. Perhaps more serious. Before I was more smiling, more joyful. I had a different pleasure in everyday life. I can't complain about anything because everything is fine, but I am more serious, I am a bit more gloomy. And does it depend on Switzerland? I don't know, there have been so many changes. The arrival in Tannay coincided with the separation, the death of my father, the loss of my job. There was a domino effect where I lost all the pillars of life: work, father, partner. And so, clearly, it was a big impact. The fact of not having this social life certainly did not help me to face this phase of restructuring my way of living, with a little more joy.

F.: Is there anything else you want to add about the migratory experience?

C. C.: I have made my life a continuous migration. I really like to arrive and depart. Even this experience in Switzerland, for me, is absolutely a positive experience, but I don't know if, going back, I would do it again.

M. C.

The 12th of November 2018

F.: Age range.

M. C.: 29–39.

F.: Country of origin

M. C.: Italy.

F.: Years of residence in Switzerland?

M. C.: 7

F.: 7, so since 2011?

M. C.: Yes, 2011.

F.: And how many family members do you have in Switzerland?

M. C.: Two, besides me, because I also count my dog. So one is my dog and the other family member is my sister.

F.: Did you migrate to Switzerland?

M. C.: Yes, yes, yes.

F.: What are the reasons why you migrated to Switzerland?

M. C.: Well, actually at the beginning I really didn't even know why. Because I was studying in Siena, and then I had finished the exams of the specialisation, but I had never had an experience abroad. So I went to my professor and told him that I would have liked to write the specialisation thesis abroad. And he told me: 'look, I know someone in Geneva, if you want, if you speak a bit of French…'. I at the time spoke a little bit of French. He told me: 'if you want, in short, I can put you in contact with someone and you can go and do your thesis in Geneva'. So, I accepted because in the end it was not so far from Italy, and I knew the language. Anyway, Geneva is small, so I said to myself: 'ok, fine, why not.' And so this was, let's say, the trap.

F.: So, let's say, for study reasons at the beginning?

M. C.: At the beginning, yes, yes, yes, yes.

F.: And then why did you stay?

M. C.: Well, at the beginning I did the specialization thesis and everything went well. Then they proposed me to do the PhD and it went very badly with my thesis director, so I was fired, that's it. And then at the time I had a boyfriend from Geneva, that is Swiss from Geneva, who absolutely did not want to leave Geneva, and so I said: 'ok, then I start looking for work here'. I have a degree in communication sciences, so I started looking in agencies, many here, but I saw that, well, I didn't like the agencies' work. I have this great passion for theatre, and I found work in a theatre.

F.: And do you travel to Italy?

M. C.: Yes, yes, I travel to Italy at least twice a year. I always take my summer holidays there, in Sicily, specifically, if I can. Every time it makes me laugh the fact that here I know many local people who tell me: 'ah, we went to Bali, beautiful.' And I think that I really don't want to go to Bali, or in Thailand or India. For God's sake, they are certainly beautiful places, but I go to Sicily, that's it. Or if it's not in Sicily, maybe in Tuscany, which I also like very much. I also like Campania very much, anyway in Italy, let's say, first choice Sicily.

F.: Because you are Sicilian?

M. C.: I am Sicilian, yes, from Caltanissetta, more precisely the province of Caltanissetta, a small town called San Cataldo.

F.: What does Switzerland mean to you?

M. C.: Well, Switzerland… It's hard to define it so briefly. I really don't know, because every time I think about it, there's always a mix of pleasant and less pleasant things. Certainly, there's the very painful moment of arrival, because I migrated twice, the first time from Sicily to Tuscany, and it went very well, because I was 18 years old, because you are freer, you are more reckless. The second time at 25 years old from Tuscany to Geneva, and I was really very unwell, because on one hand I clearly left the comfort of the University of Siena, which is really a beautiful city and where I had many friends. But once I arrived here it was very painful, because here at the university it didn't go very well, or at least it didn't go as I expected. Financially, to support myself at university I did 4–5 different jobs, so it was very tiring, especially because I arrived here in winter. Very cold. It was minus 11 degrees, the lake froze. In short, it was a terrible experience. And then the pain of the racism I suffered. I can say that I suffered it, every time someone asks me I say it. I say it because really, yes, I met racist people. I know what it means to be racist, maybe not at the same level as my Arab or French friends, who here are really treated very badly, especially the border workers, but I can say I suffered it. But then on the other hand there are all the satisfactions that I have taken here in Geneva, including professional ones. There's the fact of doing a job that I like 100%, that satisfies me 100%, the fact of having achieved some of my dreams. So in short, there are these two contrasting emotions.

F.: What does Italy mean to you?

M. C.: Well, there's something inside me that's Italian. There's my childhood, beautiful moments, the time of education, at university, but if I have to tell you the truth, if I feel 100% Italian, no. I am Sicilian.

When I say it, it makes people laugh, but I feel more Sicilian, then Tuscan, but I wouldn't say that I feel Genevan. I feel myself, that's it. I can say that I got a tattoo and it's a snail, and I love this animal very much, because not only is it one of the symbols of the city of Siena, of one of the districts of Siena, the snail, and the snail carries its home with it. So my home is inside me, and I wouldn't know if it's Italian or Genevan, but it's everything you have inside, really.

F.: So Italy represents childhood, education, and little more?

M. C.: Yes, but it's more complex. The last time I went to Italy it was hard. Yes, very hard. I was in Florence for 24 hours. It had been a long time since I had been to Florence, I think at least 4–5 years for sure, and I don't know, there was something really strong in the air. I saw some friends and this always makes me very happy. I miss them a lot. But there was really something in the air, in the earth, in the scent, something that really grabbed my stomach, and yes, then I was there with my partner, we were at Santa Maria Novella, and there was a delay of our train that was supposed to take us to Milan, because then we had the Milan–Geneva train. I was hoping that this train would never arrive, so I could catch the connection to Siena at 3:15, and at 4 o'clock I would have been in Siena. Yes, there's something very deep that attracts me, and I wouldn't know exactly what it is.

F.: So is this Italy?

M. C.: Yes, Italy is this, it's a particular smell, a particular scent that makes me feel good.

F.: And these smells, because we're talking about smells, don't you have them here?

M. C.: No, no. But let's say that, to tie in with this episode, after my 24 hours in Florence, returning here to Geneva, I came back as a rational little person, which I am, and I said, look, let's do a nice exercise. Let's see if we can find a smell here in Geneva that makes you feel as good as you do in Florence. I tried and, no, nothing happened!

F.: What does the word 'integration' mean to you?

M. C.: So the word integration to me means being at ease with all the elements of origin. It means feeling good about coming from a place different from the one where you live without feeling inferior, without feeling judged, without fearing the gaze of others and this is what integration means. I also like the word inclusion more than integration because in integration for me there is only an effort on the part of those who arrive while in inclusion there is an effort from both the parties of those who welcome and those who arrive.

F.: What are your strongest memories of when you moved to Switzerland?

M. C.: When I moved to Switzerland I remember that I arrived at the station with my dog and a huge suitcase. The lady who was hosting me, that is, with whom I had rented a room for only 800 francs, very kindly came to pick me up and said: 'look now we stop at the supermarket so you can shop for what you need to eat tonight.' I was shocked because at my house, even if I rent a room, it can happen that at least the first night we eat together. I already understood from there that things would not be very easy. Another dear memory is about a friend of mine from Florence who arrived two days after me by bus loaded with all the things that I had not been able to bring. So I brought a suitcase and the dog and she brought the other two suitcases two days later.

F.: What are the effects on you of living in Switzerland?

M. C.: Certainly Switzerland has opened up many horizons for me in the sense that thanks to Switzerland I have learned to be braver, to aim higher, to have more aspirations, so to believe more in myself and believe that with some sacrifice you can also aim for something big. And to also have an openness towards others that I didn't have because I was in Italy and so I had never travelled so much. Getting to know many different cultures, well, certainly opens up the spirit, in short, the mind.

F.: Is there anything else you would like to add about your experience with migration?

M. C.: There is always this feeling of contrast when you return to Italy and you would like to stay, but you know that it is very difficult to find a job. Now in Geneva I have many contacts thanks to the work I do. How could I do the same in Florence? I really wouldn't know where to start because having never worked in Italy I absolutely have no experience or, let's say, no idea of how to make a CV, how to present yourself at a job interview. So it would be very difficult. Every time I go to Italy there is always this sort of schizophrenia of 'yes, I'll stay, but, no, I can't'. My dream is to buy a house in Siena or nearby. Yes, definitely. But then I say to myself 'damn maybe I have all my family here and how can I leave them?' But I also know of other migrants who anyway returned to their home country when they retired. On one hand the dream would be this: a house in Siena and another holiday home in Sicily.

B. S.

The 23rd of April 2021

F.: Age range?

B. S.: 40–49.

F.: How long have you been living in Switzerland?

B. S.: Since 2008.

F.: How many family members do you have in Switzerland, if any?

B. S.: Four.

F.: Did you migrate to Switzerland?

B. S.: Yes.

F.: For what reason?

B. S.: Initially it was for love. My boyfriend was already working in Geneva so I joined him. Then today he has become my husband.

F.: Do you often travel to Italy?

B. S.: Yes, before becoming a mother, I went down about every two months then, when the children arrived, only a few times a year.

F.: What was and what is the purpose of your trips to Italy?

B. S.: Family reunion, and to feel that air, that scent that Rome has unlike Geneva. Then the food, the friends. For pleasure, not for business. For pleasure, yes.

F.: What does Switzerland mean to you?

B. S.: Stability.

F.: Is that all? What does stability mean?

B. S.: It makes me feel safe from a medical point of view. I feel that if something were to happen I immediately have the means to solve the problem or at least have immediate help. Here there are many cases, compared to Italy, of heart attacks that have been treated immediately precisely because everything is organised differently while in Italy many did not get to the hospital because it is not well managed.

F.: So stability from the point of view of health?

B. S.: Health and salary. Then it's also a safety for the children. My son today at ten years old went out with his little friends on the bus around Geneva. I feel calm, something I would never do in Rome. I wouldn't even let him go down to play in the street. And I was born and raised in Rome, central Rome. Switzerland represents, therefore, security, stability, serenity. I have positive affirmations to give, but it's because I've been here for a long time. If you had asked me this question after a year I was here, the answer would have been different.

F.: And what would it have been?

B. S.: What was Switzerland to me when I first arrived? Sadness, loneliness, nostalgia, not being integrated, not understanding the language.

F.: And why is it no longer sadness and loneliness today?

B. S.: Because I have integrated, because now I speak the language, I speak two unlike before. I didn't even speak one! Now I feel an integral part, I like how it is structured. Now when I go to Italy I find it difficult because certain rules are not followed so for me it is difficult to return to the context in which I was before.

F.: So what does Italy mean to you?

B. S.: Italy is home, Italy is holiday. Italy right now means holiday, home, escape. Escape means to take off the weight of the hard work that Geneva, Switzerland, Geneva in particular, as much as I love it, still leads you to have. It's a very tight work rhythm precisely because you have to produce, you have to produce because the cost of living is very high so to always maintain this status you have to work hard. You always have to be on the ball. In Geneva you have to prove, you always have to produce. You have to prove it continuously.

F.: Do you think this demonstration discourse applies to everyone?

B. S.: I see it a lot in Italians and less in the Swiss because they grew up in a safe, calm environment. We are used to a fast pace. When I came here and saw how they did their work, I felt like super-woman. I felt very strong, but not because I was strong. I had an advantage: I came from the jungle and so I made a career. I made a career as if it was due to my own abilities. In Italy I would be one of many others. Here I have exploited this potential that Italy has given me and that Italians obviously have. I have many Italian colleagues, many people I know and they all confirm this: they really see the difference between us and the others, but not because they have less than us. It's because they were educated differently. They didn't have to struggle to find food. We did, our history is like that.

F.: What does the word integration mean to you?

B. S.: Integration… Let me explain well, at least as far as I am concerned. For me, integration is when you are in a group of people who do not speak the same language and you tell a joke hoping that the others will laugh. They laugh even if they don't understand the language because we mime. But it means that you are part of a group. And you are an active part in that group.

F.: You told me earlier that when you arrived you felt homesick, a bit of sadness. What is, then, the strongest memory that you still carry with you from when you arrived?

B. S.: When I arrived, I went to live in a small village nearby called Ferney Voltaire. It's a town between Geneva and France. This house was in the middle of the green with a strong smell of cow. So coming from Garbatella, coming from a place in the city where the tram passed below me and going to an area where there was a smell of cow all the time, it really upset me.

F.: So you mean it in a negative sense?

B. S.: In a very negative sense. I am a city mouse. I like being in nature, of course, but I need the city.

F.: What effect does living in Switzerland have on you?

B. S.: If there is an effect it is that when I go on holiday to Italy I feel misunderstood. When I go down there and explain what we do here where you have to stop the car to let people cross on the zebra crossing and respect certain rules, I am misunderstood. I am an alien. So for me the effect that Switzerland has had on me is as if I have two lives. It's as if before, in Italy, I was one person and now, here in Geneva, another. So I feel that I received a very positive effect. I feel evolved, I feel good. I like being more Swiss, being more respectful towards others. In short, to live without having that feeling of having to cheat others to survive. I no longer have to elbow my way through. For me it's important because I lived in a society where you had to elbow your way all the time. It was tiring.

F.: Is there anything else you would like to add about your experience as an migrant?

B. S.: I feel that many of my fellow countrymen say: 'ah, when I retire I will go to Italy because enough, I can't take it anymore here'. No, for me it's not like that. I will not go to Italy when I retire.

F.: Where will you go?

B. S.: I will stay here. I will enjoy it here because this is a city made for the elderly. Here everything is at hand. If at 70 years old I have to go to Rome in the middle of the chaos, well, better not to move!

5

Cultural Identity and Photographic Portraiture: Methodological Challenges and the Creative Process

Abstract This chapter questions the methodological challenges that the practice-based research has posed and explains the creative process that supported the development of the photographic work. The theoretical background led me to reflect on practical and creative solutions when producing portraits, and a series of key points about this visual journey is developed. The challenges of the representation of a group of people with individual photographic portraits are discussed. The chapter underlines how previous work and the understanding of a creative process can be precursory of later research and why the inclusion of the landscape versus maintaining a neutral background has links with paintings from the Italian Renaissance.

Keywords Creative process • Italian renaissance • Portraiture • Cultural identity • Photography

F. Arese Visconti, *The Invisible Diaspora*, Palgrave Studies in Creativity and Culture,
https://doi.org/10.1007/978-3-031-74925-4_5

Introduction

Reflecting on the results of research conducted on illustrated publications from the 1960s to 1970s and from 2006 to 2019, I will now offer a better understanding and clarity of the creative process and its methodology which served as the basis for the creation of the photographic portraits of recent Italian migrants living on the *Arc Lémanique*. The entire production has followed theoretical reasoning and practical experience and has moved from one part to the other back and forth in a continuous exchange which is at the base of attempts and successful results. In this chapter, then, key points that need to be considered while looking at the photographic work are introduced and developed. In the first instance, inspired by the reflections of Ariella Azoulay on the civil contract of photography and the value of the gaze, particular attention will be given to the psychological challenges which are the result of the encounter between the photographer, the sitter and the spectator. The second part of the chapter will investigate the challenges of the representation of a group of people through individual photographic portraits: while arguing that seriality can be one of the solutions, this choice will be supported giving some examples of photographers who have produced bodies of work in archival forms. This part will be followed by the story of my works which led the photographic practice of this research to represent the cultural identity of the recent Italian diaspora in Switzerland. It will, then, be crucial to explore the reasons behind the decision to include the landscape in the photographs instead of having a seamless background and the connection of the photographic portraits of this research to Italian Renaissance portrait paintings. Finally, the chapter will conclude with the critical analysis of the exhibition and the reasons behind the choices taken for the final display. The purpose of this ending will be to explain how to plan and show the photographic portraits of contemporary Italian migrants in the Swiss Confederation in a way that can lead the visitor through an intimate visual journey.

The Gaze, the Face and the Mask

In his essay '*La questione del ritratto*', Georg Simmel in 1901 stated that in visual arts the first impact that the viewer has with a portrait is optical, just mechanical (Simmel 1985: 51–53).[1] Nonetheless, he explained that in everyday life we realize that human contact is not limited only to an optical connection but it is actually multi-sensorial. However, considering the non-human nature of a painting, it is inevitable in Simmel's opinion that the first impact with a painted portrait is merely optical. The first role of a portrait is to portray the simple visible side of a human being. The spectator is not in front of a physical body (a human being) depicted as a whole. Is there going to be a relationship with the spectator? If we are referring to photographic portraits, how is the encounter of the photographer and the sitter going to generate a communication with the viewer? This was one of the first points that needed to be understood while undergoing the production of the photographic portraits of recent Italian migrants in Switzerland. The value of the gaze in photographic messages given by Ariella Azoulay (2012) in *The Civil Contract of Photography* has a special value here. Azoulay states that the denotation of a photographic portrait goes beyond its material appearance. When looking at a photograph, we see a frame which contains a message implying reflection. As users of images, we are part of a civil contract and universal spectators (Azoulay 2012: 339). What does Azoulay mean when she describes a photographic image as the result of a civil contract? Each photographic image is the witness of the meeting of the photographer and the subject portrayed. None of them has control on what will happen as the result of this encounter and its consequences. Each photographic act includes a photographer with a camera, a subject frozen in the image and the viewer. The moment when the photographer presses the shutter, he/she is performing an act, a civil act. This act will trigger a series of reactions which involve the subject portrayed and the universal spectator. The photographic camera is between the actors of this encounter and it 'embodies a gaze' (Azoulay 2012: 333), 'the gaze by which we are surprised' (Azoulay 2012: 333). Who is the final user of the image? To whom is this image

[1] Italian translation from (Simmel 1901).

addressed? The message produced by the civil act of photography involves the presence of a viewer. An image is universally addressed to spectators. 'What is imprinted in the paper of the photograph', Azoulay (2012: 337) clarifies, 'is never completely circumscribed by what the photographer meant, and always includes something requiring clarification'. The spectator will interpret individually the image with the details that even the photographer didn't realize that they were going to be included. This is the reason why the images of this project portray subjects with neutral expression and in a frontal position. These are all aspects which intend to offer the universal spectator space for reasoning. The photograph is silent but invites the spectator to take a position. Therefore, as stated by Azoulay (2012: 340), 'the spectator is an effect of the act of photography' and photographic portraiture is a place of dialogue between the photographer, the sitter and the universal spectator. Photographic portraits can, thus, assume the role of a mirror for recognition, self-recognition, and self-misrecognition and become a multi-directional dialogue between the photographer, the sitter, and the spectator. The question is, then, about which means can be used in photographic narratives to deliver a specific message which in my case is related to the visual representation of a specific cultural identity.

The human face is one of these elements of communication and it is quite complex to define. In German 'face' is translated as 'Gesicht' which means *being seen*. This concept evokes the idea of being seen by the viewer. It is, thus, a passive action that the sitter is receiving. In ancient Greek, the theatre mask and the face had the same name: πρόσωπον (prosopon). This term has its etymology from the verb ὁράω (orao) which means 'to see'. Πρόσωπον (prosopon) includes the sense of seeing and being seen and involves the idea of the others' gaze. If the face and the mask in Greek have the same term, do we have to assume that the face and the mask also had the same value? Romans had two different terms to identify the face. While *facies* means *form, configuration, external aspect* (Collatinus-web 2019a), *vultus* signifies *an expression of countenance, the countenance* (Collatinus-web 2019b). As far as the mask is concerned, in classical theatre Romans had fixed types. The Roman mask was called 'persona ', and these masks had one fixed expression. An interpretation of the face is also given by Gilles Deleuze and Félix Guattari. In *A Thousand Plateaus*, Deleuze and Guattari (Deleuze and Guattari 1987) discuss faciality, significance and subjectivity. According to the philosopher and the psychoanalyst, a system of expression is called a regime of signs. A regime of signs is a semiotic system. The substance of expression for Deleuze and Guattari is faciality (Deleuze and Guattari 1987: 115). Language is always linked to facial expressions and the face receives and produces signs which signify. The face is like a body unto itself. The authors state that 'it is a whole body unto itself'. It is the *icon* of the signifying regime. It is what gives substance to the signifier. 'It is what fuels interpretation, and it is what changes, changes traits when interpretation reimports signifier to its substance' (Deleuze and Guattari 1987: 115). In being so, there is no idea of the mask. The mask does not cover the face. In Deleuze and Guattari's opinion, the mask is the face (Deleuze and Guattari 1987: 115). The face is the meeting point of significance and subjectivity. Significance (which they call *semiotique de signifiance*) is represented by the social messages projected onto different social surfaces (like signs projected on white screens) and carried by ordinary language. Subjectivity (which they call *semiotique passionelle*) is the personal consciousness and personal passions experienced in an inward dimension (like black holes of which it is not possible to determine the end). It is how the subject individually reacts to the world. These two components are always combined. Human subjectivity is never completely autonomous but is always integrated with patterns of significance. Then the face is a critical element for human communication.

Art historian Hans Belting (2017: 1) claims that a face becomes really a face after the interaction with the other's gaze. With the gaze, we invite the other to communicate with us or not. Therefore, it is with the play of facial expressions that the face comes to life. The action of seeing and being seen implies our interaction with society.[2] As described by Italian writer Luigi Pirandello in his novel *One, None and a Hundred-Thousand*

[2] On social interaction and the relationship with the other, roles assigned in life and life seen as a performance, see also (Goffman 1955, 1959, 1963).

(Pirandello 2017), we have private and public faces.[3] If seen as masks, we are influenced by society. Do we do the same when we look at photographic portraits? Do we assign roles? Is the photographer transmitting a message about these roles? Do we read the image with our interpretation as we do when we meet people in person? What drives the practice part of this research is the face in the context of photographic portraits to be interpreted as a mask. French anthropologist Marcel Mauss (1938) discussed the notion of person (also mentioning the Latin *persona*) in connection with a social meaning of mask. He develops considerations on the individual, the sense of 'me', the person and the mask in societies through history. Belting (2017: 7) stated that 'when we let our whole face become expressionless, we allow our face to become indecipherable and stiffen into a mask'. Do the portraits of this research have to be interpreted as mask? Are we then our own masks? As already mentioned in Chap. 4, Barthes (1980: 35) states that photography can only achieve significance when it shows a mask. In order to better understand this point, we can look at the work of August Sander (Sander and Keller 1980; Sander 2008) as a photographer who portrayed people as masks of his time and society. While French photographer Nadar (2004, 2007) represented the French bourgeoisie of the nineteenth century, Sander portrayed the people of the Republic of Weimar (Sander and Keller 1980). They all reproduced masks of their time and society. The camera produced masks of someone who is now not there anymore.[4]

In 1934, in *Antlitz der Zeit*, Sander (2008) represented a series of portraits of Germans.[5] Immortalizing his subjects from close-up to full length, Sander aimed to represent social types and classes in their collective roles. The Nazi Ministry of Culture banned *Antlitz der Zeit*. This series of images was later expanded in the famous *Menschen des 20. Jahrhunderts* (Sander and Keller 1980). In his work, Sander has

[3] Published in 1926, *One, None and a Hundred-Thousand* is the story of the introspective analysis of an ordinary human being. Just merely looking at his image reflected in a mirror, Vitangelo Moscarda starts a journey into himself which he calls 'my sickness' (Pirandello 2017: 17). He understands that he is not what he thinks he is and that others see him differently. Others, as society, assign him different roles (masks) which he accepts changing role each time.

[4] Belting calls it the *thanatos effect* (Belting 2017: 160)

[5] For readings on August Sander, note Baker (1996) and Jones (2000).

individual portraits, then couples and then groups—they are not snapshots. The subjects are portrayed in full length or three-fourths with a severe attitude in their environment. Sander's idea was to have a series of images structured in the form of an archive. The archival system applied by Sander recalls a sense of typology: there are always four individual portraits of male farmers, four corresponding female farm wives, one other photograph of a woman, two portraits of couples and one family portrait. The four men represent the earthbound man, the philosopher, the revolutionary and the wise man. The same system is applied to the female portraits.[6]

In his analysis of Sander's work, American documentary photographer Walker Evans claimed that *Menschen des 20. Jahrhunderts* was a 'cultural necessity' and 'photographic editing of society' (Evans 1931: 128). Walter Benjamin (1980: 211) highlighted the fact that Sander's work is organized as a series and exactly because of this reason becomes 'a training manual.' This serialization gives Sander's work the value of masks evoked by Barthes. Living in the same years of August Sander, Erna Lendvai-Dircksen (1932) had a similar view and mentioned that the face is an essential element for the identity representation of a country. Although she was a Nazist and Sander was progressive with different points of view on society, they both shared this idea of using photography to represent the face of a nation. As the portraits of this research are doing representing the cultural identity of recent Italian migrants in Switzerland, Lendvai-Dircksen produced portraits of people that could communicate the context they had lived in. She represented the face of rural Germany. She stated that the face is like a landscape on which the real landscape is imprinted (Lendvai-Dircksen 1933: 84). These photographs are an attempt to read the characteristics of a country through the physiognomic aspect of the faces of the people who lived in it. In his introduction to Sander's *Antlitz der Zeit*, Alfred Döblin (2012) is convinced that, in creating identifiable social types, Sander develops a sort of sociology through images rather than through words. Döblin (2012: 12) explains how faces and images can be levelled by universal forces such as

[6] Referring to Atget photographs , Rosalind Krauss (1982: 316) called this type of archival structure a 'repetitive rhythm of accumulation', which is typical of the Neue Sachlichtkeit.

death and human society. For levelling, Döblin intends the cancellation of diversity. As far as the first case is concerned, the levelling caused by death, Döblin refers to the death masks. Once dead, all the faces, in his opinion, have the characteristic of having lost expressivity. He defines, then, the death masks as the final product of life consumption on body and mind. To underline how life has an essential impact on these faces, Döblin compares these post-mortem faces to pebbles eroded by the endless action of the sea. Death mask captures a face for eternity. If, with Deleuze and Guattari (1987: 115), Agamben (2000: 98,9) and Cousin (AA 2017) we assume that the face is the carrier of expressions, we can think that a mask is when an individual is liberated from every psychological origin. The death mask has no expression, or better the expression is no longer linked to life; therefore, the death mask becomes the image of the 'authentic' face (Belting 2017: 21).

In the portraits of Italian migrants in twenty-first-century Switzerland, we intend to compress and include all the expressions of one person's life in a mask-like effect. Durs Grünbein (Davidis and Dessoff-Hahn 1999: 12) in the catalogue of the collection of the Schiller National Museum in Marbach, Germany, said 'whatever can be read from the face of a dead person is now left up to the meditations of the viewer'. We can identify this viewer with Azoulay's spectator (Azoulay 2012: 340). Moreover, here this blank expression of portraits can generate communication between the sitter and the beholder. The photographic portraits of this research have blank expressions to communicate through a mask. They invite the other to dialogue and suggest an interpretation of whom the spectators have in front of them. These images evoke a mask. In European culture, the portrait assumed the role of the mask and became the memory of the face (Belting 2017: 92). The photographic portrait gains a mimetic meaning: it is the presence of an absence. It is the imitation of the face. These expressionless portraits become an alternative to the death mask. However, differently from the death mask, they have the gaze, the gaze of the sitter which engages the spectator. This interaction frees the sitter from the plane and allows the represented subject to claim a presence. The gaze creates a direction and places the subject in the world and gives to the portrait the value of a real face establishing a connection with the viewer. The photographer proposes the dialogue but the spectator chooses the role: 'the sight

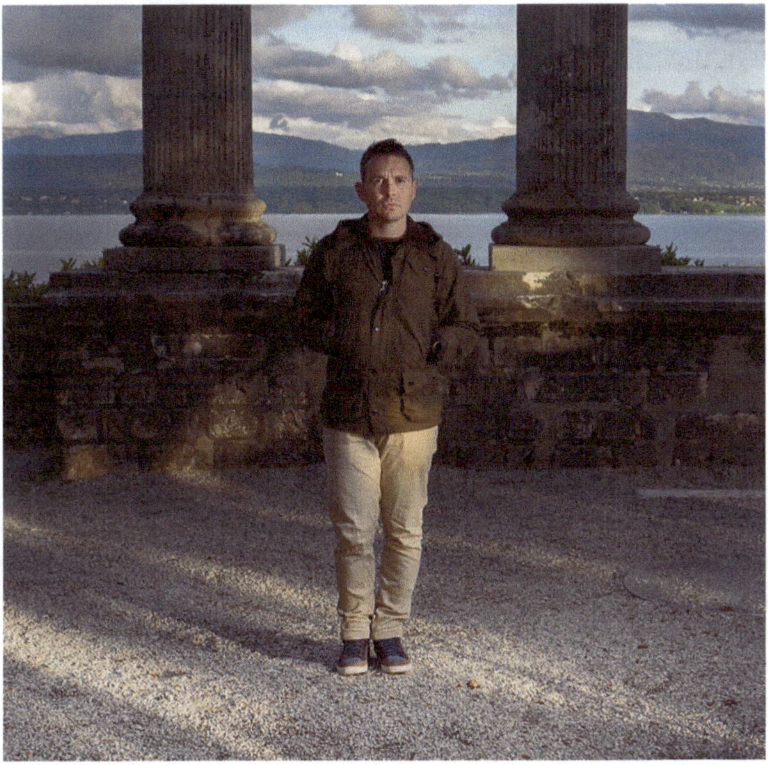

Fig. 5.1 Francesco Arese Visconti, *YD*, 2021

of the true spectator is supposed to be free of any personal interest save the common interest in the civil contract of photography' (Azoulay 2012: 340). The timeless and authentic face presents living subjects in a frozen form and, by doing so, tries to communicate a mimetic meaning of the face like in a catalogue with a series of death masks (Fig. 5.1).

Seriality

These timeless and authentic faces assume particular relevance once presented as a series. This part of the chapter argues why seriality was identified as the main approach to represent with photographic portraits a specific group of people. We can see seriality as a sort of inventory, a catalogue of individuals which form, all together, a group, almost like an identification system. There was a moment in time when photography was used with a pseudo-scientific approach to record individual characteristics and develop identification systems. In their book *The Beautiful and the Damned*, Peter Hamilton and Roger Hargreaves (Hamilton and Hargreaves 2001) trace an exhaustive history of how the nineteenth-century society used portrait photography to record information on individuals.[7] Images have always attracted the attention of science but until the advent of photography everything related to diagrams, maps, paintings was based on human drawing skills (Hamilton and Hargreaves 2001: 57). From the sixteenth century, observation was central to scientific research. With the invention of photography, there was a paradigm shift: it was believed that pure objectivity was introduced in the way of thinking (Hamilton and Hargreaves 2001: 58). It was the time for social inventory with the intersection with other systems of identification. Photography was applied to physical anthropology in relation to Darwin's (2018) evolutionism and to control the population. It was used by the British Empire to document the colonial exploration (as in the case of David Livingstone in Zambesi between 1858 and 1864) (Hamilton and Hargreaves 2001: 86–87). In his essay, *The Body and the Archive*, American critic and photographer Allan Sekula (1986) describes the birth of archival photography as a branch of portrait photography and how it was used to develop police archives from the 1840s until more recent years. The diffusion of photography was linked to the nineteenth-century rise of the middle classes and portrait photography became a new mass phenomenon. Sekula identifies two aspects of portrait photography: while in its honorific role photography was used to represent the self of the middle classes (bourgeoisie), it was also clear that its repressive side played an important role in criminals' identification. Photographic documentation of prisoners was not completely embraced until the 1860s but the potentiality of its use in possible archival systems was already recognized in the 1840s.[8] Allan Sekula (1986: 6) calls it 'legalistic truth'. In the United

[7] On this topic see also (Sekula 1986; Tagg 1988; Phillips 1998).

[8] William Henry Fox Talbot presented his calotype 'Articles of China' from the book 'The Pencil of Nature' as a good example of visual document (Schaaf 2003: 192–193).

States, police began to use photography as a means of identifying criminals and to develop a social and moral hierarchy, identifying the betters (in the case of the bourgeois self) and the inferiors (criminals). Sekula explains that in these terms we can talk about a 'social archive' which highlighted the distinction between the bourgeoisie and the criminal body.

By 1880 and 1890, police work moved to a more professional and technological level in identifying criminals and archiving their profiles with the inclusion of photographs (Sekula 1986: 17). The photographic archive became a fundamental tool of detection and control of criminality. The photographic representation of the criminal body mainly followed two different systems. First, according to a realist approach, the aim was to identify reality of species and types through a theoretical and scientific methodology. The final result was to define the general criminal type. Second, the nominalist approach wanted to generate large categories and mental constructs with a practical and technical system to study individual criminals. These two systems were deployed in the 1880s (Sekula 1986: 22). Photography started to be used in strong connection with statistics. Physiognomic anthropologist Alphonse Bertillon (2014) developed the 'bertillonage', the first scientific, nominalist, structured system for police identification (Sekula 1986: 18). The system was coupled later with photographs of the crime's scene and images of cadavers' faces. In the 1880s in Paris, Alphonse Bertillon was the Director of the Identification Bureau of the Paris Prefecture of Police where he attempted to rationalize the volume of images which were produced every day and created a system of criminal identification. There were, nevertheless, several issues he had to face: the problem of classification and the organization of individual cards. This standardized system was based on three actions: after having identified eleven bodily measurements, he realized that it was almost impossible that two individuals might share the same series of these measurements and then calculated that they were constant in every adult body. Bertillon was possibly the first one to understand the value and complexity of the photographic documentation and its archiving. In Bertillon's view the photographic document was merely a morphological registration which was considered globally useful also for the telegraphic transmission of suspects. His system was widely exploited, paralleled and surpassed by the fingerprint system, which needed less technical skills to be applied. Sekula (1986: 37) states that photographic documentation was well accepted by the majority of the practitioners even if in the late nineteenth century there was a large discussion about other factors that could determine criminal action (Sekula 1986: 40). Francis Galton contributed to this search with a realist method of composite portraiture to define the criminal type (Galton 1998; Stimson 2006). He tried to work on a different level than on just singular cases. Compared to Bertillon, Galton was not a systemizer and used composite images to identify types of criminals. Known in particular for the development of the first statistical method applied to heredity, Galton's peculiarity is the so-called *composite images* realized overlapping multiple exposures on one single plate. The result allowed him to create types with no subjective characteristics. In his 1869 work 'Hereditary Genius', Galton attempted to highlight the quality of human intelligence building a hierarchy and applying it to racial groups through quantification, numerical ranking and physiognomic description. He found it impossible to follow Bertillon's method of individual classification and believed the representation of general types to be more productive. Even though the two systems applied by Bertillon and Galton might seem totally different in their final goal, they both represented positivist attempts to regulate criminal body identification and were based on Adolphe Quetelet's (1991) theory of the 'average man:' through a deep study of recurring births, deaths and crimes, Quatelet's final aim was to create an exact science based on social phenomena. While, as seen before, August Sander is an example of a photographer who accepted and continued the tradition of the archival approach, Walker Evans can be considered a representative of anti-positivism and anti-rationalism documentary photography. In his 1938 work *American Photographs*, Evans (2012) revamped the archival model adding a poetic structure. With the dry documentation of his photographs taken in the subway (Greenough and Evans 1991), he was very close to police photography. Nevertheless, in a 1971 interview (Katz 1971: 87) Evans described the difference between his 'documentary style' and the 'literal document' as we consider a police photograph of the murder's scene. He highlighted the importance of the poetic experience beyond the normal and physical level in each image.[9] This poetic experience added to the archival approach was at the basis of previous photographic works that I have produced and are the prelude to the current research.

From Africa to Europe: A Prelude

'New World—Stories of African Immigration and Integration in Switzerland' (Arese Visconti 2012) and 'We, Prato' (Arese Visconti 2015) are two migration-related photographic projects that were completed in 2012 and 2015 (Figs. 5.2, 5.3, 5.4, and 5.5). In different ways, they both had a significant impact on my photographic research on recent Italian migrants in Switzerland. Being a migrant myself, I decided in 2010 to start researching the integration process of migrants with photographic portraiture. I was not interested in the migration process *per se* but rather in the moment of settlement when a person establishes in a country and starts the process of integration. In 2012, I worked on a project on the African immigration and integration in Switzerland and later, in 2014, on the Italian-Chinese community of Prato (Italy).

'New World—Stories of African Immigration and Integration in Switzerland' is a photographic documentary project that I developed in 2012 intending to raise awareness about the global issue of migrants' identities. I contacted twenty-eight subjects from eleven different African countries who had legally migrated and were permanently resident in Switzerland. The work, also presented on an online platform,[10] eventually became a book and an exhibition which was shown at the *Salon des artistes indépendants* at the Geneva Palexpo in November 2012 and at the *Université Ouvrière de Geneve*[11] in February 2013. Short texts were displayed next to the photographs. After a brief description of the migratory experience, the text included a one-sentence advice offered by the subject

[9] See the following portrait photographers who are known for their archival style: (Greenfield-Sanders et al. 2001; Dijkstra 2003; Greenfield-Sanders and Vidal 2005; Schöller and Abramović 2012; Schöller and Funderburg 2013; Taylor-Lind 2014; Hussain 2014, 2017; Serrano n.d.).

[10] newworldproject.wordpress.com

[11] www.uog.ch

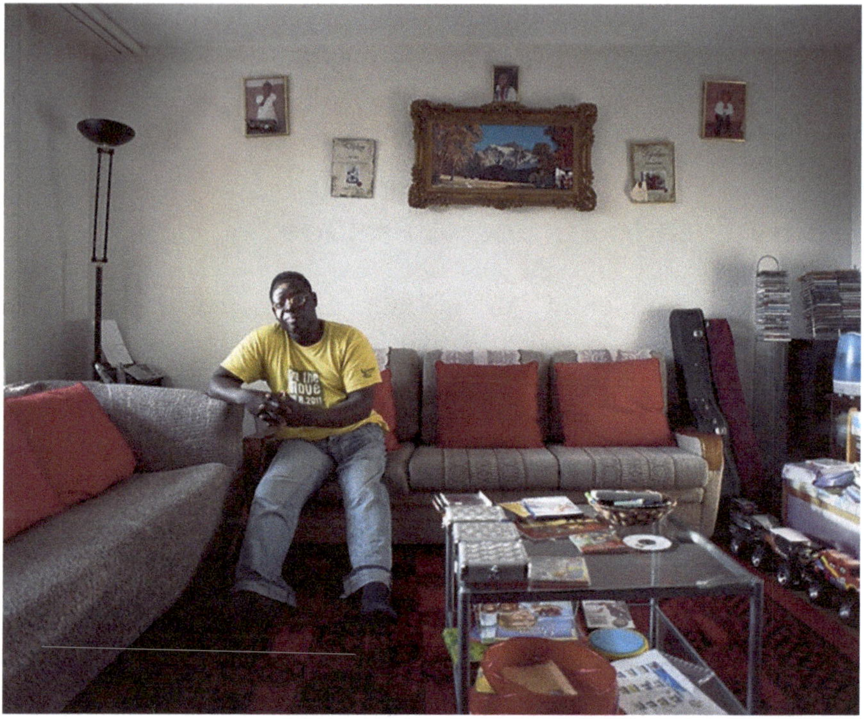

Fig. 5.2 Francesco Arese Visconti, *AA*, 2012

portrayed, for people who might want to migrate to Switzerland. The subjects are photographed in their living spaces. The resulting environmental portrait includes personal details which narrate a richer story of the sitters. The images were taken with color film to have additional information. These images refer to the tradition of documentary photography devoted to migration.[12] As mentioned above, these images are presented as a series, and this was also the method used in the exhibition.

While still engaged in 2013 in documenting similar issues, I was fascinated by the migration and integration process of the Chinese population in Prato (Italy). About thirty kilometers away from Florence, Prato hosts the largest Chinese community in terms of population density in

[12] See for example the works on Ellis Island by Lewis Hine (Sundell 1986; Szlezák 2009, 2012) and in the Eastside slums of New York by Jacob Riis (1971).

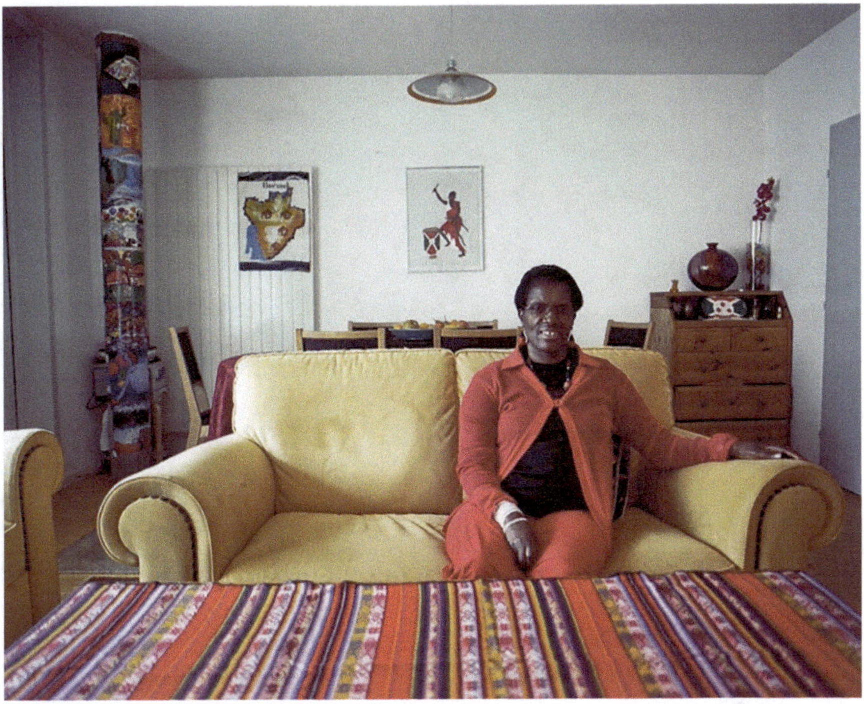

Fig. 5.3 Francesco Arese Visconti, *DN*, 2012

Europe.[13] In this context, broad literature on the controversial phenomenon of integration of Chinese migrants with the local population has been produced.[14] I met the Chinese migrants' second generation, boys and girls who were born in Italy to Chinese parents but who had never been to China. I was particularly interested by the level of integration of the second under-twenty-eight-years-old generation Chinese migrants and their relationship with their Italian peers. Did they feel different from the others or rather had the perception of being part of the same

[13] The National Institute of Statistics (ISTAT 2013) in Italy published a study in December 2013 which reported that the 8.35% of the resident population in Prato was Chinese. This data shows that in the year when my research work was conducted, the Chinese community in Prato was the largest in Europe in terms of population density.

[14] See Bernardini (2014), Pieraccini (2010), Nesi (2010), Johanson Russell Smyth and French (2009).

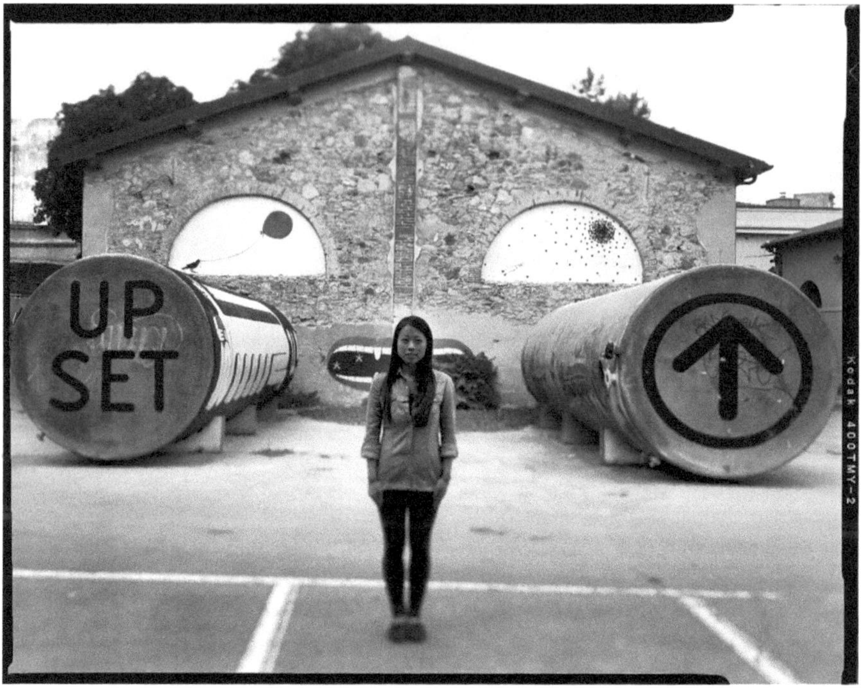

Fig. 5.4 Francesco Arese Visconti, *MMH*, 2015

community? Were they Chinese or Italians or, in certain cases, both of them? I went to local schools, associations, and cultural centres where these young people met, and I started establishing stronger connections with them. The final result of this activity are sixteen portraits of boys and girls aged between sixteen and twenty-eight years. All the photographs were taken on black & white film with a 4×5 inches large format camera to recall the long tradition of documentary photography. The environmental portraits are always horizontal with the subject standing in the centre of the composition in a location chosen by them (Figs. 5.3 and 5.4). While the focus is on the faces, the bottom of the image is blurred with the idea of melting the lower part of the bodies with the ground: the subjects become visually part of the context despite of their facial look which suggests different origins, Italian or Chinese. This technical solution helped me to visually show what I collected from the interviews that

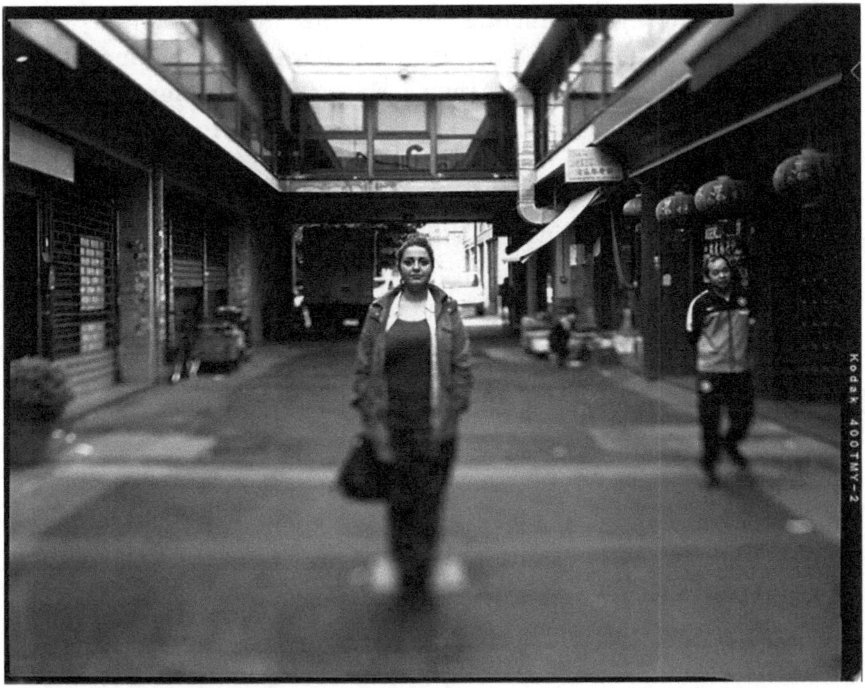

Fig. 5.5 Francesco Arese Visconti, *LL*, 2015

I ran with all the sitters: they all told me that they felt part of the same community. These subjects were all rooted in the same place. Seriality in the sense of an archival approach recurs even stronger in this work as it did in 'New World—Stories of African Immigration and Integration in Switzerland'. This photographic research became a book and an exhibition shown at the Theatre Grütli in Geneva in January 2015.[15]

Developing further my interest in the integration process of migrants' communities, in 2015 I decided to start working on the contemporary Italian diaspora in Switzerland, focusing my attention in particular on the area between Geneva and Lausanne. As anticipated in other parts of this book, the *arc lémanique* is populated by a large community of people with different nationalities (Italians included) employed in international

[15] https://aresevisconti.com/2015/01/24/we-prato-opening/

organizations, non-governmental organizations and corporations which operate on a global scale. Moreover, the Geneva and Lausanne cultural identity have been deeply influenced by the Italian migration of the 1960s and 1970s.[16] For these reasons, this geographic zone is quite peculiar in the Swiss panorama and interesting in the context of my research. While at the beginning the intention was to work on the differences between the first generation of Italian migrants who moved to Switzerland after the Second World War and the twenty-first-century Italian migrants, I realized that I had to scale down and devote my research only on recent migrants. For this project I created a page on Facebook and started to contact Italians in the area with the aim of developing new connections. As a result of the exposure due to the Facebook page, I was contacted in May 2015 by the City of Geneva, and I was asked to be included in the Swiss Pavillion at the 2015 EXPO in Milan. The Swiss Pavillion devoted specific days to three main cities of Switzerland (Zürich, Bern and Geneva) and the Administration of the City of Geneva had decided to dedicate part of the events to the Italian migration phenomenon which had deeply contributed to the development of the city in the 1960s and 1970s. Since the EXPO in Milan was centred on nutrition, my images had to portray recent Italian migrants and second-generation Italians who were working in the food industry. Through my personal connections, I contacted a list of people who I thought could be available to be photographed. The images were all taken in black & white with 8 × 10 inches film. The monochromatic tones offered a uniform and abstract approach to the project. The large format camera allowed me the opportunity to establish a certain distance with the subject in the moment of the shot, which helped to create a sense of aura. The subject had to stand in a frontal position before a white background. The light had to be soft so that the shadows didn't alter the facial expression. Sitters were represented in three/quarters and had to hold a prop which could give the viewer a hint on their personality (Fig. 5.8). The ten resulting images were printed on 80 × 60 cm fiber-based paper, mounted in large black

[16] The interest towards the Italian diaspora of those years is still strong today as witnessed by the two exhibitions on the topic held in Geneva in 2019 (Brux 2019) and in Lausanne in 2021 (Costa and Golay 2021).

wooden frames and exhibited in the Swiss Pavillion at the EXPO in Milan (Figs. 5.6 and 5.7). I wanted to replicate Richard Avedon's style of portraits which he made for his 1980s project *In the American West*. The aim of my project was to create an archive of Italian migrants of the new

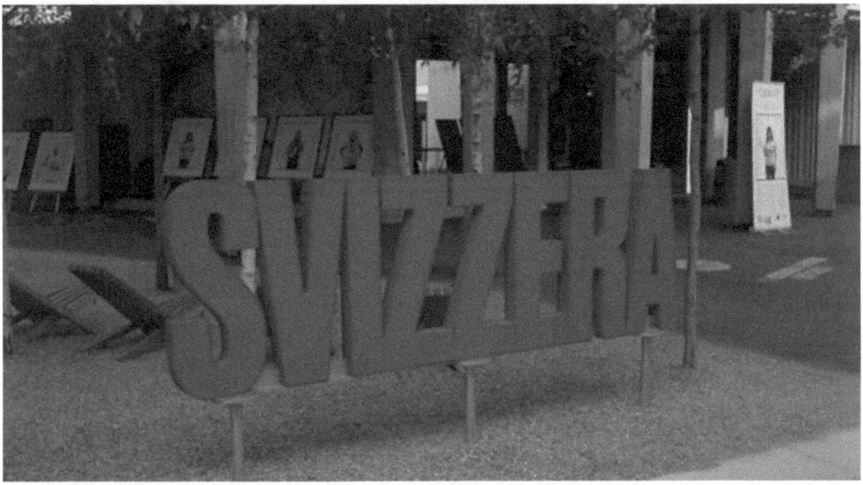

Fig. 5.6 The Swiss Pavillion at the Milan EXPO in 2015

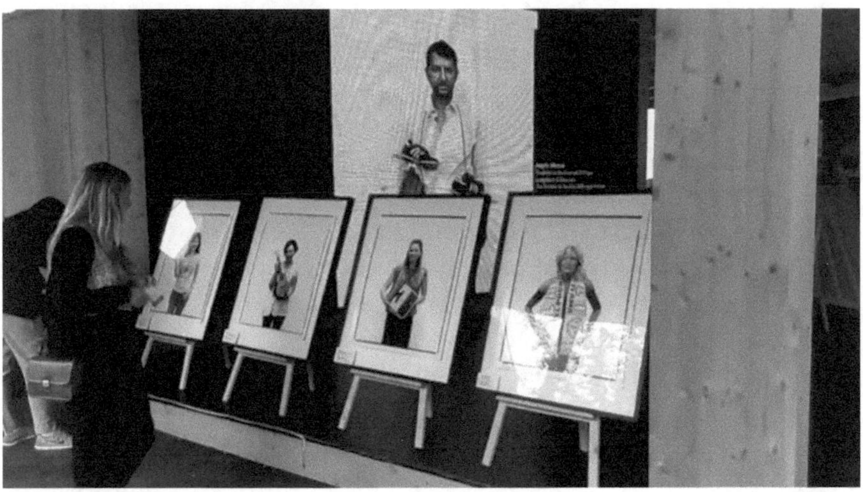

Fig. 5.7 The Swiss Pavillion at the Milan EXPO in 2015

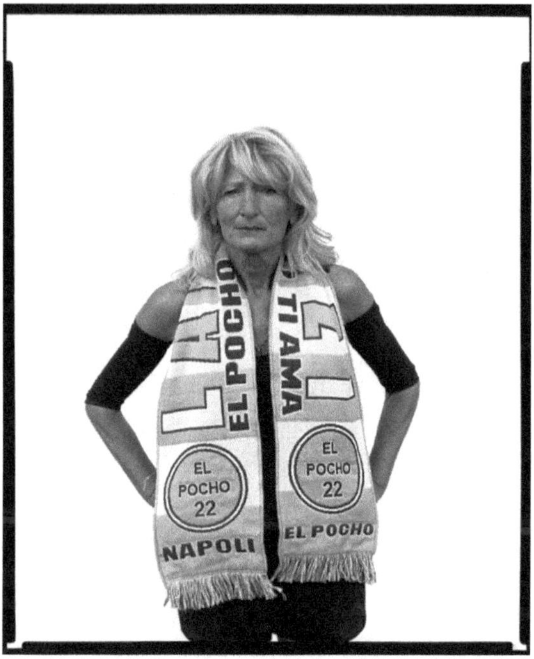

Fig. 5.8 Francesco Arese Visconti, *GCM*, 2015

millennium. I had studied how Richard Avedon had produced his portraits (Wilson 2003; Pénichon Sylvie 2012) and, fascinated by his approach, decided to reproduce the methods that he had used in *In the American West* (Avedon 1985).

Avedon said that his work was about the working class (Whitney 2002), not about the American West but taken in the American West. He was looking at people and trying to find the truth about them but these pictures were fragments of himself. In his photographic sessions, there was no space for the collaboration between the photographer and the sitter. For Avedon, it is the photographer who always has total control of the sitting session. Speaking with one of the individuals portrayed, Sandra Bennett, who was complaining with him about being put on the front cover of the book *In the American West*, Avedon said: 'you can't say you weren't there, which you have to accept, then you are there under control of the photographer. I have the control in the end but I can't do it alone.

You have a lot to say by the way you look' (theradpho 2013: 1:05:08). His sitters are objects like clay in the hands of the sculptor. Avedon photographs his subjects against a neutral white sheet of paper and away from the sunshine to avoid shadows and highlights which could lead the viewers' eyes to something which is not of any interest for the photographer. The light has to be even to 'neutralize its role in the appearance of things' (Avedon 1985: 19). He uses an 8 × 10 inches camera, standing next to it always at a determined distance from the lens and from the subject. Avedon claims that 'a portrait is not likeness. The moment when an emotion or fact is transformed into a photograph it is no longer a fact but an opinion. [...] None of them is the truth' (Avedon 1985: 21).

On the back flap of her book *Avedon at work in the American West*, Laura Wilson (2003) declared that 'as much as all these photographs may appear to be moments that just occurred, they are finally, in varying degrees, studied works of the imagination.' This idea is significant for the creative process of my research on recent Italian migrants in Switzerland because my images are not snapshots but images studied in every aspect. All the details collaborate to communicate something about people's cultural identity. There is, therefore, a similarity between my work and Avedon's images in the conceptualization of photographs. They are not examples of occurred moments but rather studied works of the imagination of the photographer. This composition is created in the case of Avedon's *In the American West* and the same process is repeated in my work. As in Avedon's work, I started to portray my subjects in front of a white seamless sheet of paper which served to isolate them from the environment. In the production of black & white images with an 8 × 10 inches Kodak MasterView camera, I always used natural soft light (Fig. 5.9). The elimination of the environment and the use of the soft light help the viewer to concentrate on the subject and nothing else. I believed that the images had to present the subjects in an archival form like in a catalogue and that the only elements portrayed had to be the subjects themselves, the clothing and the props which could add indications of the cultural identity of the individual.[17]

[17] Also see Anastasia Taylor-Lind (2014) on Maidan Nezalezhnosti (Independence Square) in Kiev.

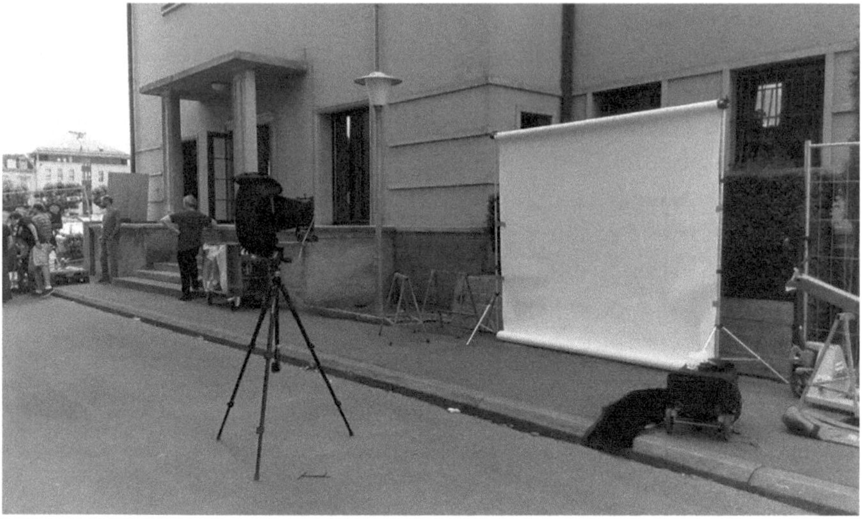

Fig. 5.9 Settings for the shooting of the first series of portraits, Nyon (CH), 2015

The interesting results achieved with these earlier projects encouraged me to develop the original idea. My research interests moved to a further understanding not only of Italian migrants in general but also in relation to the more general meaning of cultural identity. I researched the value of photographic portraiture as a means of communications between the photographer, the sitter and the viewer, and specifically the representation of Italian cultural identity in still images. I started thinking and reading about identity and all its layers, specifically about the cultural aspects which identify the individual. I thought about the elements that can culturally unify a population (and in the specific case of my research the Italians) and at the same time help others to identify that same population. From March 2017 I started working on a new set of images. While studying identity formation[18] and how photography could reflect it,[19] I

[18] See Althusser (2014), Baynham (2015), Bhabha (1984, 1990), Bourdieu (1977, 1986, 1997), Butler 1993), Hall (1989, 1990, 1996, 1997, 1999, 2003), Hall and Back (2009), Lacan (2005), Lang (1985), Merleau-Ponty (1963).

[19] See for A. Sherman, Mesenhöller (2005) and Szlezák (2012); for L. W. Hine (1909), Rosenblum (1977), Seixas (1987), Sundell (1986), Szlezák (2009, 2012) and Ureña (2009); for R. Dijkstra (2003) and (Grunberg 1997); for J. Hanzlova (2012); for M. Petruzziello (2017).

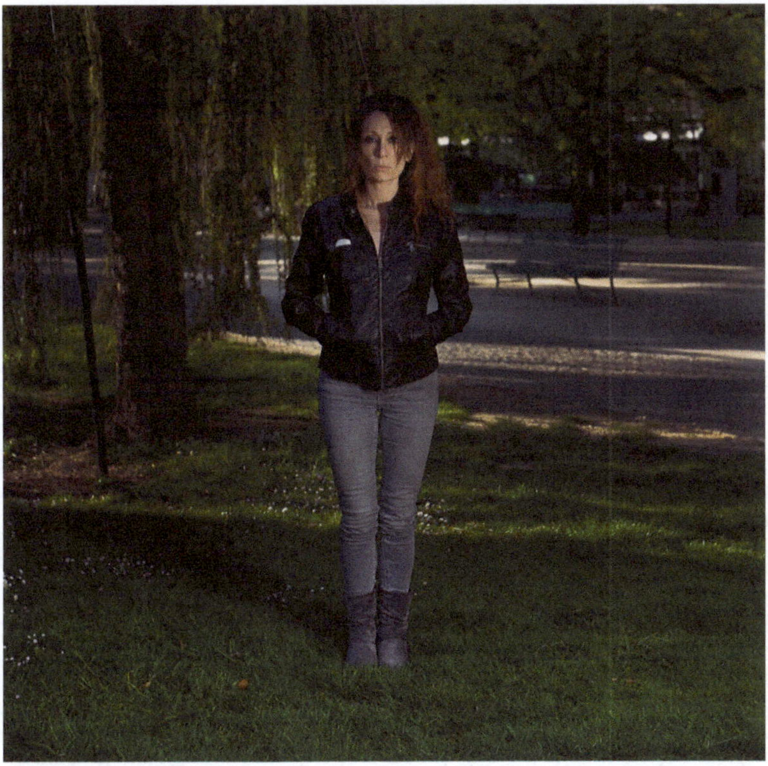

Fig. 5.10 Francesco Arese Visconti, *BS*, 2021

realized that it was necessary to change the concept of my images and decided that I had to include the full body in the landscape (Fig. 5.10).

The Body and the Landscape

The representation of the full body in the landscape suggests a relationship between migrants and the new space where they are living. The full body is the physical representation of an experience of migrating to a new place and its embodiment. I use the term embodiment in its value of incorporation. I refer here to psychologist Richard Lang's definition of incorporation (Lang 1985: 202): 'Incorporation is the initiative of the active body, embracing and assimilating a certain sphere of foreign reality to its own body. In this sense, incorporation is essentially the movement from the strange to the familiar.' In portrait photography, the sense of how bodies assimilated a foreign reality can be visualized in *Passengers*, the award-winning documentary work by César Dezfuli (2022). On 1st August, 2016, 118 migrants from Africa were rescued in the Mediterranean Sea. Spanish photographer Dezfuli portrayed them and re-photographed them after few years once the migrants had found a place to stay in Europe. The difference of the portraits is impressive. While in the second images they look relaxed, in the images taken in 2016 these migrants had incorporated their fears, abuses and humiliations. Their faces and bodies reflected their migration experience, their journey. French philosopher Maurice Merleau-Ponty (1963: 168) explains how our body lives space by means and adapts its status according to the inputs it receives from the context and the other. He uses the example of the soccer player in the playground with the adversaries and his team-mates. The field and the other players are the context in which he moves. Merleau-Ponty calls the field 'the immanent term of his practical intentions'. The structure of the context (the other players) constantly changes. The soccer player embodies the context adapting to it with his moves. We all inhabit place as the soccer player does. Inhabiting, Lang states, is 'an act of transformation where space becomes place. Inhabiting is an act of incorporation; it is a situation of active, essential acquisition' (Cromby 2015). In doing this we embrace the external impulse into our body. The space where we move does not belong to us but becomes more familiar. John Cromby states that we are, before other things, feeling bodies (Cromby 2015). Feelings are not just emotions. They are somatic experiences, and as in the case of the migrants photographed by Dezfuli, they will change and transform our bodies during our lives. Cromby states that these experiences are not easy to control. They have us before we have them and, of course, they have a direct influence in the visual transformation of our body. 'Feelings are intrinsically part of the experience', Cromby states (2015: 16). The body is an entity which is shaped by feelings. 'Feeling', continues Cromby, 'emerges as a quality or aspect of the body under certain condition' (2015: 17). 'Feeling is a phase or aspect of the body' (2015: 21). 'Feelings are emergent phases of the body' (2015: 28).

These points are essential for the development of the creative process behind the production of the photographic images of this research and their composition. I want to portray my subjects as full bodies because I am portraying the result of the emotions connected with the process of migration and integration that the subject must have experienced. The representation of the full body is the physical representation of the experience of these feelings. All the feelings connected with the experience of moving from a comfort zone (the motherland) to a new space have inevitably shaped the migrant body, maybe in almost invisible details. I want, nevertheless, to make sure that these details, no matter what they are, are recorded and documented in an image.

The representation of the body in the landscape is also one of the characteristics of Renaissance portrait painting. This is a fundamental link to the visual references that I have used to connect to a specific shared native cultural background of Italian migrants living in the *arc lémanique*.

Italian Renaissance Portrait Paintings as a Common Native Cultural Aspect

I decided to develop a photographic narrative which could suggest a correlation to a common native cultural aspect. My point was not to construct a myth of national identity that could possibly mislead the viewer of the exhibition and, most importantly, not be felt by all Italians as a common cultural background deliberately assigned by me. However, it was a way to tackle the discussion on the topic while trying to find a response to my research questions. I wanted to find a method to photographically represent a group of people who share a common native cultural background that can culturally unify a population and at the same time help the others to identify that same population As a key point for my practice, I had to choose which artistic period could represent *Italianity* in its cultural aspect in visual arts. As already anticipated, *Italianity* is a complex multi-layered concept. However, I wanted to understand what characteristics in visual arts could represent *Italianity* abroad. Therefore, I wondered what was in the opinion of Italian migrants resident in the *arc lémanique* the historical period which could be identified by them as a shared cultural common background. In particular, I was interested by these answers for their connection with painting portraiture: once understood that I could replicate some of the visual characteristics of those paintings in my photographic portraits and create a visual reference to an Italian common cultural background. This point is complicated and controversial considering the multifaceted and peculiar origin and structure of the Italian population. Being aware of this aspect, I circulated a survey among the Italian community living in the *arc lémanique* about what they thought was the most common native cultural background shared by them.[20] Acknowledging here the scientific imperfection of the tool used, the answers suggested that the period to which I should refer was the Italian Renaissance (out of thirty answers, the Italian Renaissance was the most popular response, followed by the period of the Roman Empire, Baroque and Risorgimento). I therefore focused my attention on the main characteristics of Renaissance portrait paintings and started considering how to creatively reproduce these aspects in my images. The visual link to Italian Renaissance paintings in my practice is given by the replication of some specific characteristics of Italian Renaissance portraiture. These aspects are likeness, the inclusion of the landscape as a means to describe the roots of the subject depicted, the use of perspective to involve the viewer putting the human being with its perfect proportions (like in case of the *homo vitruvianus* by Leonardo da Vinci) at the centre of the universe/painting/image. I will now expand on these points.

Likeness was not a novelty of the Renaissance portraiture of the fifteenth century (Rubin 2011). Giorgio Vasari in his *Lives of the Artists* from 1550 (Vasari 1998) stated that Giotto had been the first painter to introduce 'good drawing from live natural models, something which had not been done for more than two hundred years. And even if someone had tried it, [...] none of them had succeeded as happily or as completely as Giotto' (Vasari 1998: 16). Also, physician and philosopher Pietro d'Abano in his *Expositio in Problematibus Aristotelis* from 1310 (Thomann

[20] In the selection of subjects, I have excluded children and elderly people: I have focused my attention on people like me, part of the middle class that has migrated abroad on the *arc lémanique*.

1991) had pointed Giotto as a 'painter capable of producing a likeness in all respects' in such a way that the people who were represented were easily recognizable. One example of likeness in Italian Renaissance is the 1490 painting *An old man and his grandson* by Domenico Ghirlandaio. In this scene, the old man is represented with each detail of his face including his irregular nose. The 1425 fresco *The Distribution of Alms and the Death of Ananias* by Masaccio in the fifteenth-century Brancacci Chapel in Florence is another example of realism of architecture and landscape. The buildings represented are typical of an Italian city of the fifteenth century. The mountains in the background are the snow-capped Apennines (Casazza 2001: 52).

The inclusion of the landscape in Italian Renaissance paintings has the intent of describing the story of the subject depicted and their sense of belonging to a specific place because of what she or he did in their life. The context here has an important role. It is not just a mere background and there is a strong link between identity and belonging. The place in which the act of portraying takes place is particularly important. Francesco Sassetti was a de' Medici's banker who worked in Geneva and Lyon. In his portrait with his son Teodoro, Domenico Ghirlandaio included a city that is probably Geneva in the background because of a chapel that Sassetti had built in that city. Ghirlandaio reproduces the same detail in a fresco in the Sassetti chapel in the church of Santa Trinita in Florence. The landscape tells us something of Sassetti's life. Another example is the portrait of the Duke and the Duchess of Urbino by Piero Della Francesca. The landscape in the background describes the properties of the Lords of Urbino, from the Marche region to the Trasimeno Lake. All these paintings have an interesting light effect: the subjects in the foreground and the landscape are differently lit. There is a clear separation between the two planes. Subjects seem to be separated from the background. In my photographs I want to replicate this effect with the use of the flash (Figs. 5.11, 5.12, 5.13, and 5.14).

The relationship with the other in Italian Renaissance paintings passes through the use of perspective. The human being is at the centre of the image and, consequently, at the centre of the universe. Everything can be measured around and for him. Perspective is, then, fundamental in this process because it is the human being who defines and measures the

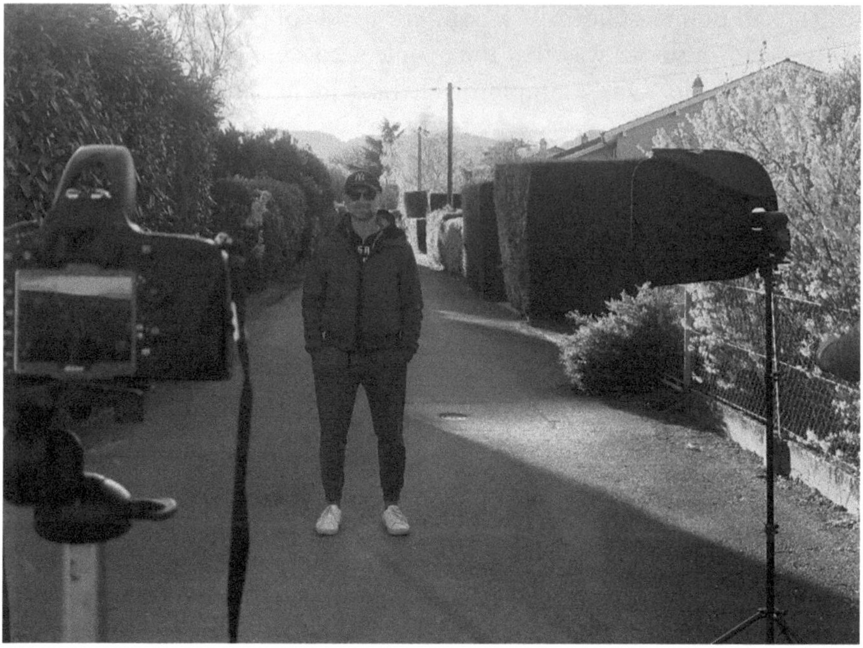

Fig. 5.11 Backstage images from a shooting session, Commugny (CH), 2021

physical space. It is an open dialogue with the viewer. In the Middle Ages, God was the centre of attention. There was no need to measure the physical space. It was important to find a way to represent the infinite and the abstract space, thus painters used gold to do it. An example is 'The Annunciation' by thirteenth–fourteenth-century artist Simone Martini. In the Brancacci Chapel in Florence there are frescoes by Masolino, Masaccio and Filippino Lippi. They are examples of the use of perspective to include the viewer in the scene. In *St. Peter Healing the Sick with his Shadow*, for instance, Masaccio deliberately alters the perception of space for the viewer. He creates the illusion of space extending out of the fresco into the real space of the spectator. Saint Peter is walking towards us as he is exiting out of the fresco and entering the viewer's space.

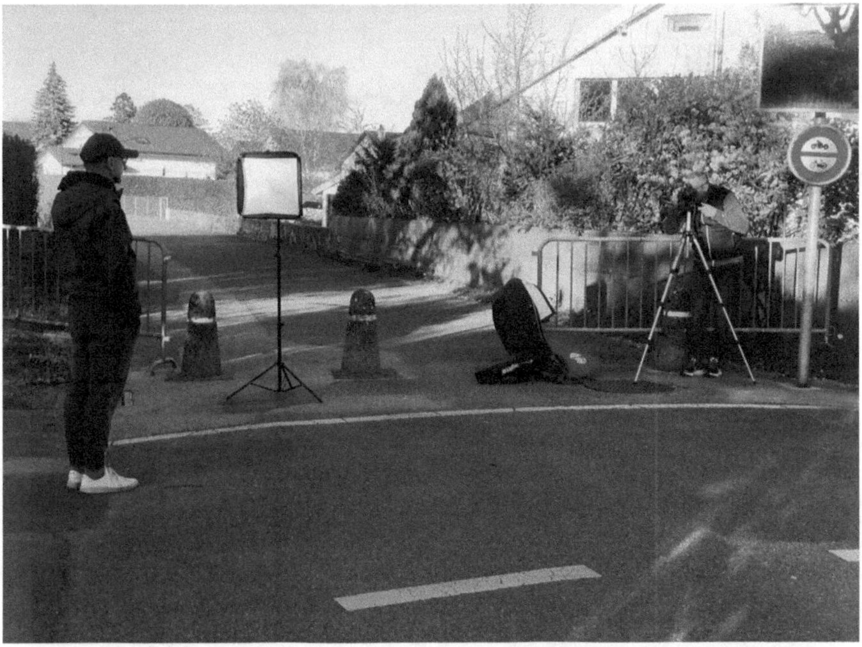

Fig. 5.12 Backstage images from a shooting, Commugny (CH), 2021

The Square

Referring to the ratio of my photographs, I created square images inspired by the *homo vitruvianus*' drawing by Leonardo da Vinci. Based on the definition of the perfect human proportions by Vitruvius, Leonardo da Vinci drew around 1490 the 'Vitruvian Man,' a pen and ink drawing kept at the *Gabinetto Disegni e Stampe* at the *Gallerie dell'Accademia* in Venice. As stated by historian Richard Kay (2012), the square represents earth and its mundane aspect and the circle represents totality and wholeness (God). Leonardo da Vinci inscribed the human body dynamically shaped inside the circle and in a very static and stable way in the square. In the *homo vitruvianus* by Leonardo, the navel of the human body is at the centre of the circle to testify the divine origin of human beings (Kay

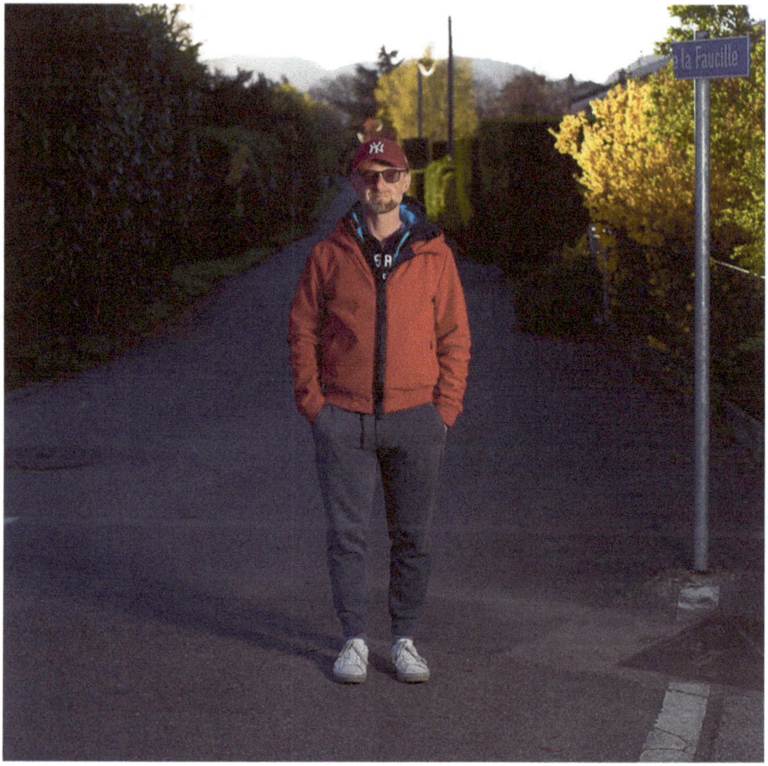

Fig. 5.13 Francesco Arese Visconti, *AS*, 2021

2012: 253). At the same time, Leonardo puts the means through which humans reproduce, the genitals, at the centre of the square. As in Leonardo's drawing, I put my subjects at the centre of the square to suggest their connection with the landscape and their belonging to a place on earth. The square, as said above, is a reference to earth. The position of the sitters in the centre of the square with their feet on the ground suggests their sense of belonging to a place. This is not the same place where they were born; it is, instead, a new country with which they now have to interact (Fig. 5.15).

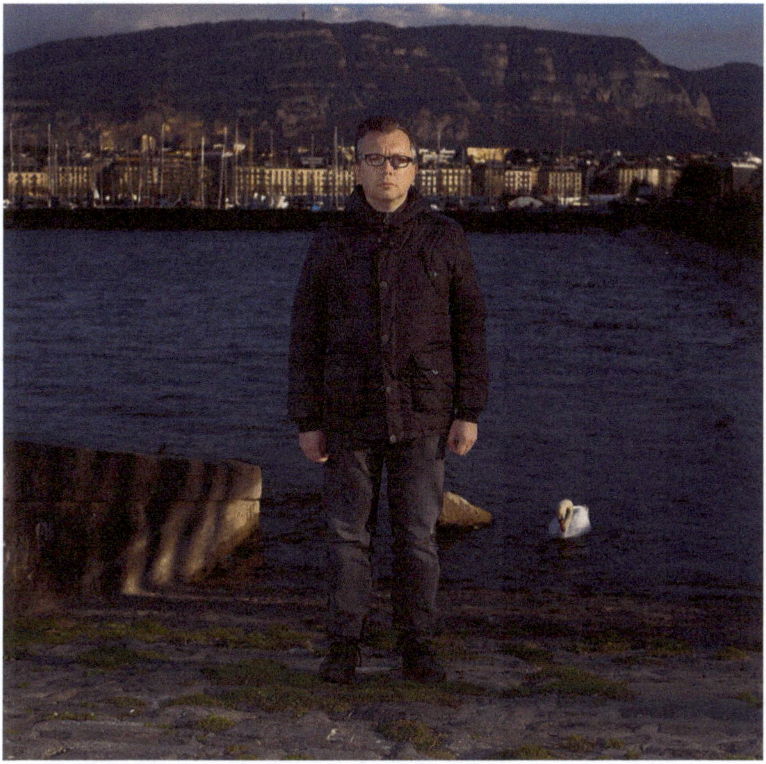

Fig. 5.14 Francesco Arese Visconti, *VP*, 2021

The Exhibition as Creative Outcome

An exhibition is the natural outcome of a photographic research. While in the creative process of developing ideas on how to showcase the portraits of twenty-first-century Italian migrants on the *arc lémanique*, some reflections had to be done. In the first stance, we have to reflect on the visual representation of migrants as a group of people which is simultaneously composed of individuals. Since the beginning of my practice, I was led by the intention to deliver the visitor of the final exhibition the perception of being in front of a diaspora, a group phenomenon, which inevitably was maintaining the characteristic of being created by the action of the single individuals.

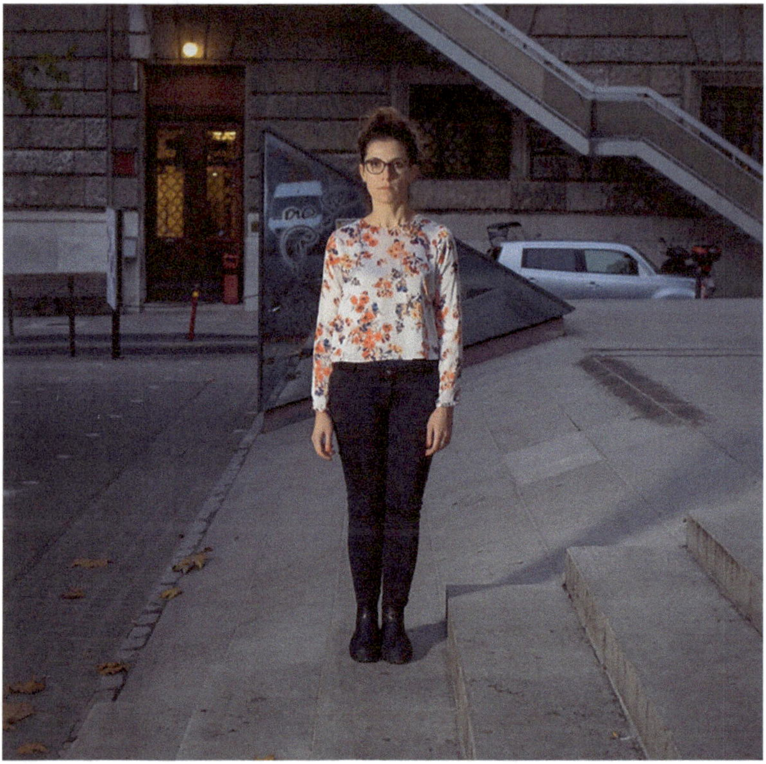

Fig. 5.15 Francesco Arese Visconti, *MC*, 2018

While, as explained in previous chapters, the 1960s and 1970s the Italian migratory process to Switzerland was composed by large groups of population coming from the same towns and villages, the recent diaspora doesn't have the same characteristics and is more individualistic. Nevertheless, we are talking about the recent Italian diaspora as a mass phenomenon. How is it possible to represent this difference through visual means? As highlighted above, seriality was the main solution but instead of having singular photographs on the walls, the images are anchored on the ceiling. They are randomly displaced in the centre of the room allowing walking space. At the bottom of the images there are QR codes that give the viewer access to text about the migrant experience extrapolated from the interviews that I have conducted with all of them

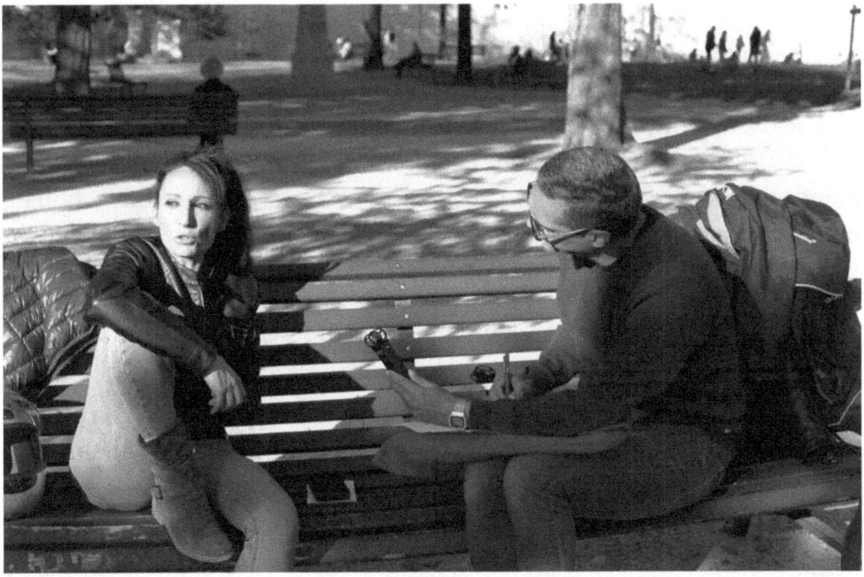

Fig. 5.16 Backstage image from an interview session on 23rd April, 2021, Geneva (CH)

(Fig. 5.16).[21] All the images face the entrance (Fig. 5.20). This visual impact entering the room gives the visitor the experience of being in front of a mass, a group of people staring at him/her and waiting to share their migratory experience. The photography exhibition is, then, moving away from the walls and occupies the central part of the space. It becomes an interactive installation and can be framed in relation to Lucy Soutter's concept of expanded photography (Soutter 2016). Referring to the idea of the 'expanded cinema' introduced by Gene Youngblood in the 1970s, Soutter looks at photography as an art medium which is part of cultural production. In this sense, photography overlaps with other art forms and moves beyond the traditional domains of the wall, the page and the

[21] I conducted semi-structured interviews with all the subjects I photographed. I asked questions about their reasons for migrating, if and how often they travel back to Italy, the purpose of their visits, the meaning that Switzerland and Italy have for them after years of residency abroad, the strongest memories related to their migration process and the effects that living in Switzerland have had on them.

screen. It overlaps with sculpture, installation or architecture developing tension 'between image and object, between craft and concept, between representation and presentation' (Soutter 2016: 42).

The display of the exhibition also gives the visitor the visual experience of less visibility of contemporary Italian migrants in Switzerland if compared to the migration of the 1960s and 1970s. In those decades, Italians had arrived with suitcases with different clothing and habits from the native Swiss population[22] and were, thus, visually different and recognizable (Fibbi 2011). As already stated before, according to the *Office federal de la Statistique*,[23] in 2022 Italians were the second largest group of migrants in Switzerland (only behind Germans). This phenomenon has, of course, an impact on different levels on Swiss society. We can then ask again the same question suggested at the beginning of this book: How can an image represent the cultural identity of a group of people whose lives have been irrevocably altered by the experience of physically moving away from their homeland and resetting in a *terra incognita*? The display of the photographs in the exhibition is an attempt to render visible the complex notion of this new migratory identity, of identity in flux which is different from the common understanding of migration. The photographs are printed on thin fabric which offers a high degree of transparency. This idea of printing photographs on textile comes from another exhibition I had in June 2018 at the Cedar Café in Bellevue (Switzerland). In order to still give the sense of transparency and less visibility of the contemporary Italian migrants in Switzerland, in this exhibition the photographs were printed on semi-translucent attachable silicon support. The images were glued directly on the windows allowing the viewer to see the images, their semi-transparency and the background through the photographs (Figs. 5.17 and 5.18). After some tests, I realized that print-

[22] A strong emphasis on the physical differences perceived in the 1970s is offered by Franco Brusati in his movie *Pane a Cioccolata* (Brusati 1973). The main character of the movie, Nino Garofoli, is an Italian migrant in Switzerland. Having migrated in the 1970s to the German part of the Swiss Confederation to find a job, Nino struggles to integrate into Swiss society and despite all his attempts, he is not successful.

[23] https://www.bfs.admin.ch/bfs/fr/home/statistiques/population/migration-integration/migration-internationale.html

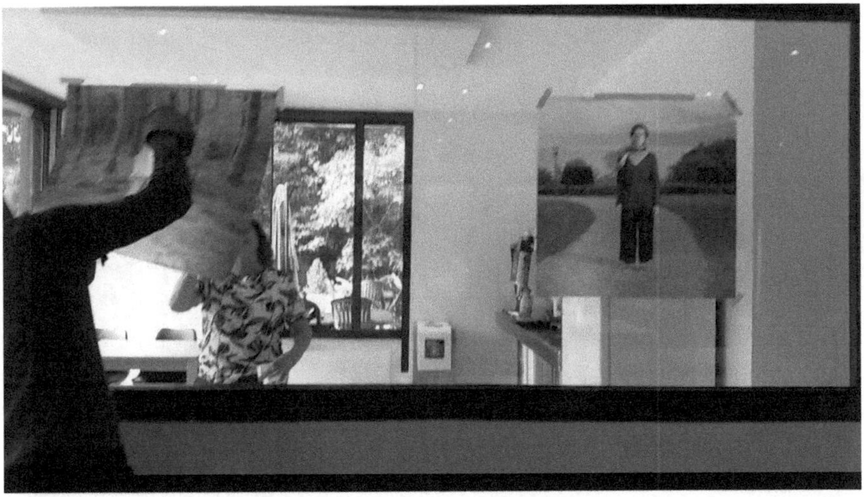

Fig. 5.17 Backstage images of the mounting of the exhibition at the Cedar Café, Bellevue (CH), 2018

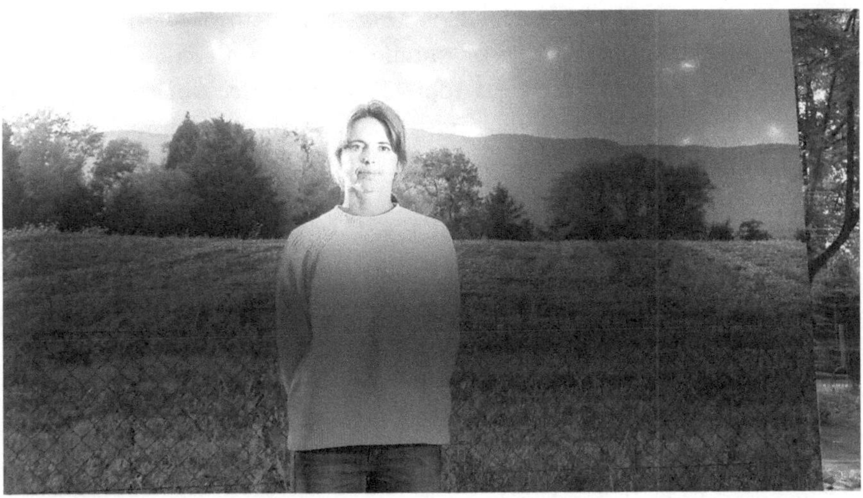

Fig. 5.18 The semi-transparency effect of the images printed on silicon support and attached on the windows. Bellevue (CH), 2018

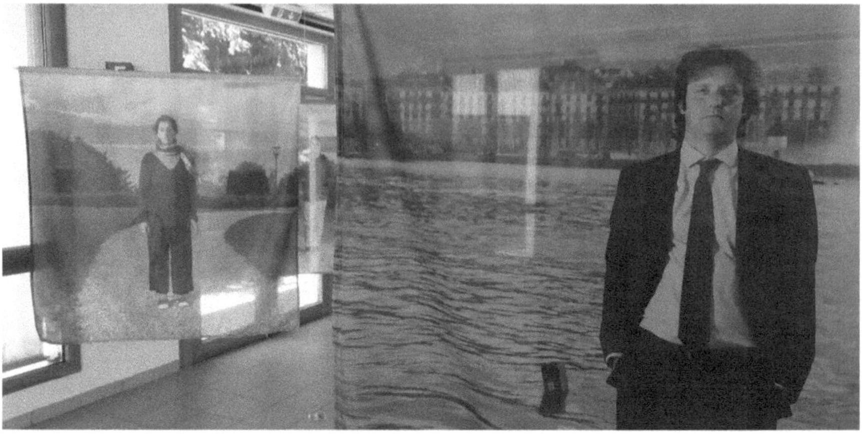

Fig. 5.19 Transparency of the images printed on textile

ing on thin textile improves the transparency effect which was only partially achieved with the silicon support.[24] The transparency and light essence of the textile is crucial here (Fig. 5.19): through this creative means I want to invite the viewer to reflect on the unseen and how photography can actually become a tool of social justice documenting the invisible (or, better, the partially visible). Referring to Samuel Aranda's work in African migrants trying to enter Melilla (Aranda 2014), therefore Spain/Europe, Tanya Sheehan (2018: 93) underlines how photography's role is to document the unseen, to become the means through which migrants can be seen in their migration process. This is a phenomenon that assigns photography the value of political intervention. 'By framing the unseen, […]', Sheehan claims (2018: 93), 'documentary photographs provide a narrative frame' and become a 'useful tools in negotiating

[24] For installations with prints on textile, see Heather Agyepong 'ego death' project or Harley Weir's work 'Homes'. With an expanded photography approach (Soutter 2016; Agyepong 2022) investigates her hidden personality discovering her Jungian shadows. She reveals her results through photographs, textiles, sound and text developing a strong visual language. Harley Weir (Fabrica Gallery 2018) presented her project on migrant camps in Calais (France) at the 2018 Biennale in Brighton (UK). In Weir's case, the semi-transparent fabric material refers to what is printed on the photographs (migrants' tents).

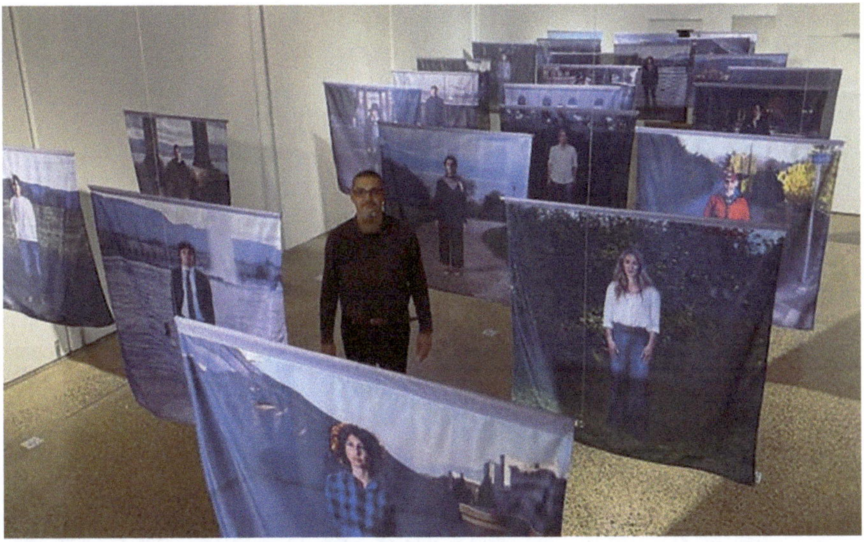

Fig. 5.20 The display of the exhibition in London

politics because they come with an aura of believability' (Levi Strauss 2003: 71). My photographs are not purely documentary in their nature; however, they aim to facilitate a discussion on a quite invisible phenomenon and stimulate a reaction.

References

AA, S. of A. (2017). "The Face and the Body - Mark Cousins." https://www.youtube.com/watch?v=UkraaawwqKs. Access 21.04.2017

Agamben, G. (2000). "The Face." In *Means without End: Notes on Politics.*, 91–102. Minneapolis: University of Minnesota Press.

Agyepong, H. (2022). "ego death." https://www.heatheragyepong.com/ego-death. Accessed 09.11.2022.

Althusser, L. (2014). *On The Reproduction of Capitalism: Ideology and Ideological State Apparatuses*. London: Verso.

Aranda, S. (2014). "Melilla: The Back Door of Europe." https://www.nytimes.com/2014/02/28/world/europe/africans-battered-and-broke-surge-to-europes-door.html. Accessed 16.09.2022.

Arese Visconti, F. (2012). *New World – Stories of African Immigration and Integration in Switzerland.* Firenze: Aión Edizioni.

———. (2015). *We, Prato.* Prato: Edizioni SUI.

Avedon, R. (1985). *In the American West.* New York: Harry N Abrams.

Azoulay, A. (2012). *The Civil Contract of Photography.* Beijin, Princeton, Woodstock: Zone Books.

Baker, G. (1996). Photography between Narrativity and Stasis: August Sander, Degeneration and the Decay of the Portrait. *October*, 76 (Spring), 72–113.

Barthes, R. (1980). *La camera chiara* . Torino: Einaudi.

Baynham, M. (2015). "Identity: Brought About or Brought Along? Narrative as a Privileged Site for Researching Intercultural Identities." In *Researching Identity and Interculturality*, edited by Fred Dervin and Karen Risager, 67–88. New York and London: Routledge.

Belting, H. (2017). *Face and Mask - A Double History*. Princeton and Oxford: Princeton University Press.

Benjamin, W. (1980). "A Short History of Photography." In A. Trachtenberg (ed.), *Classic Essays in Photography* (p. 314). New Haven: Leete's Island Books.

Bernardini, G. (2014). *Chen contro Chen. La guerra che cambierà Prato.* Rome: Round Robin Editrice.

Bertillon, A. (2014). *Alphonse Bertillons Instructions: For Taking Descriptions for the Identification of Criminals and Others, by Means of Anthropometric Indications*. Whitefish: Literary Licensing, LLC.

Bhabha, H. (1984). "Of Mimicry and Man: The Ambivalence of Colonial Discourse*." In *October* 28: 125–33.

Bhabha, H. (ed.) (1990). *Nation and Narration*. London and New York: Routledge.

Bourdieu, P. (1977). *Outline of a Theory of Practice*. Cambridge: Cambridge University Press.

———. (1986). "Habitus, code et codification." In *Actes de La Recherche En Sciences Sociales*, 64, 40–44.

———. (1997). *Méditations Pascaliennes*. Paris: Seuil.

Brusati, F. (1973). *Pane e cioccolata*. Italy: Lucky Red.

Brux, T. (curator). (2019). "Nous, saisonniers, saisonnières…Genève 1931–2019." http://rosabrux.org/category/saisonnier-ere-s/. Access 11.01.2021.

Butler, J. (1993). *Bodies That Matter*. London: Routledge.

Casazza, O. (2001). *Masaccio*. New York: Riverside Book Co.

Collatinus-web. (2019a.). "Vultus." https://outils.biblissima.fr/fr/collatinus-web/. Access 19.11.2021.

———. (2019b.). "Facies." https://outils.biblissima.fr/fr/collatinus-web/. Access 19.11.2021.

Costa, S. and Golay, L. (curators). (2021). "Losanna, Svizzera. 150 ans d'immigration italienne à Lausanne.". https://www.lausanne.ch/vie-pratique/culture/musees/mhl/expositions/expositions-passees.html#losanna-svizzera-150-ans-d-immigration-italienne-a-lausanne-00. Access 11.01.2021.

Cromby, J. (2015). *Feeling Bodies: embodying psychology*. London: Palgrave Macmillan

Darwin, C. (2018). *The expression of the emotions in man and animals*. Mineola, New York: Dover Publications.

Davidis, M., and Ingeborg Dessoff-Hahn. (1999). *Archiv der Gesichter: Toten- und Lebendmasken aus dem Schiller-Nationalmuseum*. Marbach am Neckar: Museum für Sepulchralkultur Kassel.

Deleuze, G., and Félix Guattari. (1987). *A Thousand Plateaus*. Minneapolis: University of Minnesota Press.

Dezfuli, C. (2022). "Passengers." www.worldphoto.org. Available from https://www.worldphoto.org/sony-world-photography-awards/winners-galleries/2020/professional/finalist-passengers-cesar-dezfuli. Access 08.04.2022

Dijkstra, R. (2003). *Rineke Dijkstra: Beach Portraits*. Chicago: LaSalle National Bank NA.

Döblin, A. (2012). I volti, le immagini, la loro verità. In *Uomini del ventesimo secolo* (pp. 11 – 16). Milano: Abscondita.

Evans, W. (1931). The Reappearance of Photography. *Hound & Horn*, *1*(October/December).

———. (2012) *American Photographs. Seventy-Fifth Anniversary Edition*. New York: The Museum of Modern Art.

Fabrica Gallery (2018). "Homes by Harley Weir." https://www.youtube.com/watch?v=iVmBCGyYZG8. Accessed 20.10.2022.

Fibbi, R. (2011). Come siamo diventati biondi: L'immigrazione italiana in Svizzera. *Limes. Rivista Italiana Di Geopolitica (L'importanza Di Essere Svizzera. I Quaderni Speciali Di Limes)*. No. 3, Pp.211–220.

Galton, F. (1998). *Inquiries into human faculty and its development*. Bristol: Thoemmes Press.

Goffman, E. (1955). "On Facework." In *Psychiatry*, 18, 3, 213–231.

———. (1959). *The Presentation of Self in Everyday Life.* Garden City: Anchor Books.

———. (1963). *Behavior in Public Places.* New York: The Free Press.

Greenfield-Sanders, T., Francesco Clemente and Demetrio Paparoni. (2001). *Timothy Greenfield-Sanders.* Milano: Alberico Cetti Serbelloni Editore.

Greenfield-Sanders, T. and Gore Vidal. (2005). *XXX: 30 Porn-Star Portraits.* New York: Bulfinch Press.

Greenough, S. and Walker Evans. (1991). *Subway Photographs and Other Recent Acquisitions.* National Gallery of Art: Washington, D.C.

Grunberg, A. (1997). "Out of the Blue: The Photographs of Rineke Dijkstra." *Artforum* 36 (9).

Hall, S. (1989). "Ethnicity: Identity and Difference." *Radical America* 23 (4): 9–13.

———. (1990). *Cultural Identity and Diaspora. Identity: Community, Culture, Difference.* Vol. 2.

———. (1996). "The Question of Cultural Identity." *Modernity: An Introduction to Modern Societies* 4: 596–632.

———. (1997). "Who Needs Identity." *The British Journal of Sociology* 48 (1): 208.

———. (1999). 'Thinking the Diaspora: Home-Thoughts from Abroad.' *Small Axe 6*, September (1999). 1–18.

———. (2003). "Introduction." In *Representation: Cultural Representation and Signifying Practices*, edited by Stuart and Jessica Evans and Sean Nixon Hall, 1–11. Thousand Oaks: Sage Publications.

Hall, S., and Les Back. (2009). "At Home and Not at Home: Stuart Hall in Conversation with Les Back." *Cultural Studies* 23 (4): 658–87.

Hamilton, P. and Roger Hargreaves. (2001). *The Beautiful and the Damned: The Creation of Identity in Nineteenth Century.* London: Lund Humphries Publishers.

Hanzlova, J. (2012). *Jitka Hanzlova.* Madrid: TF Editores.

Hine, L. W. (1909). "Social Photography: How the Camera May Help in the Social Uplift." In *Proceedings of the National Conference of Charities and Correction at the Thirty-Sixth Session*, edited by Alexander Johnson, 357. Fort Wayne: Print of Fort Wayne.

Hussain, M. (2014). "The Commonality of Strangers." www.mahtabhussain.com. https://www.mahtabhussain.com/work/the-commonality-of-strangers/. Access 08.04.2022.

———. (2017). *You get me?* London: MACK/Light Work.

ISTAT 2013. "Popolazione ufficiale (ISTAT) – Residenti al 31 dicembre a Prato e in Italia." www.comune.prato.it. https://www.comune.prato.it/it/statistica/popolazione-ufficiale-31-dicembre/popolazione-totale/pagina2325.html. Access 11.09.2023.

Johanson Russell Smyth, G. and Rebecca French (eds.). (2009). *Living Outside the Walls: The Chinese in Prato.* Newcastle upon Tyne: Cambridge Scholars Publishing.

Jones, A. (2000). Reading August Sander's Archive. *Oxford Art Journal, 23*(1), 3–21.

Katz, L. (1971). Interview with Walker Evans. *Art in America*, vol. 59, no. 2 (March-April 1971).

Kay, R. (2012). "Vitruvius and Dante's Imago Dei." *Word & Image*, 21 (3): 252–60.

Krauss, R. (1982). Photography's Discursive Spaces: Landscape/View. *Art Journal, 42*(4), 311–319.

Lacan, J. (2005). "The Mirror Stage as Formative of the Function of the I as Revealed in Psychoanalytic Experience." In *Écrits*, 502–9. New York: W. W. Norton & Company.

Lang, R. (1985). "The Dwelling Door: Towards a Phenomenology of Transition." In *Dwelling, Place and Environment*, edited by David et al. Seamon. Dordrecht: Martinus Nijhoff Publishers.

Lendvai-Dircksen, E. (1932). *Das Deutsche Volksgesicht.* Berlin: Kulturelle Verlagsgesellschaft m.b.H.

———. (1933). Über deutsche Porträtphotographie. *Das Atelier Des Photographen*, 40 (6–7).

Levi Strauss, D. (2003). *Between the Eyes: Essays on Photography and Politics.* New York: Aperture.

Mauss, M. (1938). Une Catégorie de l'Esprit Humain: La Notion de Personne Celle de "Moi." *The Journal of the Royal Anthropological Institute of Great Britain and Ireland*, 68 (Jul.–Dec.), 263–281.

Merleau-Ponty, M. (1963). *The Structure of Behaviour.* Boston: Beacon Press.

Mesenhöller, P. (2005). "Augustus F. Sherman: Ellis Island Portraits 1905–1920." In *Augustus F. Sherman: Ellis Island Portraits 1905–1920*, 4–21. New York: Aperture.

Nadar, F. (2004). *Quando ero fotografo.* Milano: Abscondita.

———. (2007). *Ritratti.* Milan: Abscondita.

Nesi, E. (2010). *Storia della mia gente.* Milano: Bompiani.

Pénichon, S. (2012). "The Making of In the American West." In *Journal of the American Institute for Conservation*, 47, 3 – 2012: 175–182.
Petruzziello, M. (2017). "MICHELE PETRUZZIELLO GOOD BYE MY LOVE SAT 2000 YouTube 36." https://www.youtube.com/watch?v=hHJuTGUSjzk. Access 21.09.2022.
Phillips, S. S. (1998). *Police Photography: The Photograph as Evidence*. San Francisco: Chronicle Books.
Pieraccini, S. (2010). *L'assedio cinese*. Milano: Il Sole 24 Ore Libri.
Pirandello, L. (2017). *One, None and A Hundred-Thousand*. New York: E. P. Dutton & Co., Inc.
Quatelet, A. (1991). *Sur l'homme*. Paris: Fayard.
Riis, J. (1971). *How the Other Half Lives. Studies Among the Tenements of NY.* New York: Dover Publications
Rosenblum, W. (1977). "Foreword." In *America and Lewis Hine*. New York: Aperture.
Rubin, P. (2011). *The Renaissance Portraiture from Donatello to Bellini*. New York: Metropolitan Museum of Modern Art.
Sander, A. (2008). *Face of our times*. München: Schirmel Mosel.
Sander, A. and Ulrich Keller (ed.). (1980). *August Sander - Menschen Des 20. Jahrhunderts: Portraitphotographien 1892-1952*. München: Schirmer/Mosel.
Schaaf, L. J. (2003). *The Photographic Art of William Henry Fox Talbot*. Princeton and Oxford: Princeton University Press. 192–193).
Schöller, M. and Lise Funderburg. (2013). 'Changing Face of America.' *National Geographic*. October. 224. 76–91.
Schöller, M. and Marina Abramović. (2012). *Identical: Portraits of Twins*. Kempen: teNeues.
Sekula, A. (1986). "The Body and the Archive." *October* 39 (Winter): 3–64.
Seixas, P. (1987). "Lewis Hine : From "Social" to "Interpretive" Photographer." *Americana Quarterly* 39 (3): 381–409.
Serrano, A. (n.d.). "Made in China." www.andresserrano.org. http://andresserrano.org/series/made-in-china. Access 18.11.2021.
Sheehan, T. (ed.) (2018). *Photography and Migration*. London and New York: Routledge.
Simmel, G. (1901). "Die ästhetische Bedeutung des Gesichts." In *Der Lotse. Hamburgische Wochenschrift für deutsche Kultur.* 1. Jg. 2. Band (Heft 35 vom 1. Juni 1901), S. 280–284 (Hamburg).
———. (1985). *Il volto e il ritratto: saggi sull'arte*. Bologna: Il Mulino.

Soutter, L. (2016). "Expanded Photography: Persistence of the Photographic." In *PhotoResearcher*, 26, pp. 36–43.

Stimson, B. (2006). *The Pivot of the World: Photography and its Nation.* Cambridge, London: MIT Press.

Sundell, M. (1986). "Golden Immigrants at the Gold Door : Lewis Hine's Photographs of Ellis Island." *Social Text* 16 (16): 168–75.

Szlezák, K. S. (2009). "The Ellis Island Experience: Through the Eyes of Lewis Hine." *Aspeers*, no. 2: 71–89.

———. 2012. "The Issue of Americanization in Photographs by Augustus F. Sherman and Lewis W. Hine." *American Studies* 57 (1): 9–29.

Tagg, J. (1988). *The Burden of Representation: Essays on Photographies and Histories. Cultural Politics.*

Taylor-Lind, A. (2014). *Maidan Portraits from the Black Square.* London: Gost Books.

theradpho (2013). "Richard Avedon Darkness and Light." https://www.youtube.com/watch?v=4XElT1udbFM&t=3942s. Accessed 20.09.2022.

Thomann, J. (1991). "Pietro d'Abano on Giotto." *Journal of the Warburg and Courtauld Institutes.* 54: 238–244.

Ureña, L. J. (2009). *Lewis Hine at Ellis Island: The Photography of Immigration and Race, 1904–1926.* Northwestern University.

Vasari, G. (1998). *Lives of the Artists.* New York: Oxford University Press.

Whitney, H. (2002). *Richard Avedon: Darkness and Light.* New York: Wellspring Media.

Wilson, L. (2003). *Avedon at work in the American West.* Austin: University of Texas Press.

6

Conclusions

Abstract This is the closing chapter of the book with personal reflections as the result of the research conducted and explained in the previous chapters. Particular attention is dedicated to the creative outcomes of this work, the final exhibition of the photographic portraits of twenty-first-century Italian migrants on the *arc lémanique*.

Keywords Expanded photography • Arc Lémanique • Cultural identity • Italian migrants • Photographic dialogue

The purpose of this book was to demonstrate how a creative process that intertwines theoretical framework and practical solutions, can develop a methodology to portray through photographic means the cultural identity of recent Italian migrants living on the *arc lémanique* area in Switzerland. In the elaboration of this process, this work links the experience of this large community with the personal one of myself as a photographer but, mostly, as a migrant. Through the years of study, I have developed an understanding of the philosophic, psychological, sociological and political implications of photographic portraiture in history and

F. Arese Visconti, *The Invisible Diaspora*, Palgrave Studies in Creativity and Culture,
https://doi.org/10.1007/978-3-031-74925-4_6

the photographic representation of the Italian migrants in Switzerland. I have never been a migrant before 2007 and I never thought I was going to be when I was still living in Italy. Studying the visual representation of the migrant of the past and that one of the new Italian migrant in Switzerland has led me to understand better my personal experience, and better comprehend my personality. My migratory adventure is similar to that of a 100,000 Italians who decided to migrate to the *arc lémanique* in Switzerland since 2007. Therefore, the valuable contribution to knowledge of this work is about a phenomenon that is happening now, and it is crucial on a global scale but also on a more intimate, personal level. As anticipated in other parts of this text, Italians are today the second largest community of migrants in Switzerland.[1] This aspect has consequences on Italian and Swiss society. For these reasons, this research is very timely: it discusses aspects of a phenomenon, the twenty-first-century Italian diaspora in Switzerland, which has important numbers and has an impact on the political decisions taken by the Swiss governments. Furthermore, the practice side of the project has a specific aspect of originality because it carried out an empirical work that (to my knowledge) has not been done before. It is the result of a very interdisciplinary approach which has collected and combined theories, concepts, ideas from different fields. This perspective gives access to a deep analysis of the phenomenon and at the same time offers a personal perspective of a migrant (myself) who is trying to understand the phenomenon and portrays it through photographic portraiture. While recognizing that this process is not perfect, it is nevertheless an answer that offers something unique: there is not to my knowledge any systematic photographic production representing the cultural identity of recent Italian migrants on the *arc lémanique* in Switzerland other than the one reproduced in this book.

This work has also brought me to reflect on my position as an independent cultural producer and the freedom that I had to maintain while working on the project. In the prospect of taking decisions for my practice, I had to understand the differences between photographic images produced for newspapers and those for magazines. While the first

[1] https://www.bfs.admin.ch/bfs/fr/home/statistiques/population/migration-integration/migration-internationale.html

ones have to be contingent and strictly related to the news (Hall 1972), magazines photographs have to illustrate the articles and therefore be a generic reference to the topic (Boltanski 2018: 369).[2] As a consequence of the analysis of these processes, I realized that I had to move away and beyond these definitions with the aim of being original and innovative. I, therefore, diverted from the voyeuristic[3] photojournalistic (Newton 2001) style but also from the documentary approach in the strict sense (Lugon 2008: 172). In the back flap of his book *Lo stile documentario in fotografia – Da August Sander a Walker Evans 1920 – 1945*, Olivier Lugon states that in the documentary photographic practice the artist disappears to give space to authentic realistic copies of the world. I move away from the two definitions of photojournalism and documentary photography given above, maintaining an independent point of view. I photographed the subjects in the context that they chose, in the clothes that they decided to use but with the lighting, the posture and the facial expression that I have asked them to take. I have the authority of choosing the instant when to press the shutter. That is the moment when I claim my independency as a cultural producer with the freedom of interpreting reality with a specific result in mind.

The experience gained through previous photographic projects and new experiments led me to take decisions that deeply influence the final result of this exciting, demanding but, eventually, rewarding research. Since the beginning of the project in 2016, my interest expanded from the specific understanding of the Italian diaspora in Switzerland to the larger meaning of cultural identity and the value of photographic portraiture as a means of communications between the photographer, the sitter and the viewer. Inspired by the work of portrait photographers,[4] I reflected on which elements the genre of photographic portraiture can find its contribution to culturally unify a population (and in the specific case of

[2] See the example of *L'Illustré* n. 14 of the 2nd of April 1970 (SCOPE 1970) where the images are not related to the subjects interviewed in the article.

[3] The subject doesn't look into the camera and the photographer/viewer of the images witnesses what is happening in the photograph without having any visual connection with him/her.

[4] To mention some of the photographers that I have studied: August Sherman, Lewis W. Hine, Sam Ivin, Michele Petruzziello, August Sander, Erna Lendvai-Dircksen, Walker Evans, Richard Avedon, Irving Penn, Timothy Greenfield-Sanders, Rineke Dijkstra, Jitka Hanzlova, Martin Schöller, Anastasia Taylor-Lind, Andres Serrano, Diane Arbus.

my research, Italians) and, at the same time, help others to identify with that population. I based my reasoning on Stuart Hall's (1989, 1990, 1996, 1997, 2003) concept of cultural identity as never shaped in a fixed form and being part of a long process of identification, on how it can be influenced by society (Bourdieu 1977, 1986, 1997) and the meaning of being part of a common imagined group which shares the same values (Anderson 1991). The theoretical framework supported the creative process on producing images that represent the Italian cultural identity. I chose to identify a period in history which still clearly influences the cultural background of Italians today. I circulated a short survey through my network (associations, friends and relatives) and the main answers indicated the Renaissance period. I, therefore, decided to focus my attention on Italian Renaissance portraiture and see how I could creatively draw a link between that period and my images. I had to consider the main characteristics of Renaissance portraiture and how I could have applied them in my photographs. The realistic representation of the sitter is one of the main characteristics of Renaissance portraiture: subjects were portrayed as they were. In my photographs, I wanted to reproduce all of these details so that they could be discernible and recognizable. In Italian Renaissance arts, the human being was at the centre of the visual representation. I, then, started placing my subjects at the centre of the composition. The landscape assumed an important role in the Italian Renaissance portraits, and it is often well recognizable (like in the portrait of Federico da Montefeltro by Piero Della Francesca). The sitter is often immersed in a geographically recognizable landscape. Subjects were always lit with a different light which separated them from the background as if they were portrayed in a room with a window behind them. In my photographic portraits, I, thus, included the landscape and used a mix of artificial and natural light to replicate the light effect visible in the Renaissance paintings. The strong use of perspective was also an important aspect of Italian Renaissance. It was used as a way to define and measure the physical space in which human beings live. In placing my subjects at the centre of the image, I want to emphasize the effect of perspective and suggest an open dialogue with the viewer. I started portraying my subjects within a square frame which is connected to the Vitruvian man (Leonardo da Vinci, *Homo Vitruvianus.* Gallerie delle Accademie,

Venice. 1490 c.). In Leonardo's drawing, the human being is represented inside a square ('homo ad quadratum') and inside a circle ('homo ad circulum'): the human being becomes a bridge between God and Earth and unifies the two elements. The circle is the divine and the centre of the circle is the umbilicus of the man. The square is the symbol of earth. The square framing of my photographs suggests this link to earth. Through this means, I want to emphasize the sense of belonging of the migrant to the land and the contrast in living in a different country which is not the motherland. In the migrants' experience, while Switzerland cannot be the motherland, it becomes nevertheless a known place of comfort zone after years of residency. I also had to think about how to develop a dialogue between the sitter and the viewer and developed my practice around David Bate's (2016: 89) considerations on the key elements of a photographic portrait (face, pose, background, clothing and props). The facial expression often suggests a mood. In my images, faces have a blank expression. The blankness is an open invitation for the viewer for an active inclusion (Van Gelder 2012). As far as the pose is concerned, the frontal position of the body suggests an openness.[5] Being in a frontal position, the subject is open to the dialogue with the viewer as usually happens in society. We see and we are seen by the other. This connection develops a dialogue and an interpretation with and by society. I developed the idea of representing the full body so that we can see it all and interpret it. We see the entire body well rooted on earth (see the Vitruvian man, the landscape and place/motherland). Due to experience, the body has incorporated feelings and emotions (linked to migration) and, thus, it is the explicit representation of feelings as a result of identity formation (Cromby 2015). The background represents the landscape in which the subject/migrant is immersed. Clothing was chosen by the subjects and no props were included in the images. I guided the shooting sessions asking the subjects not to smile and look straight into the camera being in a static frontal position. In this way, faces became masks. As Barthes argued (1980: 35), photography can only achieve significance when it shows a mask. Photographed and exhibited in a way which aims to recall a type of archive (Sekula 1986), these portraits have a deadpan expression. However, they are real faces of living people, and their gaze engages the

[5] See Susan Sontag on Diane Arbus (Sontag 1990: 38, 60).

spectator (Azoulay 2012: 340). The photographer proposes the dialogue with the sitter but the spectator chooses the role based on their personal background.

The outcome of my photographic production was an exhibition. Between 2nd February and 18th February, 2024, the Galata Museo del Mare in Genoa (Italy) hosted my exhibition 'The Invisible Diaspora – Re-thinking Photographic Portraiture of 21st Century Italian Migrants on the Arc Lémanique Area' (Arese Visconti 2024) . The exhibition was organized by the Museo Nazionale dell'Emigrazione Italiana (Genoa, Italy) (Fig. 6.1). Initially thought of as a photographic show traditionally exhibited on the walls, it became progressively clear that this work had to go beyond the photographic itself and be something more articulated. As already mentioned above, we refer here to the concept of expanded photography formulated by Lucy Soutter (2016). It is very challenging for photography to represent a cultural background. While acknowledging

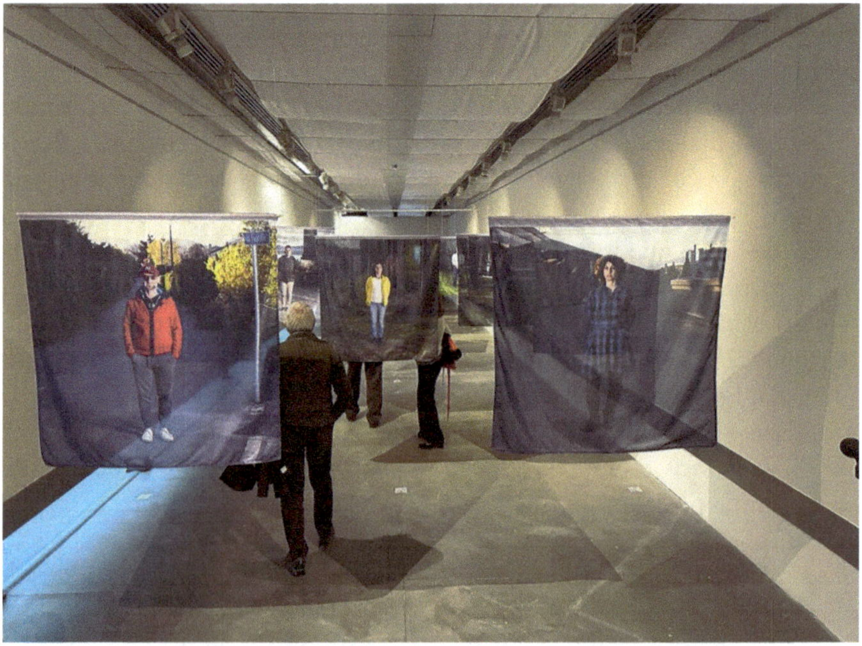

Fig. 6.1 The exhibition in Genoa at the Galata Museo del Mare

that the photographic is still fundamental, it is however true that we need more elements contributing to the narrative to enrich the beholder's experience. The expansion of photography to other fields (in this case installation and texts available through QR codes linked to a website) can help to better understand the message and avoid remaining on a superficial level. Certainly, this process has helped to deepen my knowledge on my cultural identity. Hopefully, the beholder will develop this understanding when put in front of these photographic portraits and will wonder about the complicated, diverse, multifaceted cultural identity of these Italians, as well as about his/hers.

References

Anderson, B. (1991). *Imagined Communities: Reflections on the Origin and Spread of Nationalism*. London: Verso.

Arese Visconti, F. (2024). "The Invisible Diaspora – Re-thinking Photographic Portraiture of 21st Century Italian Migrants on the Arc Lémanique Area." https://areseviscont i.com/2024/02/15/solo-exhibition-the-invisible-diaspora-re-thinking-photographic-portraiture-of-21st-century-italian-migrants-on-the-arc-lemanique-area/. Access 25.07.2024.

Azoulay, A. (2012). *The Civil Contract of Photography.* Beijin, Princeton, Woodstock: Zone Books.

Barthes, R. (1980). *La camera chiara* . Torino: Einaudi.

Bate, D. (2016). *Photography: The Key Concepts*. London: Bloomsbury.

Bourdieu, P. (1977). *Outline of a Theory of Practice*. Cambridge: Cambridge University Press.

———. (1986). "Habitus, code et codification." In *Actes de La Recherche En Sciences Sociales*, 64, 40–44.

———. (1997). *Méditations Pascaliennes*. Paris: Seuil.

Boltanski, L. (2018). "La retorica della figura." In *Un'arte media – Saggio sugli usi sociali della fotografia*, ed. Pierre Bourdieu. Milano: Meltemi.

Cromby, J. (2015). *Feeling Bodies: embodying psychology*. London: Palgrave Macmillan

Hall, S. (1972). "The determinations of news photographs." In *Working Paper in Cultural Studies*, n. 3 (autumn), pp. 53–87. Reissued: Stanley Cohen and Jock Young (eds.), *The Manifacture of News: social problems, deviance and the mass media.* London: Constable, pp. 176–190, 1972.

———. (1989). "Ethnicity: Identity and Difference." *Radical America* 23 (4): 9–13.

———. (1990). *Cultural Identity and Diaspora. Identity: Community, Culture, Difference*. Vol. 2.

———. (1996). "The Question of Cultural Identity." *Modernity: An Introduction to Modern Societies* 4: 596–632.

———. (1997). "Who Needs Identity." *The British Journal of Sociology* 48 (1): 208.

———. (2003). "Introduction." In *Representation: Cultural Representation and Signifying Practices*, edited by Stuart and Jessica Evans and Sean Nixon Hall, 1–11. Thousand Oaks: Sage Publications.

Lugon, O. (2008). *Lo stile documentario in fotografia – Da August Sander a Walker Evans 1920 – 1945*. Milano: Mondadori Electa).

Newton, J. (2001). *The Burden of Visual Truth: The Role of Photojournalism in Mediating Reality*. New York: Routledge.

SCOPE. (1970, April). Les étrangers - Au pays de la solitude. *L'Illustré*, 4–14.

Sekula, A. (1986). "The Body and the Archive." *October* 39 (Winter): 3–64.

Sontag, S. (1990). *On Photography*. New York: Picador.

Soutter, L. (2016). "Expanded Photography: Persistence of the Photographic." In *PhotoResearcher*, 26, pp. 36–43.

Van Gelder, H. (2012). "Aesthetic Equality." www.fotomuseum.ch. http://www.fotomuseum.ch/en/explore/still- searching/articles/26927_aesthetic_equality. Access 13.05.2018.

Portfolio

F. Arese Visconti, *The Invisible Diaspora*, Palgrave Studies in Creativity and Culture,
https://doi.org/10.1007/978-3-031-74925-4

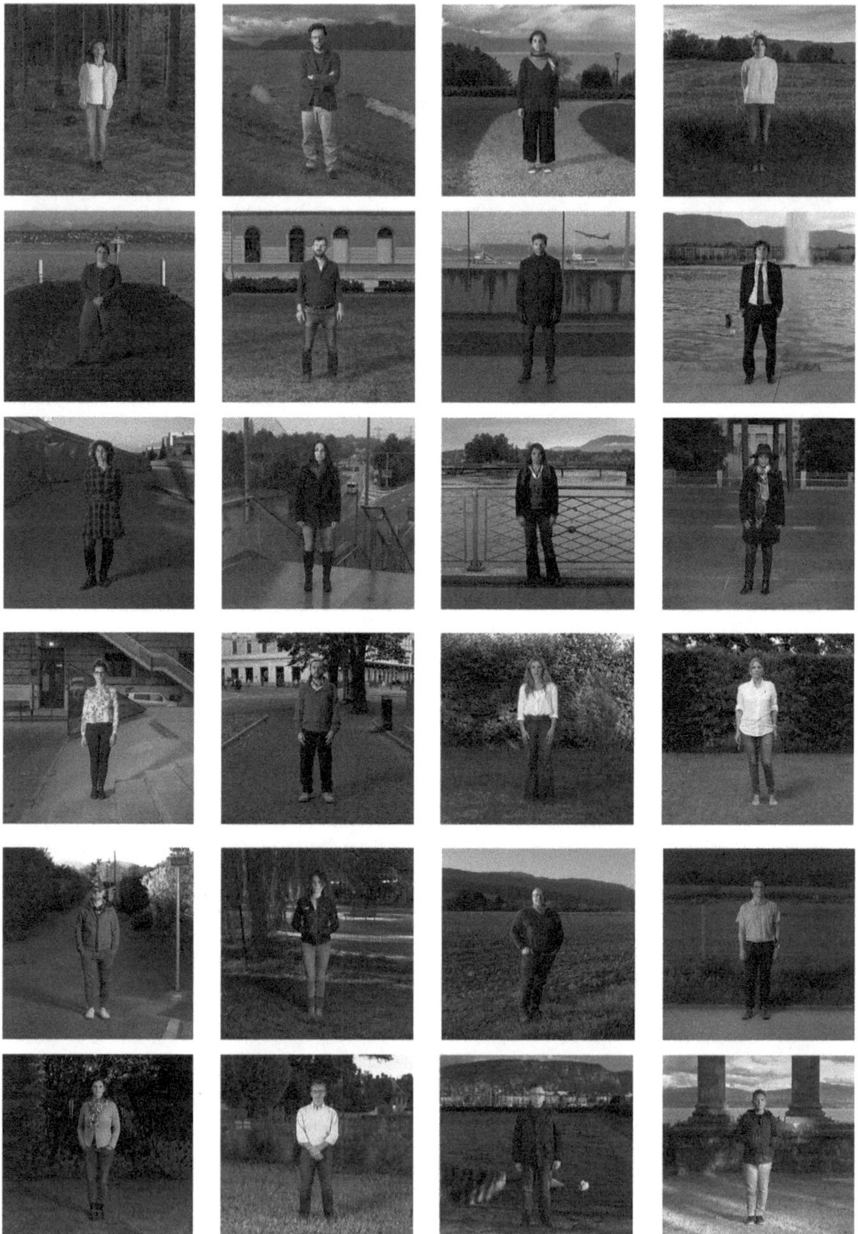

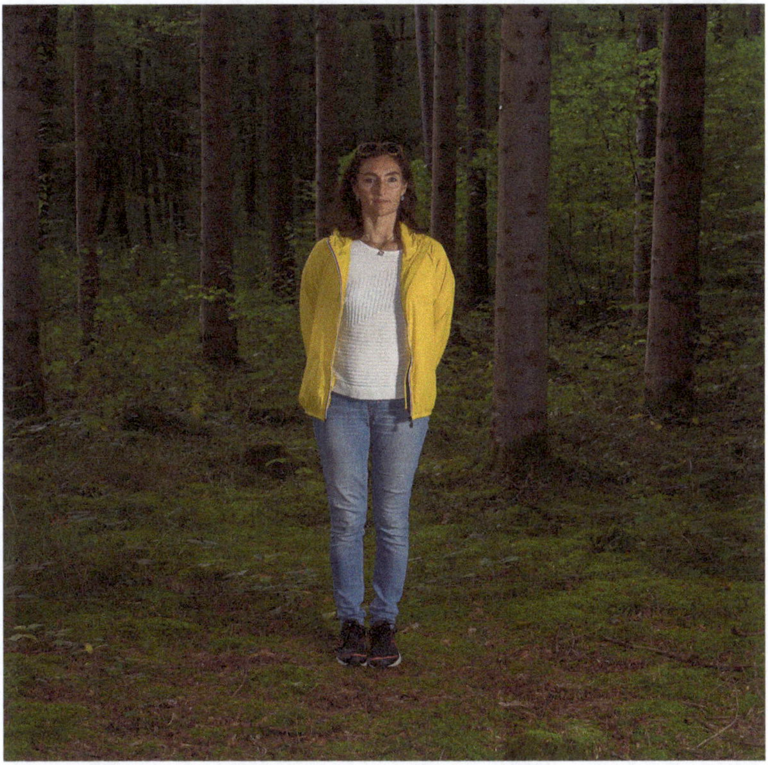

Francesco Arese Visconti, *ADM*, 2017

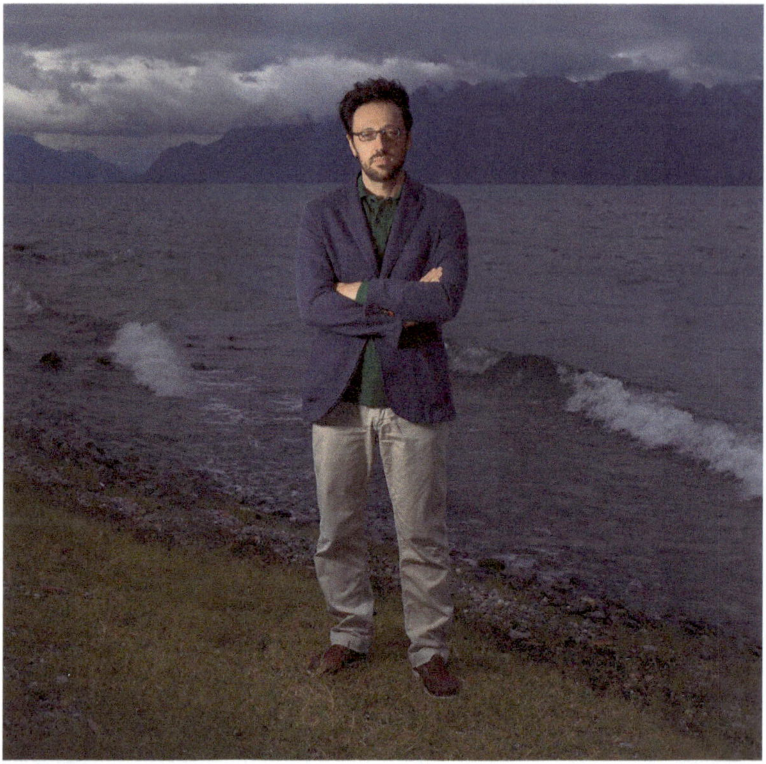

Francesco Arese Visconti, *AV*, 2017

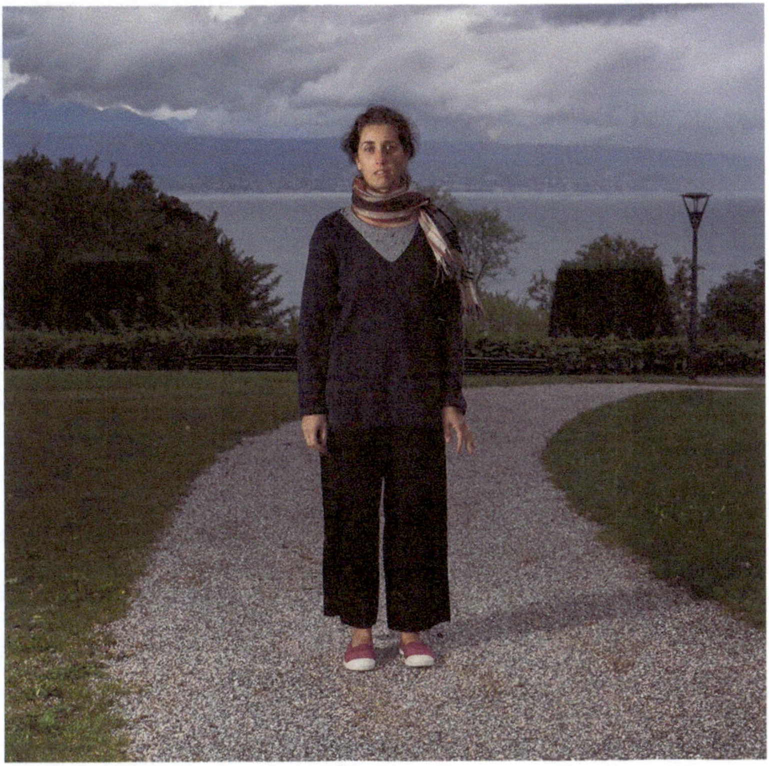

Francesco Arese Visconti, *LP*, 2017

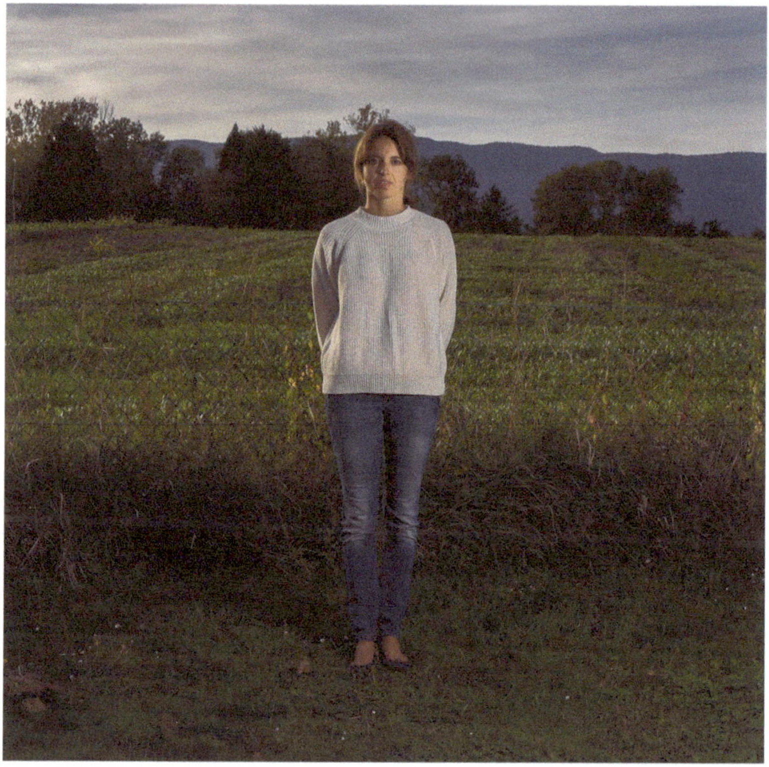

Francesco Arese Visconti, *OM*, 2017

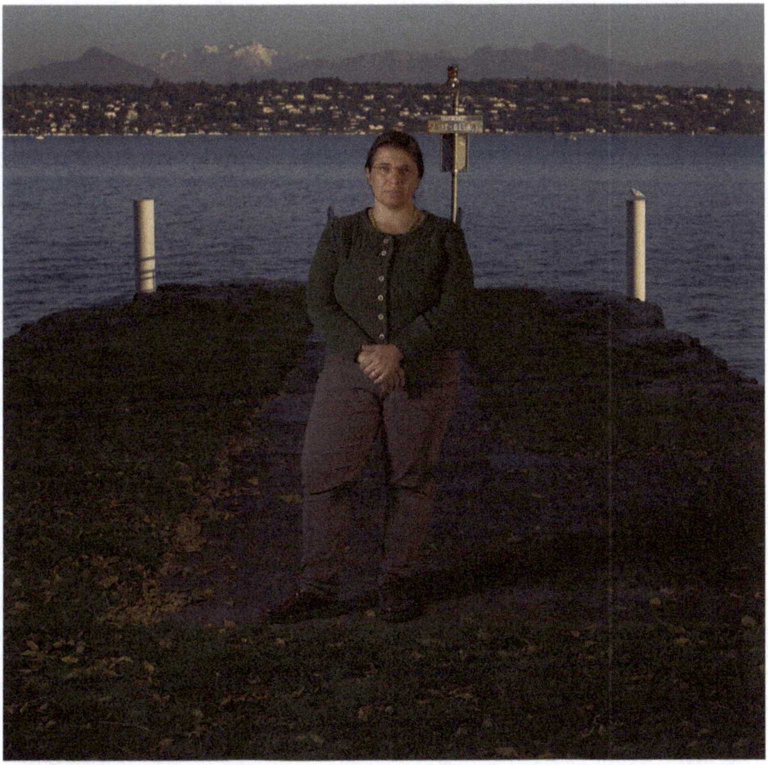

Francesco Arese Visconti, *PDS*, 2017

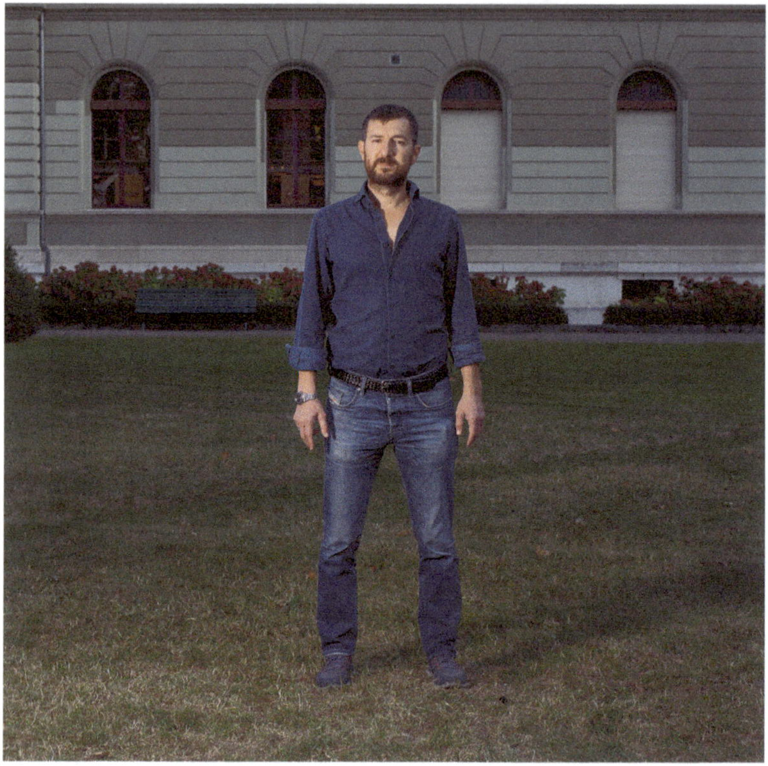

Francesco Arese Visconti, *AA*, 2018

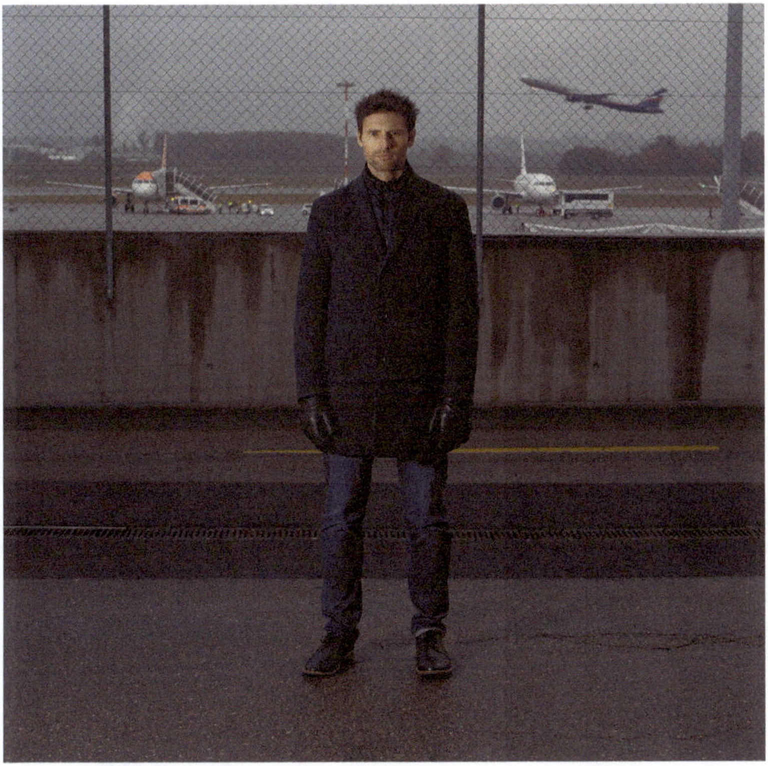

Francesco Arese Visconti, *AC*, 2018

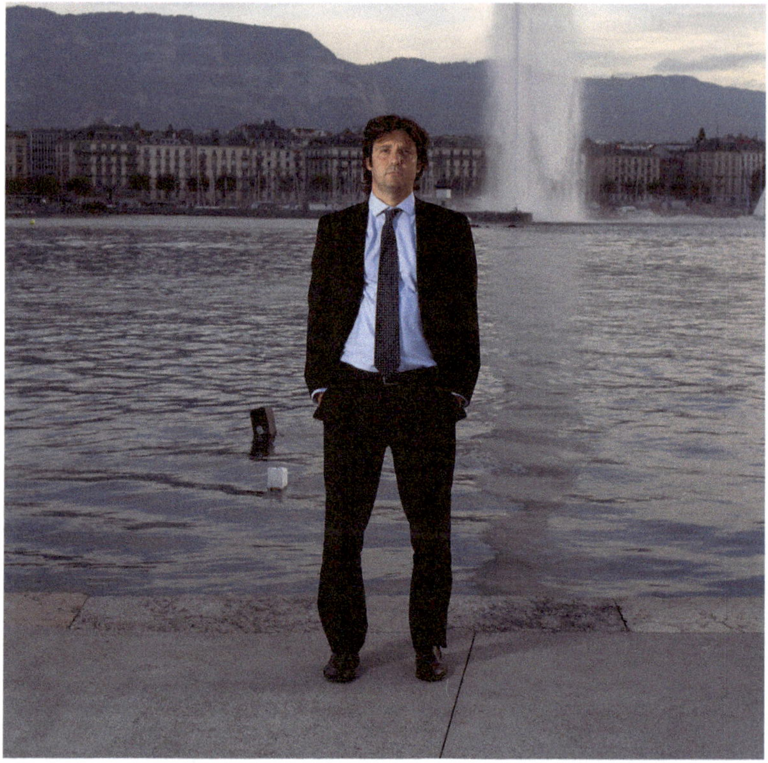

Francesco Arese Visconti, *AP*, 2018

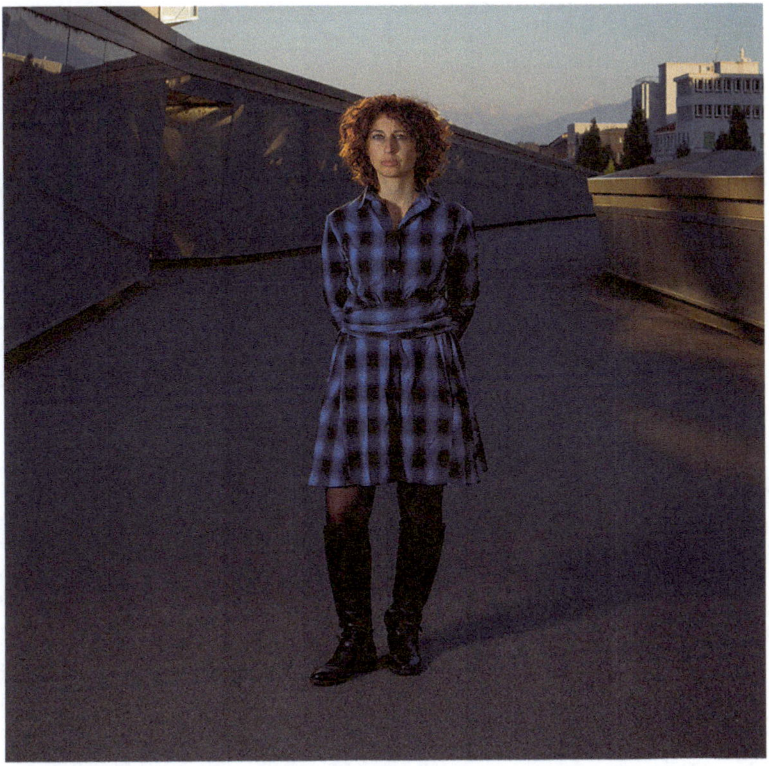

Francesco Arese Visconti, *CM*, 2018

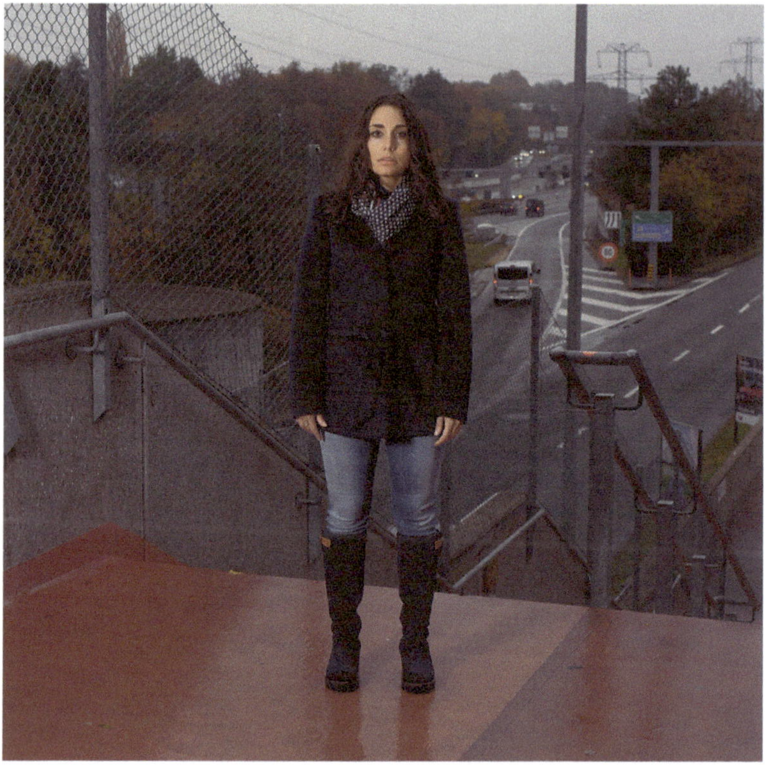

Francesco Arese Visconti, *ES*, 2018

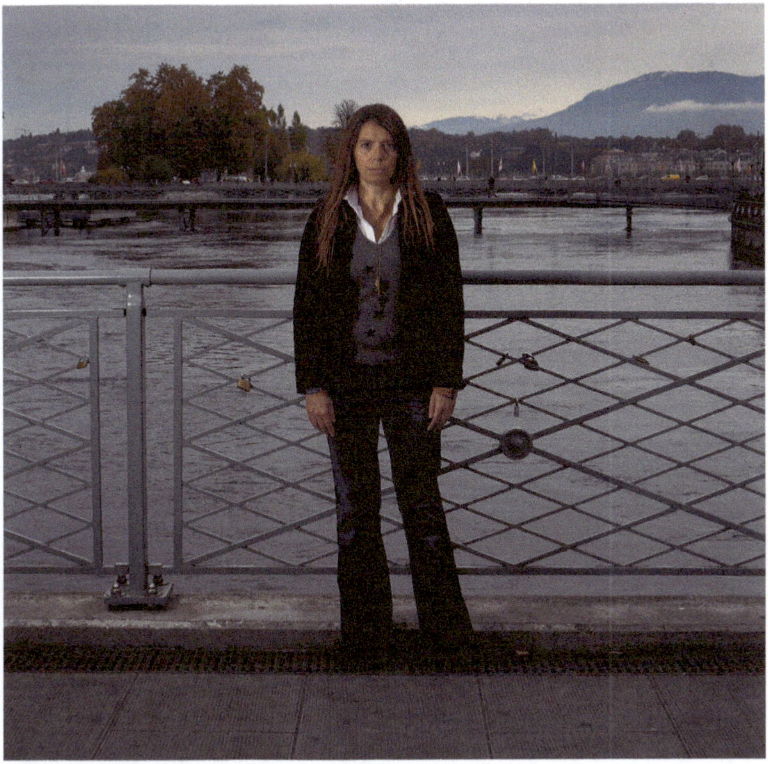

Francesco Arese Visconti, *FR*, 2018

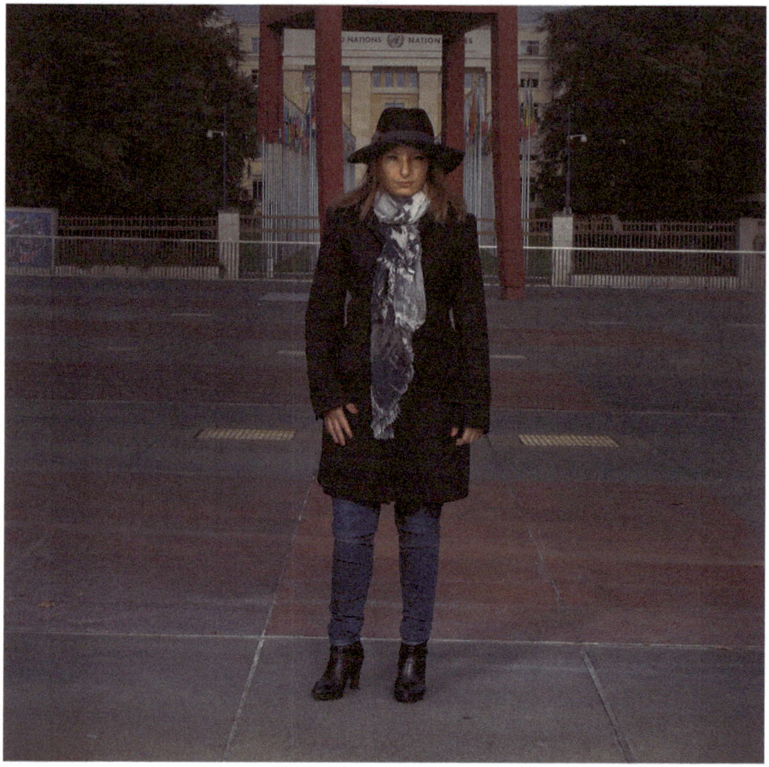

Francesco Arese Visconti, *IP*, 2018

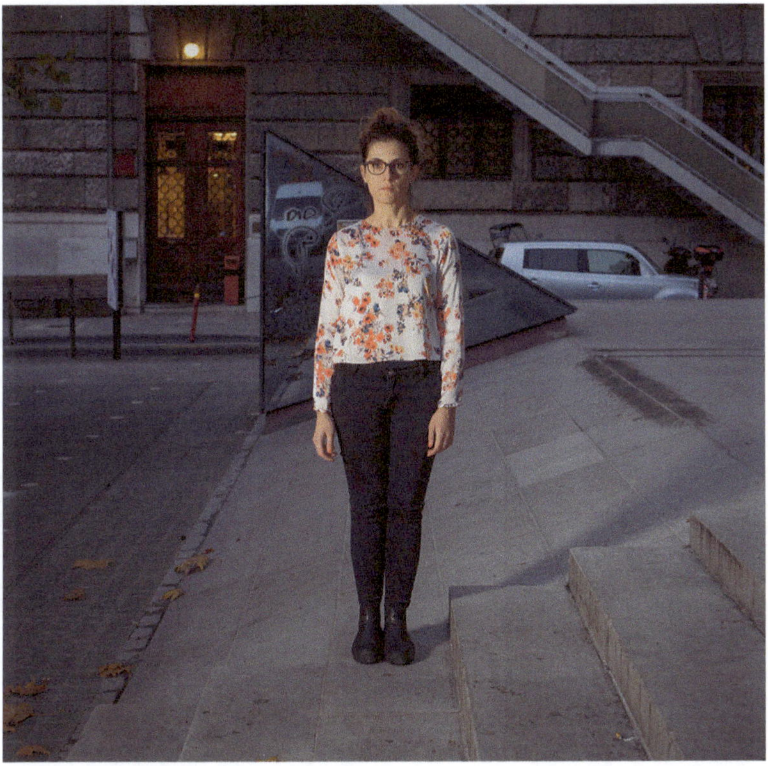

Francesco Arese Visconti, *MC*, 2018

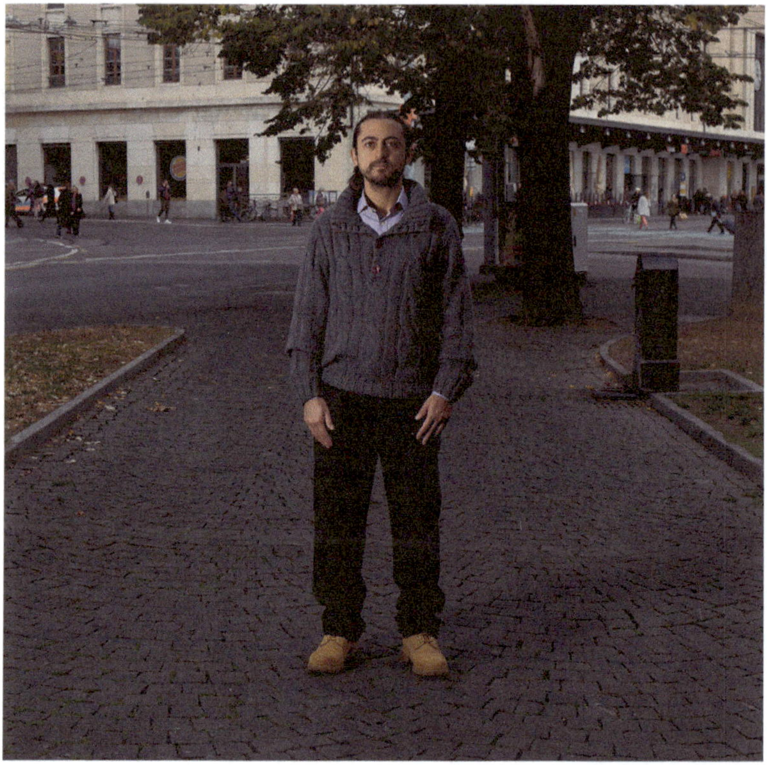

Francesco Arese Visconti, *NC*, 2018

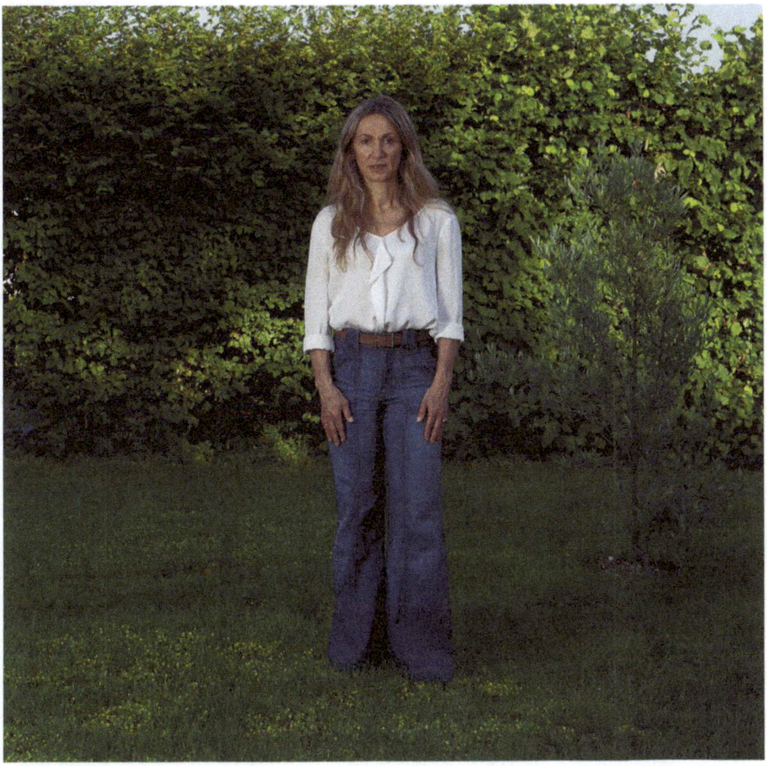

Francesco Arese Visconti, *CC*, 2019

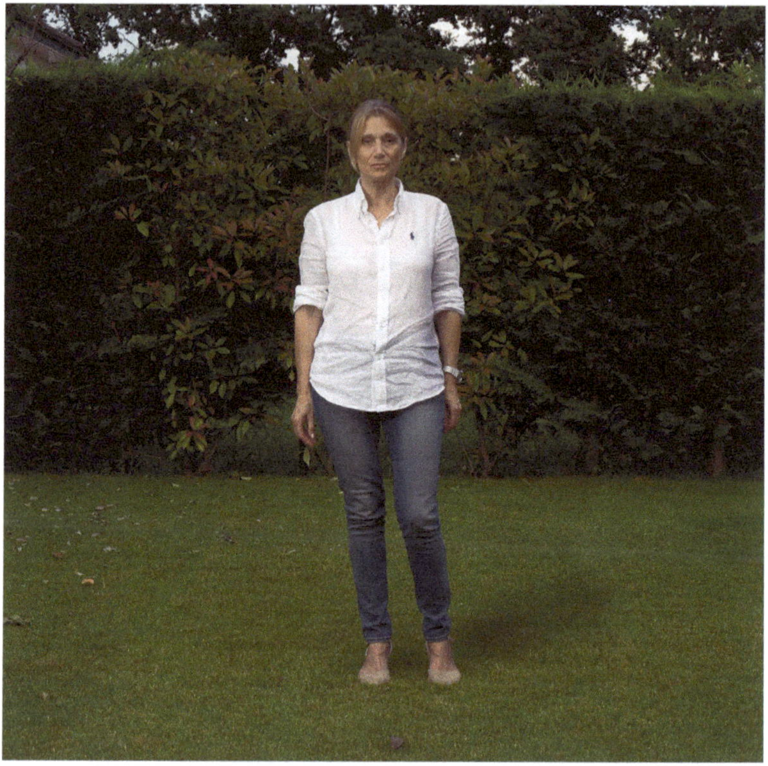

Francesco Arese Visconti, *RL*, 2019

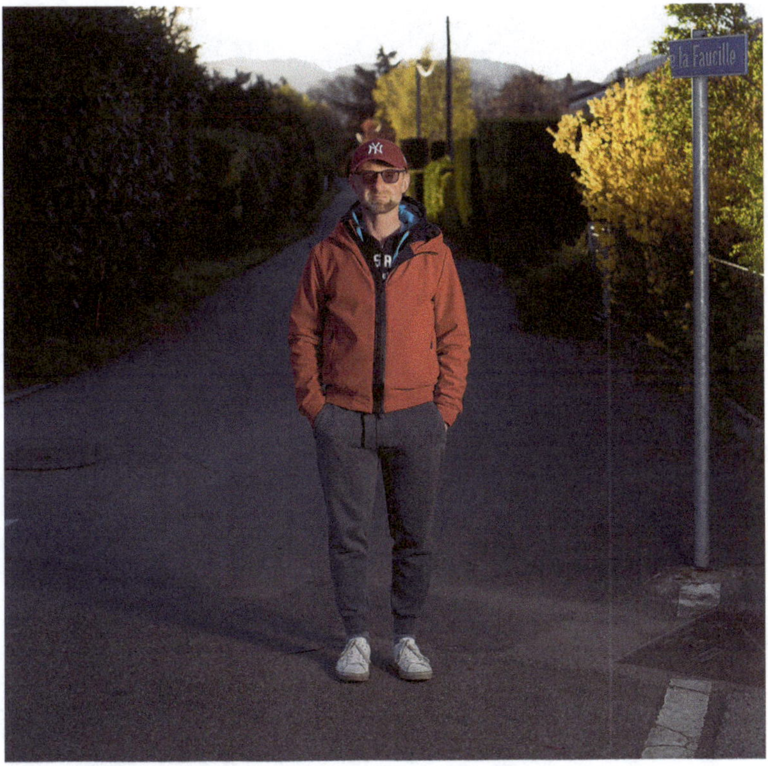

Francesco Arese Visconti, *AS*, 2021

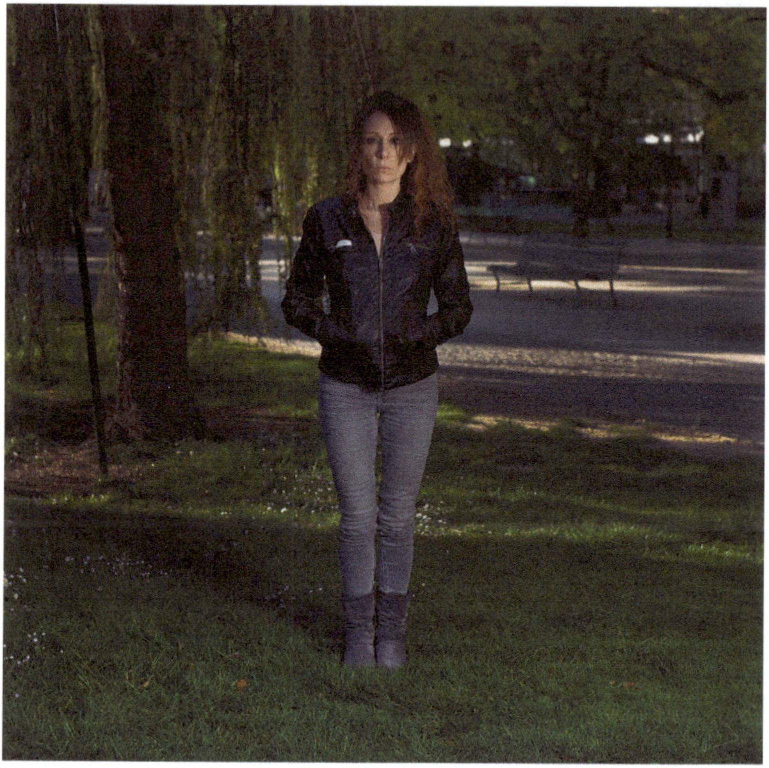

Francesco Arese Visconti, *BS*, 2021

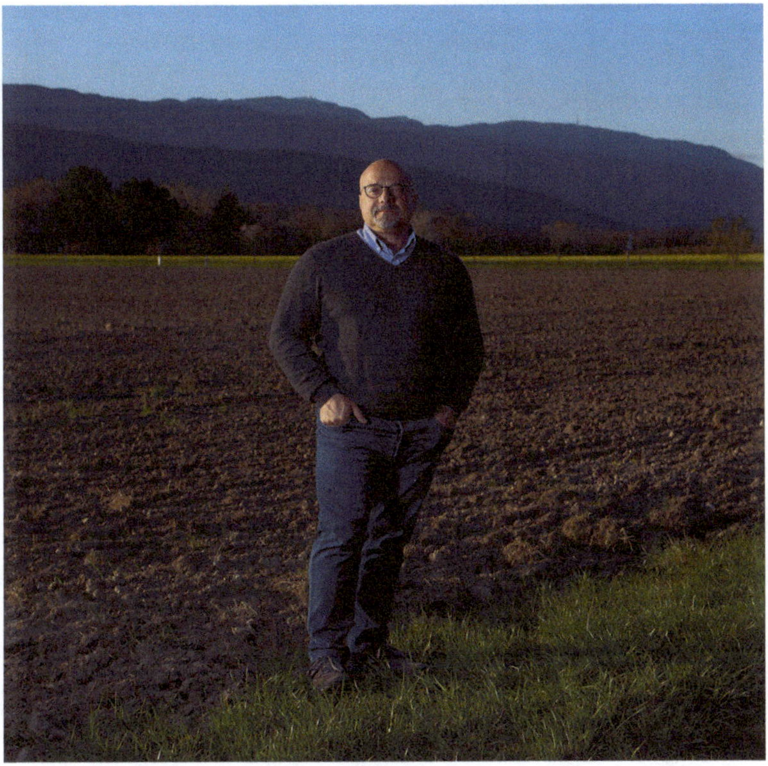

Francesco Arese Visconti, *CDS*, 2021

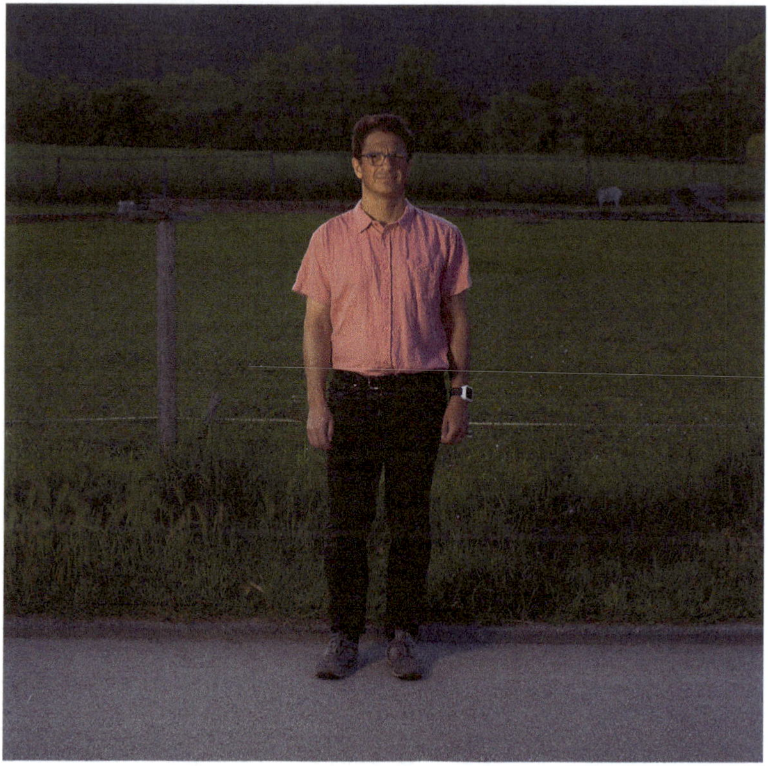

Francesco Arese Visconti, *CF*, 2021

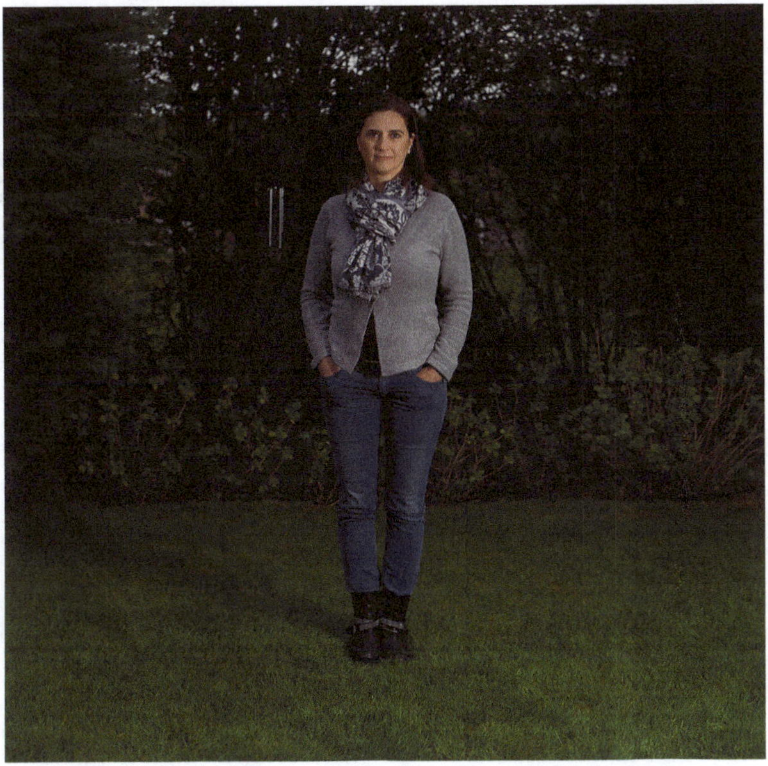

Francesco Arese Visconti, *FL*, 2021

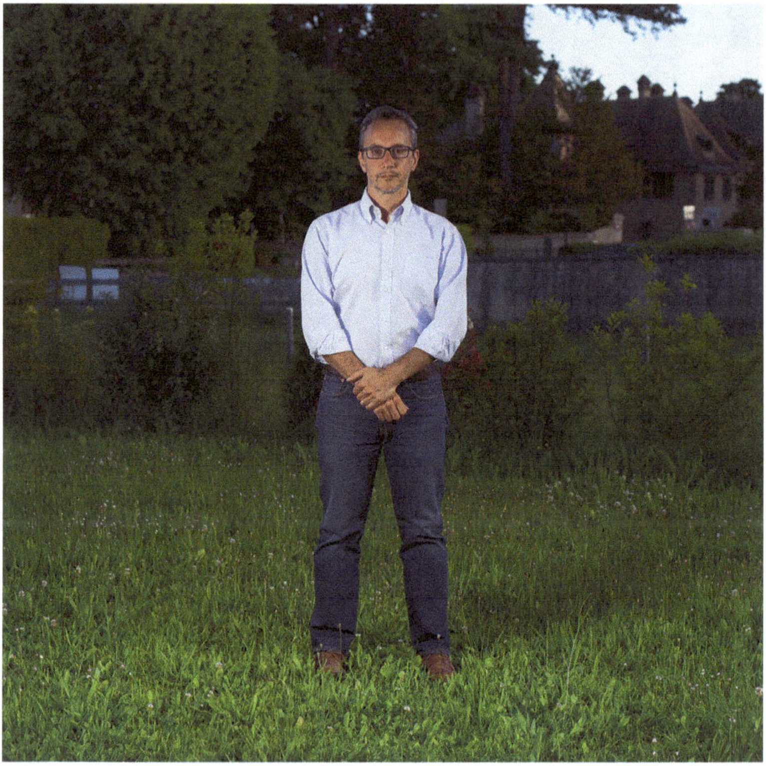

Francesco Arese Visconti, *MM*, 2021

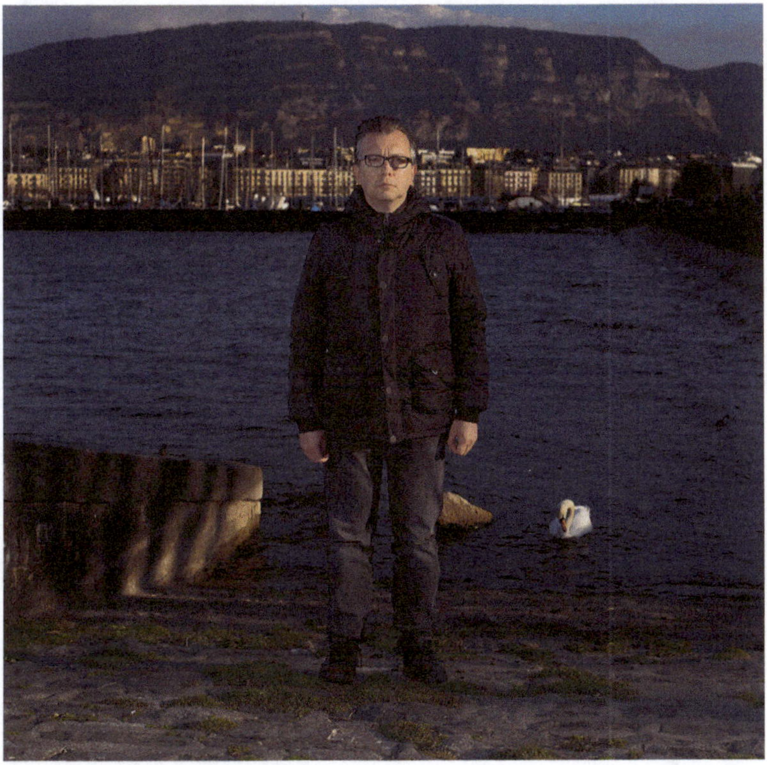

Francesco Arese Visconti, *VP*, 2021

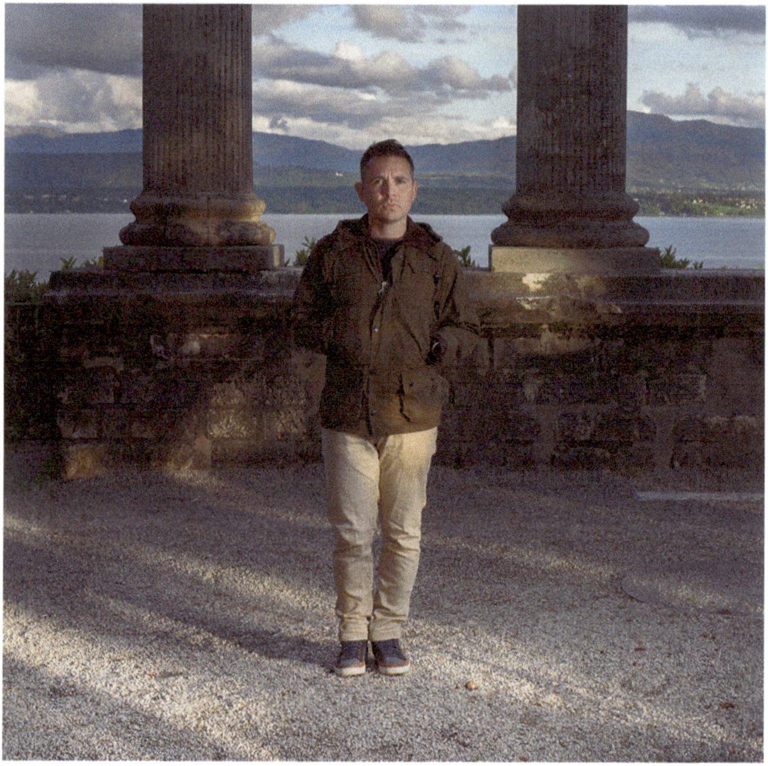

Francesco Arese Visconti, *YD*, 2021

List of References for Figures

Fig. 2.1 L'Illustré - n. 10 of March 7th, 1963, pp. 28–29
Fig. 2.2 L'Illustré – n. 13 of March 28th, 1963, pp. 28–29
Fig. 2.3 L'Illustré – n. 45 of November 5th, 1964, p. 81
Fig. 2.4 L'Illustré – n. 14 of April 1st, 1965, pp. 22–23
Fig. 2.5 Unknown, Travailleurs étrangers, 1965
From L'Illustré – 14 of April 1st, 1965. p. 22. Left
Fig. 2.6 Unknown, Travailleur étranger, 1965
From L'Illustré – 14 of April 1st, 1965. p. 22. Right
Fig. 2.7 Unknown, Celui qui part. Ceux qui restent, 1965
From L'Illustré – 14 of April 1st, 1965. p. 25
Fig. 2.8 L'Illustré – n. 14 of April 2nd, 1970, p. 4
Fig. 2.9 Unknown, Au pays de la solitude, 1970
From L'Illustré – n. 14 of April 2nd, 1970. p. 4
Fig. 2.10 Unknown, Au pays de la solitude, 1970
From L'Illustré – n. 14 of April 2nd, 1970. p. 6
Fig. 2.11 L'Illustré – n. 19 of May 11th, 1967, p. 93
Fig. 2.12 Unknown, Les petits enfants de la frontière, 1967
From L'Illustré – n. 19 of May 11th, 1967. p. 93
Fig. 2.13 Unknown, Les petits enfants de la frontière, 1967
From L'Illustré – n. 19 of May 11th, 1967. p. 94

F. Arese Visconti, *The Invisible Diaspora*, Palgrave Studies in Creativity and Culture,
https://doi.org/10.1007/978-3-031-74925-4

Fig. 2.14 Unknown, Les petits enfants de la frontière, 1967
From L'Illustré – n. 19 of May 11th, 1967. p. 95. Top
Fig. 2.15 Unknown, Les petits enfants de la frontière, 1967
From L'Illustré – n. 19 of May 11th, 1967. p. 95. Center
Fig. 2.16 Unknown, Les petits enfants de la frontière, 1967
From L'Illustré – n. 19 of May 11th, 1967. p. 95. Bottom
Fig. 2.17 Unknown, Les petits enfants de la frontière, 1967
From L'Illustré – n. 19 of May 11th, 1967. p. 96. Bottom
Fig. 2.18 Unknown, Les petits enfants de la frontière, 1967
From L'Illustré – n. 19 of May 11th, 1967. p. 96. Top
Fig. 2.19 L'Illustré – n. 19 of May 7th, 1970, pp. 26–27
Fig. 2.20 L'Illustré – n. 19 of May 7th, 1970, pp. 32–33
Fig. 2.21 Unknown, Ceux du sud chez ceux du nord, 1970
From L'Illustré – n. 19 of May 7th, 1970. p. 29. Left
Fig. 2.22 Unknown, Ceux du sud chez ceux du nord, 1970
From L'Illustré – n. 19 of May 7th, 1970. p. 29. Right
Fig. 2.23 Unknown, Ceux du sud chez ceux du nord, 1970
From L'Illustré – n. 19 of May 7th, 1970. p. 27
Fig. 3.1 Unknown, Filomena Giannini and Enzo Lasprogata in an interior color portrait, 2012
From L'Hebdo – n. 46, 15th of November 2012. p. 45
Fig. 3.2 Readers Digest – July, 2012, front cover
Fig. 3.3 Unknown, Untitled, 1965
From L'Illustré – n. 14, 1965. p. 23
Fig. 5.2 Francesco Arese Visconti, *AA*, 2012
From Arese Visconti, F. (2012). New World – Stories of African Immigration and Integration in Switzerland. Firenze: Aión Edizioni. p. 37
Fig. 5.3 Francesco Arese Visconti, *DN*, 2012
From Arese Visconti, F. (2012). New World – Stories of African Immigration and Integration in Switzerland. Firenze: Aión Edizioni. p. 51
Fig. 5.4 Francesco Arese Visconti, *MMH*, 2015
From Francesco Arese Visconti. (2015). We, Prato. Prato: Edizioni SUI. p. 51
Fig. 5.5 Francesco Arese Visconti, *LL*, 2015
From Francesco Arese Visconti. (2015). We, Prato. Prato: Edizioni SUI. p. 63

Index[1]

[1] Note: Page numbers followed by 'n' refer to notes.

F. Arese Visconti, *The Invisible Diaspora*, Palgrave Studies in Creativity and Culture,
https://doi.org/10.1007/978-3-031-74925-4

Kolibri 360 GmbH
Ferdinand-Jühlke-Straße 7
99095 Erfurt, Deutschland
produktsicherheit@kolibri360.de